Advance Praise for *An American Radical*

"Susan Rosenberg's *An American Radical* is remarkable—and terrifying. In taut, unadorned prose, she recounts her sixteen years imprisoned in American jails, much of that time spent in isolation and high-security units. That she survived at all is something of a miracle. Her stark, harrowing story is all at once mesmerizing, horrifying, and deeply saddening. Her revelations about the U.S. prison system and its various forms of torture and diminishment should forever prevent glib distinctions between our 'democratic' system and that of totalitarian countries. Rosenberg herself emerges as an admirable, remarkably resilient, and honorable figure."
 —Martin Duberman, Distinguished Professor of History Emeritus, City University of New York, and author of more than twenty books

"Walt Whitman wrote: 'My call is the call of battle, I nourish active rebellion.' Our dear sister Susan Rosenberg did just that in the 1960s. And her journey is part of this American history/herstory of radicalism. We thank her for sharing her life of introspection, activism and resistance. And we thank her for resisting . . . resisting . . . resisting."

—Sonia Sanchez, poet

"Susan Rosenberg's struggle as an American radical is retold in this story of her life and those of her 'sisters in punishment' as political prisoners here in the U.S. Incarcerated in some of the worst prisons, Rosenberg documents not only the oppression of women in prison but also the great strength and courage she and her politically oppressed sisters demonstrate in these penal colonies. She is simultaneously aware and respectful of the awful situation of the majority of women—black, brown, and poor—who are incarcerated in the U.S. today. As she grows and changes, she does so as *An American Radical*. A must-read book to understand prisons in America today."
 —Natalie J. Sokoloff, professor of sociology,
 John Jay College of Criminal Justice

"This book is for every American—one woman's story that puts us all on trial. 'I have met death in the cold / of this prison,' Susan Rosenberg writes, and shows us forty pounds of shackles on her hundred-pound body and how it feels to struggle for years against abuse and deprivation, how it feels to change, to find purpose, solace, even love. Executive clemency from the President of the United States finally freed Susan Rosenberg. You won't want to believe her words on these pages, but they're both true and truly well written, and none of us is free to ignore them."

—Hettie Jones, author

"In the decade of the '90s, Nelson Mandela was freed, apartheid was ended, the Soviet Union collapsed, and most Americans talked about a world led by a well-intended, peaceful United States. Susan Rosenberg witnessed these developments from the vantage point of a tiny cell in America's most notorious prisons. A political prisoner in her own country, Rosenberg endured the most heinous conditions, designed to break her will. As in the most backward nations, renunciation of her political beliefs was the price of decent conditions. Rosenberg never surrendered. Her haunting memoir vividly depicts what life is like for a radical woman in maximum security. Rosenberg also gives voice to the tens of thousands of female prisoners, mostly Black and poor, who lived and died through the AIDS epidemic that ravaged America's incarcerated. It is bitterly ironic that Rosenberg, an activist who tried to change the world, found herself in conditions where even the smallest change requires intense struggle. Her battles to change the lives of the women around her are inspiring; this book is a testament to the strength of the human spirit."

—Ron Kuby, civil rights and criminal defense attorney

"Surviving oppression is, as Susan Rosenberg shows us in this powerful prison memoir, a creative act of camaraderie and solidarity. Even in the face of the unfathomable brutality, the nonstop assault on humanity that is the American prison system, Rosenberg shows us how women prisoners took care of each other in their battles against AIDS, sexual violence, police brutality, and political repression.

Rosenberg's evocative prose, interspersed with poems she wrote in prison, demonstrates that we must celebrate humanity in order to dismantle mass incarceration."
—Dan Berger, editor of *The Hidden 1970s: Histories of Radicalism*, and author of *Outlaws of America: The Weather Underground and the Politics of Solidarity*

"Rosenberg tells a compelling story in *An American Radical*—an intimate portrayal of life as a political prisoner and a potent analysis of the ongoing failures of the American form of incarceration and punishment. She inspires with her story of active resistance to really tough conditions at a time when the label and preoccupation with 'terrorist' is again a collective obsession, as it was in the early 1970s in America. *An American Radical* will rouse readers to forge ahead with their own commitments to genuine patriotism through opposition to oppression."
—Don Hazen, executive director of the independent Media Institute and executive editor of Alternet.org

"In her powerful and harrowing quest, Susan Rosenberg's amazing story drives us to examine our own relationship with justice. You can feel the heat coming off the pages of this book as it bears witness to the industry behind our wretched penal system—while at the same time her odyssey leads us to discover unforgettable places within the human heart and soul. This is a journey that most Americans could never even imagine, let alone take."
—Jackson Taylor, director, PEN Prison Writing Program

"Anyone teaching a course relating to the American prison system will obviously find Susan Rosenberg's *An American Radical* to be a fine choice as a required text. But the book would also have great relevance in any course exploring our epoch of America's permanent wars. Rosenberg's odyssey takes us from the liberation movement of the 1960s, through the nightmarish worlds of federal prisons, into a twenty-first century where the American prison has expanded into a global gulag of secret prisons and unspeakable torture, government secrecy, and a culture that defines radical dissent as beyond the bounds of American normality. It's hard to imagine a classroom where this book would fail to provoke invaluable discussion."

—H. Bruce Franklin, John Cotton Dana Professor of English and American studies at Rutgers University, Newark

"Susan Rosenberg takes us on an astonishing journey—from a tiny underground revolutionary cell into the vast underground of the American penal system. En route, we see the desperate, isolated idealism that led to her prison term become grounded and compassionate, centered on the cruel plight of her sister inmates. Her lifelong commitment to racial equality and justice bears fruit in this impassioned memoir. 'Write it down for the record,' her lawyer insisted when she and other women political prisoners were subjected to experimental torture techniques. *An American Radical* is indeed that intimate record of the suffering and solidarity of women in America's toughest prisons."

—Bell Gale Chevigny, professor emeritus of literature, Purchase College, SUNY, author and editor of *Doing Time: 25 Years of Prison Writing*, a PEN American Center prize anthology

"The bravery and courage, and the original voice of Susan Rosenberg carries the reader with it—every moment of her sixteen years in prison. Her deep self-analysis for precious sanity, in search of truth—past, present and future—for herself and the world, is nothing less than astounding. The book's gift redefines radicalism itself. It also elicits that rare, silent 'Ah!' of unexpected recognition experienced in compelling theater and art."

—Doris Schwerin, author and composer

"Susan Rosenberg has gone into the hell of the American prison system and come back miraculously unembittered, her soul intact and bringing us the news that Abu Ghraib and Guantanamo are not aberrations but business as usual. What 'we' did to foreign terrorists 'we' do to our own every day of the year. America is a one-eyed jack, but Rosenberg has seen the other side of its face."

—Henry Bean, writer and director

"In this gripping book, Susan Rosenberg tells a harrowing story that is painfully personal and an important part of American history. The psychological torture and physical cruelty of American prisoners can so often seem abstract. But not when you read *An American Radical*; its pages are packed with adventure, claustrophobia, heartache, constant political struggle, and Rosenberg's indomitable will to survive."

—Christian Parenti, author of *Lockdown America* and *The Soft Cage*

"Windowless underground prisons, unfounded charges, years in solitary confinement with no clarity on when that will end have been American practice well before Guantanamo. This is the story of a woman, imprisoned for a crime, sentenced for her politics, and treated horrifically in U.S. prisons. It describes a journey that is both personal and political. It reveals how the American criminal justice system has little to do with justice. It undermines our notion that our current human rights violations, so vividly demonstrated by the War on Terror, are recent overreactions to the threat of international 'terrorists.' Susan Rosenberg was considered a 'terrorist' in the early 1980s. Her story gives us perspective. It reminds us that these rights violations are not idiosyncratic of a failed Bush policy. Perhaps most important, however, through the clarity of her vision and relentless spirit, Susan Rosenberg gives us hope."

—Jane H. Aiken, professor of law,
Georgetown University Law Center

An American Radical

Radical

Political Prisoner in My Own Country

Susan Rosenberg

CITADEL PRESS
Kensington Publishing Corp.
www.kensingtonbooks.com

CITADEL PRESS BOOKS are published by

Kensington Publishing Corp.
119 West 40th Street
New York, NY 10018

All Kensington titles, imprints, and distributed lines are available at special quantity discounts for bulk purchases for sales promotions, premiums, fund-raising, educational, or institutional use. Special book excerpts or customized printings can also be created to fit specific needs. For details, write or phone the office of the Kensington special sales manager: Kensington Publishing Corp., 119 West 40th Street, New York, NY 10018, attn: Special Sales Department; phone 1-800-221-2647.

Some names of individuals have been changed to protect their privacy.

First printing: March 2011

10   9   8   7   6   5   4   3   2   1

Printed in the United States of America

Library of Congress Control Number: 2010931894

ISBN-13: 978-0-8065-3304-9
ISBN-10: 0-8065-3304-8

This book is dedicated to my loving parents, Bella and Emanuel Rosenberg, and to all the people who have been disappeared and exiled in U.S. prisons.

[This] is sent out to those into whose souls the iron has entered, and has entered deeply at some time in their lives.

—THOMAS HARDY,
Jude the Obscure

The degree of civilization in a society can be judged by entering its prisons.

—FYODOR DOSTOEVSKY,
The House of the Dead

Contents

Foreword

by Kathleen Cleaver

THE MASSIVE PROTEST movements and freedom struggles of the 1960s mobilized young people all over the world. Thousands were injured, arrested, jailed, and killed; thousands more watched, and millions of young people were inspired to act. Mass social movements surged during those days, marked by urban riots and insurrections, guerilla uprisings, and the scandalous murder of leaders such as Malcolm X, Martin Luther King, and Fred Hampton. Evening news broadcasts showed horrendous scenes of warfare in Vietnam, while thousands of young men were drafted to fight there. My conscience was seared when four young girls were murdered at the 16th Street Baptist Church bombing in Birmingham, girls who were part of the children's campaign of constant protest marches during 1963. It happened in Alabama, my home state, the year I started college. For Susan Rosenberg, who grew up in New York, watching the televised National Guard assault at the Attica prison in New York State, which left 29 prisoners and 10 hostages dead in 1971, had a life changing impact. The massacre happened during her junior year in high school.

The prison memoir had not attained recognition as literature when Susan Rosenberg entered Barnard College two years later, but the political prisoners taken during insurgent independence movements or revolutionary uprisings were making a profound impact on our generation's world view. The leaders of Third World national liberation movements had spent time in colonial prisons, and if not captured or killed, after independence was won some of them became the leaders of their countries. The startling rise of Patrice Lumumba to prime minister in the formerly Belgian Congo during 1960 set off waves of liberation struggles to end imperial white rule in Africa; that, combined with the revolutionary struggles we learned about in South Asia and South America, helped inspire our own brand of radicalism. In the United States, the most confrontational leaders of our black liberation struggle were being arrested, tried, and sent to prison—if not shot in the streets.

In 1967, at the height of antiwar protest, we saw world champion boxer Muhammad Ali ordered to prison for refusing to fight in Vietnam. UCLA professor Angela Davis was hunted and jailed on charges of assisting the escape of a prisoner, during which a judge was killed, from the Marin County Courthouse in 1970. Just as years later demands that ANC leader Nelson Mandela be free circled the world, young African American revolutionaries launched the "Free Huey" campaign and spread the Black Panther Party across the country. Both at home and at school, Rosenberg was sensitized to challenge fundamental wrongs, her consciousness nurtured in New York's liberal political culture during a decade when race, economic injustice, and the Vietnam War were polarizing the entire country.

I met Susan Rosenberg at a crowded welcome home party held in New York City in 2001. The event was at the Walden School on the Upper West Side, where Susan had graduated from high school. Before her time, Andrew Goodman, one of the three civil rights workers murdered in Mississippi in 1964, had graduated from this progressive school. It was a damp winter evening, the gathering of many supporters and activists filled the hall in clumps and rows around small tables. I loved the festive air the bouquets of flowers gave to the room, and the feeling of joy that everyone radiated. The guests buzzed with the warmth of reunions, like families and old friends coming back together. I saw some faces from the political prisoner movements I'd worked with before, but most of the guests I did not recognize. After the formal part of the program ended, I had a chance to see Susan for the first time. I was excited—she looked more frail than I had imagined her—but we shared friends and comrades. The one I knew best was one of her codefendants, Marilyn Buck, who was still behind bars, which gave us a special bond. We hugged each other, spoke briefly, and agreed to meet later in the month.

The party was pulled together within weeks after President Bill Clinton commuted Rosenberg's sentence in January 2001, during those same last days when the rumored pardon for Leonard Peltier never materialized and the controversial pardon of Marc Rich generated frenzied news coverage. Outraged cries against Rosenberg's parole back then originated within the police and the FBI, but they never provoked a national controversy. In 1984, then-U.S. attorney in New York Rudolph Giuliani had withdrawn the indictment against her for participating in the Brink's robbery in Nyack, New York, but that legal fact never prevented the local press from vilifying her as a "cop killer" along with those who had been convicted, nor did it stop the fraternal organizations representing New York police from hounding her and her family for being a "terrorist." Thankfully, President Clinton had commuted her sentence months before the anti-terrorist political obsession gripped the city in the wake of the destruction of the World Trade Center that September.

Rosenberg's arrest in 1984 while driving a truck loaded with hundreds of pounds of explosives on the New Jersey Turnpike led to her conviction in a possession of weapons and explosives case in 1985. "I knew . . . I had a fifty-eight-year sentence and a minimum of twenty years. But it wasn't life," she wrote. "Though it seemed unlikely, I had an outside chance of parole. I couldn't allow myself to think of dying in jail." Her memoir details the sixteen years she spent in women's prisons as a political prisoner.

A deep tone of solidarity, commitment, and love that the revolutionary women prisoners shared vibrates through these lines, as Rosenberg tells about their fight to save their sanity and each other's lives. She writes from the shadowy underbelly of prison, those dungeons within federal prisons created for specified prisoner types. She and the other radical women were confined away from the rest of the prisoner population in places labeled "high-security unit," "control unit," and other euphemisms. They provided structured conditions of psychological deprivation and torture to force the prisoner to renounce her ideological convictions or political views. This treatment reserved for the revolutionary or "subversive" prisoner reads like some secularized version of the Inquisition. While Rosenberg was incarcerated in Kentucky at the federal prison in Lexington, a report the ACLU issued on its high-security unit stated that when the measures fail to produce in prisoners "the state of submission essential for ideological conversion," the unit's "next objective is to reduce them to a state of psychological incompetence sufficient to neutralize them." These facilities were designed and functioning before the current use of Guantanamo Bay as a prison for captives in the "War on Terror" for similar purposes.

A lawsuit against the conditions Rosenberg and other political prisoners were subjected to in Lexington eventually led to her transfer to the women's prison in Marianna, Florida. About Marianna, she wrote, "One of the deepest commitments I had made to myself was that I would not allow prison or repression to erode my soul, and I felt that my soul was more deeply threatened than at any time before. For the first time, I felt that my political will was not enough to give me the daily strength to survive." Susan's inner balance was shattered; she plunged into the deepest place of her creative being, and resurfaced with a new consciousness of herself.

The voice you hear in *An American Radical* did survive the barbaric cruelty of her maximum-security hell holes, and it is clear, fierce, and compassionate—a voice that continues in these pages to speak truth to power.

KATHLEEN NEAL CLEAVER, a senior lecturer at Yale University and at Emory Law School, has been involved in the human rights movement since high school. She quit college in 1966 to work full time in the Student Nonviolent Coordinating Committee (SNCC) and then joined the early Black Panther Party in California, where until 1971 she was the party's communications secretary. She has worked to free many imprisoned political activists, including Geronimo (Pratt) ji-Jaga, released after serving 27 years for a crime he did not commit, and Mumia Abu-Jamal, who remains on death row. Cleaver and George Katsiaficas co-edited *Liberation, Imagination and the Black Panther Party* (2001), and she edited *Target Zero: A Life in Writing* (2006) by Eldridge Cleaver. She is currently completing a memoir entitled *Memories of Love and War*.

Acknowledgments

TO ALL THE prison writers everywhere.

To all who encouraged me to write, Sue Gambill, Bell Chevigny, Fielding Dawson, Professor Floyd R. Horowitz, Susie Waysdorf, Henry Bean, Doris Schwerin.

To all who relentlessly fought for my release, thank you.

To Mary O'Melveny, for whom there are no adequate words.

To Blue Mountain Center, who provided invaluable support.

To PEN American Center Prison Writing Program.

To Professor Donald Goodman, Dr. Richard Korn, Buzz Alexander, Rabbi Joshua Saltzman, Rabbi Rolando Matalon, Ron Kuby, Kathleen Cleaver, Jane Aiken.

To Ona Mirkinson, whose research and notes completed the historical record.

To Shirley Cloyes, my friend and editor who worked from beginning to end, without whom this book would not have been written.

To my editor Richard Ember, who made it happen.

To Marilyn Buck and Dr. Alan Berkman, in loving memory.

To my mother, Bella Rosenberg.

And to Molly and Dawn, who continue to make it all worthwhile.

Part One

Arrest and Trial

Chapter 1

Explosives

DANGER, HIGH WINDS. The signs on the New Jersey Turnpike were flashing red-and-yellow directions to all the motorists. It was cold and getting dark and the road was filled with post-Thanksgiving traffic. Cars swerved from one lane to the other and then crawled past us as the speed limit got lower and lower. I was frightened. Our twenty-foot U-Haul truck, filled with guns and dynamite, was swaying back and forth in the wind. I looked at Tim as he gripped the wheel and he didn't look like his usual calm and collected self. While the brush of his crew cut was gleaming and his suit and tie were perfect, there was sweat glistening on his upper lip, wetting his small brown mustache. As I scrutinized him, he was almost unrecognizable in his "Officer Bill" disguise, as he had jokingly nicknamed himself after recoiling from a look in the mirror. "What are we doing here?"—the question kept whirling around in my head. What we were doing was driving hundreds of pounds of dynamite, fourteen guns, and hundreds of pieces of false identification to a storage space in Cherry Hill, New Jersey.

"Bill, shouldn't we get off the highway?" I asked. I was calling him "Bill" because that was his illegal name. The name he used in the underground. It seemed silly, because he was indelibly Tim to me, but for security purposes I complied. "Jo," he answered back, "I think we should stay on this road until we have to get off, even if we have to drive slowly. I think that the back roads will be worse and filled with lots more people." "Okay, but the space will be closed. We're pretty late," I answered. "You have the storage combination, right?" Tim asked. I nodded yes.

"This is awful. I wish we could go back," I whispered. But we could not go back; there was no place to go back to. We had been driving for twelve hours and had crossed state lines. We had to make it to the storage place and get all the stuff put away. We could not keep driving around with it. If we got hit by another vehicle, in the windy weather, well, it wasn't just us who would be killed. It was impossible to think about that.

After another forty minutes and fifteen miles, Tim said, "Maybe we should get off. Look at all these troopers; maybe there will be fewer off the highway." My scalp was itching under my wig and I envied Tim's short hair. I thought of Tim five years earlier when we had first met and he had had long blond hair and a quiet beauty about him. He looked his age then, twenty-two. Before all the weight training and iron pumping, he had a lithe dancer's body. Now he looked older than his years. He had been a progressive social activist and a student leader at a college in the northeast valley in Massachusetts. I had gone there to organize a public meeting against the Ku Klux Klan. He was part of the group of students who wanted help organizing a national movement. I was a member of a small group called the John Brown anti-Klan committee, which had developed to stop the KKK from organizing guards in the New York state prisons. Our very first conversation had been about Latin American literature. I liked him from the moment we met. His smile was glorious and his sense of humor alternated between high sarcasm and whimsy. We had flirted a lot, but we ended up being friends with bonds that deepened over time. This dangerous mission made them even deeper. The U-Haul lurched again in the wind. We looked at each other and without speaking, Tim moved us toward the exit ramp.

It was 1984. Anyone who was black or a political activist knew that the New Jersey State Troopers had the highest arrest rates of black drivers in the nation. It was a bad road to be on. I had been underground for two years. I was on the Federal Bureau of Investigation's most wanted list. In 1982, I had been indicted in a federal conspiracy case, charged with participation in the prison break of Assata Shakur (Joanne Chesimard)[1] and the Brink's robbery. I was accused of being part of a group of white radicals who aided and abetted a group of black revolutionaries in their attempt to build a revolutionary organization. The Brink's robbery had been a devastating blow to the Rockland community, where two local police officers, Edward O'Grady and Waverly Brown, died along with a Brink's guard, Peter Paige. The subsequent investigation into this robbery and multiple deaths led to several prosecutions, grand juries, indictments, trials, and convictions. Many people who were both remotely and closely connected to the events were targeted and I was one of them. The government was looking for me. And the FBI orders for all of us were "considered dangerous, shoot to kill."

I had been a political activist for fifteen years, from the time I was a teenager in the late 1960s. I had been in the anti–Vietnam War movement as I believed that, as an American, I was responsible for the acts of my government and that voting for politicians who were against the war had not been enough to stop the war. I did not accept the U.S. claim that what was happening in Vietnam was a civil war between the North and South. I thought that the Vietnamese people were fighting a just war of national liberation. Seeing the B52s dropped from planes, watching the burning of civilians with napalm and Agent Orange, reading about the incarceration of Vietnamese militants in cages only big enough for tigers made me furious. In watching the terrible violence of the war against Vietnam and hearing Vietnamese people talk about the war, my consciousness and understanding of the way to end the war led me to believe that opposing the war simply by demanding U.S. troop withdrawal would not by itself be enough to end the war. I believed that one had to try to stop the machinery of war. There had been a call stemming from the earlier student movement that I had agreed with: "You've got to put your bodies upon the gears and upon the wheels, upon the levers, upon all the apparatus, and you've got to make it stop."[2]

Later, I worked with some of the most radical people in the Black Panther Party, the Young Lords,[3] and the Weathermen. I had been a part of the political and social movement that developed throughout the 1960s and 1970s. It was a worldwide revolutionary movement for peace, equality, and liberation. Everywhere one looked in those years, there were counters and alternatives to the predominant culture. People were challenging the draft, the war, their social relations, gender roles, and all the norms of society. There were popular movements in almost every country. Revolutions that had begun in the developing world in the 1950s actually succeeded in the next decade. Countries were throwing off colonialism and building independence. All over Western Europe, students and workers were taking over universities and factories. It actually seemed possible to challenge the power of the rulers and the governments and bring about a different and better world. The civil rights movement showed us, showed me, that we lived in a segregated society, in a divided country where black people were still slaves and millions of poor people were unemployed and went to bed hungry. The power of the black struggle woke up my generation to look around and see the divisions and the injustice. Sit-ins, marches, boycotts, and demonstrations were responded to with water hoses, jailings, and killings by racists with direct ties to the police. In turn, revelations of the true conditions in the Southern United States exposed the myth of the country's rhetoric about democracy. It moved a whole generation to act. I considered myself an ardent supporter of revolution and was under the influence of people like Franz Fanon, a psychiatrist, revolutionary, and one of the twentieth century's most important theorists of the African struggle for independence,[4] and George Jackson,[5] an American revolutionary who had become a member of the Black Panther Party while in prison, where he had spent the last eleven years of his life. Jackson was one of the founders of the U.S. prisoners' rights movement. His books, *Soledad Brother* and *Blood in My Eye*, were read around the world.

As a result of the investigation by the FBI, I was indicted in 1982, and rather then stand trial, I fled and disappeared into the underground. My indictment pushed me in a direction I had been going in for several years—embracing the illegality of a revolutionary movement. The repression by the FBI and Joint Terrorist Taskforce (a newly formed law enforcement group) was tearing apart the aboveground movement. They had deemed whole segments of the radical left to be "terrorists," and they were surveiling, phone tapping, infiltrating, and harassing people who were carrying on legal work, such as community organizing. There was enmity by law enforcement officials against all of us in the left who had exposed them for their own violations of our constitutional rights and who had organized against them. The COINTELPRO (Counter

Intelligence Program) program[6] was in full force. I decided that rather than go to what I presumed would be a rigged trial, I would follow my revolutionary heart and risk all.

The underground, becoming a fugitive, being on the run, however one describes it, is both a physical and mental state of being. The underground, not unlike the French resistance movement during World War II, consisted of a network of people who thought enough like you to risk opening their lives and homes to fugitives in order to protect them from capture by the authorities. In the language of criminal law, their help is defined as "harboring." In wartime, it would be called "aiding the enemy."

By the time I fled, however, whatever underground had existed as a result of the anti-war movement, the anti-draft movement, and the movement to give illegal immigrants sanctuary had all but disappeared. There was nothing romantic or fun about it. The lack of a vital and thriving network of committed radicals willing to sacrifice their careers and possessions should have been enough of a warning to me that I was incorrectly reading the mood of the country. The election of Ronald Reagan to the presidency in 1980 by an overwhelming majority should have been further proof that our view of American society was deeply skewed. But I saw only what I wanted to see. I was blinded by my own dedication and extremism. Life underground was lonely and isolating, and this should have been another signal to me that something was wrong with the path I was treading. But, because I had lived through the rise of a mass movement and had felt the power of collective action once before, I still believed it could happen again. And so all the signs that I was moving in the wrong direction didn't stop me.

As the country moved to the right, some of us in the radical left went further afield and were increasingly polarized and far from the mainstream. I had been in various projects and organizations over the course of my life, including student groups at Barnard College and later at the City University of New York, as well as solidarity organizations that supported Puerto Rican independence and African liberation both in South Africa and in the United States. The overlapping core of people who built these organizations and many others grew increasingly frustrated with the inability to organize and grow or effect change in U.S. policies.

It was this core of radical activists that I joined to build the ranks of the underground. We hoped that our actions would help galvanize a militant mass protest against repressive U.S. policies in Central America, in Africa, and at home. We thought that by taking armed actions against government property (including bombing unoccupied government buildings), we would show that despite the power of the state, it was possible to oppose it.

In order to build an underground, we had to retreat further and further away from our public lives and psychologically further into our own political thinking and commitment than any of us had before. Although living in obscurity was difficult and tedious, there was a feeling of power that came from invisibility. Anonymity was often invigorating and chilling at the same time. For so many years in the left we had been trying to be different, to present an alternative to the norms of regular society. We were in the broadest sense part of the counterculture. This meant that we looked different, acted different, and were different from the accepted models of behavior. So, by our own definition we attracted attention. Going underground demanded a completely different discipline and relationship to our public appearance. Here the goal was to look exactly like everyone else around you so that nothing stood out, so that nothing would be a visual cue to anyone to remember anything about you. Leave no trace, we said to ourselves, blend in and glide along. We dyed our hair and straightened the curls, bought dresses and skirts and suits and ties and applied makeup and play-acted that we were straight, in all senses of the word. For some of us this was easier to do than for others. But all of us found it was a difficult life and dramatically different from how we had formed our identities. We had been organizers, we had been in the public movement, and we had been speechmakers and workers. We had been living our lives for the purpose of helping people and ending society's inequities. Once underground, we could no longer talk to people or engage in any social work. Suddenly our lives had become the very antithesis of our beliefs, the embodiment of the social alienation that we had been trying to redress. And so, we made jokes to cope with the loneliness and pain. We laughed when the first time we dyed our hair it turned orange, a long-honored tradition of underground participants around the world. The color was called "underground orange" because it would take several attempts to get the color right. While we laughed, nothing about our lives was funny. We were trying to create lives and structures that were in no way connected to the world. We were trying to build identities that could coexist while there was a manhunt in progress for all of us. We were trying to create a look that would never be remembered and with it a capacity to appear anywhere. We were erasing our own identities in an attempt to be invisible.

When the mother of one of our members died, we had a big debate about whether or not she should attend the funeral. We all had seen the movies where the FBI was crouching behind tombstones waiting for a fugitive to show up. Several years earlier when I had been aboveground, I had attended the funeral of a member of the Black Panthers who had been in a terrible gun battle with the NYPD. FBI agents in helicopters surveilling the people followed the funeral procession to the cemetery in attendance. We had worked so hard to create a clandestine space with a network of apartments, cars, and contacts that we were loath to take the risk. But in the end, she went. It was the right decision, it was the humane decision. Her father was very glad that she came. And she was not put in jeopardy. There were no police or FBI at the funeral, no overt or covert surveillance of any kind.

It was hard to let down the wall that we had constructed between our past and present lives. I missed my parents and wanted to see them. Through an elaborate maze of procedures that included lipstick scrawled on a hotel mirror, indicating that it was safe to go, we contacted my parents and invited them into the underground. They came for a weekend. My mother said that all the precautions were right out of a John Le Carré novel. We shared our world over two days, talking inside an upscale motel. My parents were worried for my safety. They were afraid that someone would get hurt. They vehemently disagreed with the choices that I had made, and they urged me to leave the country. They had been visited by the FBI and threatened with jail themselves if they failed to turn me in. And yet, they risked themselves for their love of me.

I did not leave the country. Instead, I kept going. On that awful and cold day in November when I was on the New Jersey Turnpike with Tim, there was no immediate, specific plan to use the explosives. We were moving them into storage for an unspecified future time and purpose. We were stockpiling arms for the distant revolution that we all had convinced ourselves would come soon.

I ended up on that highway because I had been a part of something that had taken hold of my imagination and heart, a world of infinite possibility that would free us all. I believed that there was no other more appealing avenue in life than to be an activist, a revolutionary who worked for justice. I knew from my reading of history that it was only through people actively trying to change the balance of forces, or a war, that made power concede to a demand. Intermixed with what I saw as lofty goals were other psychological factors. I wanted to be loved, to be rewarded, to be an outlaw, and to reject conformity. Was it rebellion or a rejection of authority, or had I fallen in love with the romantic idea that justice was pure and that goodness would not be affected by the means? Was all this intense activism a way to fill the spiritual hole that I felt from being born in America, which I considered to be a morally empty landscape? No matter what, I could not see the long distance I had traveled from my commitment to justice and equality to stockpiling guns and dynamite. Seeing that would take years.

That night on the New Jersey Turnpike, I still believed with all my heart that what Che Guevara[7] had said about revolutionaries being motivated by love was true, and that by being willing to die for the cause we were simply embodying the ideals that we were striving for. I also believed that our government ruled the world by force and that it was necessary to oppose it with force. I felt that we lived in a country that loved violence and that we had to meet it on its own terms. This is why I was moving explosives on the New Jersey Turnpike with Tim Blunk.

Chapter 2

Arrested

AS IT GOT darker and darker that cold and blustery evening, I was filled with a terrible sense of foreboding. It was mad to be moving so many weapons all at once, in bad weather, by ourselves, and especially when I was on the most wanted list. My bad feeling grew worse and worse. Weighing the danger to others and ourselves, Tim and I debated whether to stop at a motel and wait until daylight before moving on. We kept going because we did not want the explosives to sit in the U-Haul any longer than necessary. Leaving the turnpike, we took the back roads, away from people.

The hours that followed are a blur in my memory. But what happened that evening after Thanksgiving was the end of one lifetime and the beginning of another. My mistake leading to our arrest was simple. It was so simple that I have never been able to get over it. I had rented the storage place with an ID card that I had found in a wallet left mistakenly in a phone booth. Instead of using the name and changing the address, I used the ID itself. When the storage company called the number on the card to confirm the rental, they were told that no one by that name had rented any such space. The company had then notified the police, and when I

called again to confirm the arrangements, they insisted on knowing the exact time of our arrival.

When Tim and I finally pulled in, it was pitch dark and very
cold. The storage space was deserted and we could not get the combination to the front entrance to work. I had to get help from the
manager to open the lock. It was a large place with rows of sheds.
The whole area was isolated from any residential neighborhood
and surrounded by a fifteen-foot-high chain-link fence topped by a
small row of razor wire. As we were unloading the U-Haul, a lone
police car cruised down our aisle. Out came one police officer, who
proceeded to walk into the shed.

The rookie officer who questioned us was as scared as we were.
I had left a gun in the car while we were unloading the U-Haul and
I knew that if we were going to control the situation I had to go
back to the car and get it. I told the officer that I wanted to show
him my ID, but I had left it in the car. I nearly begged him to let
me get it. Tim stood in the storage space, trying to prevent the
policeman from seeing the weapons and explosives. The policeman
told me to get my ID. I quickly walked back to the car, opened the
passenger door, and reached down under the seat to find the gun
exactly where I had put it. My hand grasped the barrel and then the
handle. I felt the cold steel. I looked around to analyze our loca-
tion, to see if there was any place to exit. I left the gun on the floor
of the car, turned around, and went back inside. My ID had been
in my bag all along.

I could not bring myself to use the gun. For all of my bravado,
I did not want to shoot a police officer, or anyone else. I had never
shot or killed or hurt anyone, all I had done was target practice. I
did want to run or help create a diversion so that Tim could run,
but Tim was trying to pull the sheeting over several boxes on the

ground. Surprisingly, the cop did not pull his gun. As he was asking us who we were and what we were doing there, I could see that he was younger than we were. He seemed to be stalling for time, waiting for backup. It all happened so fast. The rookie had made a call, and then other police officers arrived within minutes. The moment they saw the dynamite and the guns, they went crazy. The police kept running between the shed where we had unloaded most of the dynamite to the back end of the U-Haul, which had both doors wide open. They were shouting on their car radios, while some of them drew their guns and ran off to search other aisles in the storage area. The police were yelling at us and at one another. They were afraid of the explosives and the ensuing pandemonium intensified their fear.

Several officers kicked Tim to the ground, until he lay in a pool of blood and mud. I was handcuffed, slapped, and shoved into the backseat of a police car. Seeing Tim on the ground and scores of police officers running back and forth between the U-Haul, the storage space, and us, hearing their shouts, feeling their fear and hatred, and knowing that in the chaos there was absolutely no escape, I slipped into a mental state in which I was no longer there at all. When a short man, a policeman with black hair and garlicky bad breath jammed his double-barreled pump-action shotgun into my temple and started screaming at me, the woman I was vanished. Suddenly I was surveying the scene above the action, and what I saw was a woman at the very absolute end of her life. I shut my eyes. I did not want to look anymore.

"Where the fuck is the backup? Where are the others? You cunt," he shouted hysterically, repeatedly punching me in the temple with the barrel of the gun. My eye was running, and I could not see as I turned that the barrel had turned with me and moved to the center of my forehead. I looked straight into his eyes, but he could not meet my stare. He just kept screaming, "You bitch, where's the backup?" My head was throbbing.

I felt as if I was emerging from a tunnel when I shocked myself by screaming, "Do it, motherfucker, just do it right now! Kill me and then it will be done!" I thought it, felt it, and meant it. I was calling for death, but my words had an unintended effect—they shocked him, and broke his hysteria. I wanted to die at that point. I felt everything that was happening at that moment was my fault, I wanted him to shoot me rather than be captured.

He did not pull the trigger, but he resumed hitting me, hard. First he hit me on one side of the head and then the other. Then he slid out of the seat, threw the shotgun on the ground, stuck his head back in the car, and spat on me, his saliva dripping down my cheek.

A few hours later in the New Jersey State Police barracks, the agents from the FBI and the Bureau of Alcohol, Tobacco, and Firearms (ATF), the New Jersey state troopers, and the Cherry Hill, New Jersey, police knew that they had made a significant arrest. They knew it because of the guns and dynamite they had captured. We had shotguns and automatic rifles, false identification, and explosives. There had been a three-year hunt for more than twenty different radicals, but they did not know that we were among the most wanted.

They did not know *who* we were and Tim and I would not tell them. We would not say anything. We were not cooperating. The police fingerprinted us, but they had to fly our prints to Washington, D.C., and wait for them to be identified. For some reason it took more than fourteen hours to get the results. While the police waited, we were kept in separate rooms, each of us chained to a chair. The agents from the ATF used the good cop/bad cop routine. They pummeled us with questions for hours at a time, and then offered us water (but no access to a bathroom). It was a very long fourteen hours, perhaps the longest I have ever spent. I replayed bits and pieces of my life. I was thinking about how eventually my parents would find out about my arrest and I wondered what they would do. I remembered my mother pleading with me to leave the country. Getting arrested was my fault, I thought, and I knew that everyone in my group would be angry with me. My wrists hurt from the handcuffs, my head was pounding from the earlier blows.

When who I thought was an FBI agent finally walked into the interrogation room, he stared at me so intensely that his eyes felt like they were drilling into my skull. His eyes darted back and forth across my face and then locked into mine. Then his lips curled and he said, "This bitch is a kike. Get the fugitive posters and find the kikes." As soon as he left, other agents brought a poster into the room and held it to my face, trying to find a match. Poster after poster followed, but within minutes they had identified me.

The FBI agent returned and said, "I can always tell a kike. At least now we know it's the kikes, the ones with the niggers."

As I sat chained, waiting for something else to happen, everything in the physical world receded and slow-moving pictures replaced the dirty, windowless room, the stale air, and the overwhelming ache to urinate. The sweet odor of my fear and anger filtered to my nose. My mind had retreated off again into its own world. I was on an inner journey that the police in the room could not begin to understand or even detect.

I was catapulted back to a childhood memory of my best friend's mother handing me a tuna fish sandwich, her housecoat sleeve riding up her arm to expose a tattooed number on her wrist. Eight years old, I questioned her. "What is that? Why is that on your wrist? Why don't you wash it off?"

She answered, "I can't wash it off."

I persisted. "Why?"

"It's from the concentration camp."

"What's that? Why did you go there?"

Her answer was short and clipped. "Because we are Jewish."

Later my mother explained to me what the camps were and who the Nazis were, the bad people hating us because we were Jewish. "Did we do something bad?" I asked. "Are we bad? Did we kill them first?" No. "Did you know other people in the camps?" Yes, my mom knew other people, and I knew some of them, as well. She explained that many of the people from our family had been exterminated in the camps. Exterminated? Like the termites in the house, like the TV commercial? I wondered. Her answers did not make me fully understand, but learning about genocide when I was eight years old dug into my soul so that, twenty years later, chained to a chair in the New Jersey State Police barracks, my wrists were aching and I recalled that tattoo on my friend's mother's arm.

Next in my mind, the picture of a young black man hanging by the neck appeared. I was remembering an old newspaper photograph on the cover of an album. My aunt was explaining it to me. Billie Holiday's song "Strange Fruit" about "the lynching of black people in the South and the tattoos and Nazi concentration camps were part of the same thing," she had said. White people and black people, Nazis and Jews, in my eight-year-old mind it was a strange but simple equation.

Images started tumbling, each one faster than the other, and memories of being Jewish that I had long forgotten. *Upstairs in the synagogue in the back with all the other women. Why did we have to sit behind an ugly curtain? My grandfather swaying back and forth, praying one morning while I hid behind the door and spied on him. Standing on the boardwalk watching hundreds of old people walk to the water to wash away their sins and remember the dead. (Even then I understood that sin was doing bad.) Then lighting the candles for the dead. Hearing a mix of Yiddish and English sounds both foreign and familiar, with my grandmother's sweet chicken soup spread before us.*

As I sat in the barracks under interrogation, waiting to be identified, my own relationship to my Judaism was irrevocably changed. *Calling me a kike, this is Jew hating,* I thought, *and it is the beginning of my captured life.* An internal vista opened in my head, and in that instant I owned it. I smiled at those government agents, those hateful, racist, anti-Semitic white men, because with their bigoted selves they had enabled me to shore up a wealth of inner resistance. When the FBI agent sneered, "Rosenberg," I shot back, "That's right."

I was labeled not just a "kike," but a "terrorist kike"—a label that was never to change. In the government's lexicon at the time, the only thing more extreme than a "kingpin narco-trafficker" was a terrorist, particularly a leftist terrorist. When it became known that I was a wanted fugitive in the Brink's robbery case and was on the FBI's most wanted list, my fate as far as the criminal justice system was concerned was sealed.

Chapter 3

Detention

AFTER WHAT SEEMED like an eternity, the next morning Tim and I were taken to our arraignment in Camden, New Jersey. The courtroom was filled with more armed agents than I had ever seen in any other courtroom before. We were charged with conspiracy to possess and transport weapons, explosives, and false identification across state lines. We pled not guilty and said we were revolutionaries. At first, bail was set for each of us at five million dollars, but later in that same proceeding bail was revoked and we were held over, pending a formal indictment. Some time after the arraignment was over, Tim and I were bundled into cars and driven at one hundred miles an hour to the New York Metropolitan Correctional Center (MCC) in Manhattan. The building, a large concrete structure amidst many government buildings, including the courts, sits in downtown Manhattan. Bordering it on one side is the Brooklyn Bridge and Chinatown on the other. It had a brutal appearance to me as we drove down the back street to the underground entrance. Helicopters buzzed overhead, and the blaring sirens and flashing lights pierced through the late-night quiet. Our arrival was being announced. We were the prize catch and every-one had to be made aware of it.

We had not eaten or washed our hands or been alone for two days. Tim and I had not been able to speak to each other. We had only gazed at each other in abject shame, with profound feelings of defeat and an occasional burst of defiance. We had been screamed at continuously and beaten up. We were emotionally and physically exhausted. Earlier someone had lifted me off the ground by my handcuffs, so as we stood at the elevators my arms, cuffed behind my back, were aching. When no one was looking, I slipped out of the cuffs. One hand at a time came out easily. It was my first mental game with capture, and it made me feel alive to give in to the thrilling desire to escape. Up until that moment, for most of the time, I had had the overwhelming desire to be dead.

Our identification with wanted black revolutionaries had pro-voked the police and the FBI into a state of frenzy. Their adrena-line production was in overdrive and they wanted to dispose of us so that they could get to work hunting down our associates. After we were booked, photographed, and deposited into detention, they locked us up in the bull pens. It was time for "cold cooking," a term I did not know then, but a reality that I would come to experience again and again. It meant being left to stew in a cold, isolated, and extremely uncomfortable environment. It could last for two or three days. Here I was shoved into a federal holding cell, empty, dark, and enormous. It had a closed front, the wall only marked by a heavy metal door with a very small window in it. Several marble benches, incongruous amid the dinginess, ran the length of the walls; two more sat in the middle of the room. The architecture was imperial decay, which struck me as funny, particularly when I no-ticed the steel toilet in a corner caked with urine and filth. There were messages carved wall to wall—TITO WAS HERE, SAM, SHIT, PETE FUCKS AGNES—all with distinct markings. As I examined them, it occurred to me that they were the modern equivalent of hieroglyphics. I understood the need to make a mark, to leave a message, to scream out loud in this disembodied hole, "I was here. Don't let me disappear." Then I saw one that read LONG LIVE BLACK LIBERATION. It relieved me greatly to see this one. I was not the first political person who laid on that bench. It was such a simple thing, yet it gave me much comfort. It was a sign that allowed me to temporarily put aside all the terrible feelings of pain and loss—the agony over the possibility that others would get caught as a result of our mistakes—that I had experienced since my arrest.

I inspected all the crevices and corners and saw no cameras. It was completely quiet and no one was peering at me through the slot in the door. I lay down on the bench and stretched all my muscles. Alone in that first of what would be hundreds of bull pens, I began to bargain, with whom I cannot say, but I began to talk to another party outside of myself. It wasn't prayer exactly; it was more like the beginning of what would become a mantra. I wasn't talking to God. It was not God that I prayed to; for me, it was the consciousness of being human. That was my God. The ability to locate beauty in the hideous, to create something in the face of devastation (man-made or otherwise), to determine one's own fate—those were my commitments and, in a spiritual sense, they were the things that I looked to for strength. I did not know that then, though. At the time, I drew on more radical examples of people who had been in the revolutionary struggle before me. I thought, *How do I resist?* I thought of people from the national liberation struggles who had raged throughout history, people like Bobby Sands[1], who had died on a hunger strike in prison while fighting for Irish independence; Lolita Lebrón[2], who had spent twenty-five years in U.S. prisons for the cause of Puerto Rican nationalism; and John Brown, the greatest ally to the black freedom struggle in American history, who had been vilified by the government and then hung from the neck. As I lay on that bench I retreated even further into the mental ritual I would go through again and again in the years that would follow, circling back to my beginnings in order to locate myself somewhere in the history of radicalism. And in search of an answer as to why I had made the choices that had landed me in that bullpen.

I was born in 1955, in the aftermath of the Second World War. I grew up on the Upper West Side of Manhattan, an only child. My father, known to his friends as Manny, short for Emanuel Rosenberg, was a World War II veteran and a dentist. His dental practice was in Spanish Harlem, where he worked with the most underserved and marginalized communities. There were occasions when he got paid in goods and services rather than money, and he would bring something home that had "fallen off the back of a truck." He had traveled to Selma to help during the civil rights movement and had always volunteered his skills. My mother, Bella, was a theatrical producer and former film editor. She helped struggling visual artists and writers to begin their careers. My parents believed in civil rights, the early anti-nuclear movement, and they were against the Vietnam War.

In 1964, when I was eight years old and attending the Walden School, Andrew Goodman, who was to become one of its most famous alumni, was slain by the Klan for his participation in the voter registration drive in Mississippi. Even though he was my senior by more than ten years, his younger brother was in the class ahead of me, and his family was very active in school affairs. The school became a base of support for the civil rights movement, raising money and recruiting people to go south. James Chaney was assassinated along with Andrew Goodman. His family was from Mississippi, and his brother Ben, who was twelve years old at the time, was sent north and later enrolled at Walden. He became my friend, and for the next several years I acutely watched events with the added perspective of what I imagined to be Ben's experience.

I continued at Walden through high school, during the height of the anti-Vietnam War movement. At first I went to anti-war demonstrations in New York with my parents. But, by 1970, I was attending with others from my school. That year, I went to the big anti-war mobilization in Washington and I got separated from my friend Janet and walked into a police action against people who had raised a North Vietnamese flag on the Justice Department building. I had never seen people getting beaten with clubs and dragged into wagons, except on television. Then the police let loose tear gas to disperse the crowd of thousands. I ran to get away from the gas and the police until I fell on a grassy slope and pressed my head into the grass to stop the searing pain and tears that I had gotten from just a small whiff of it. When I returned home, I discovered that other Walden students had been beaten up by the police. Furious, I joined the Student Mobilization Committee to End the War in Vietnam, an anti-war group that was organized by college students who were members of Students for a Democratic Society. My high school chapter organized teach-ins and actions against the war in schools all over the city. The Vietnam War, specifically what our government was doing against the people of Vietnam, was predominating all of my thinking about the world and my own responsibility in it. Daily, I watched on TV the carpet bombings, the napalming of whole villages, and the tiger cages that were built out of bamboo that were smaller than a bathtub and used to torture pro-Vietcong villagers. As the body counts got higher and higher on both sides, I groped for any justification that made sense.

I was fifteen in 1970, and along with millions of other people across the globe, I wanted to make change, stop war, and build a peaceful and just world. It seemed possible because there were clearly drawn sides between war profiteers and supporters of the establishment and the majority of people who were resisting and demanding transformation.

Perhaps my choices and life course were the result of a combination of nature and nurture. Despite being surrounded by middle-class privilege, I seemed to be aware of injustice and inequities around me. At the age of five I had first seen a legless man on a skateboard and refused to go into a store to buy shoes, because, as I angrily explained to my mother, how could I buy shoes when the man had no feet. Maybe from that moment when I understood the oppression of others, followed by the images from Selma, Alabama, and Haiphong, Vietnam, and the rows and rows of burned-out houses along Morris Avenue in the Bronx, my skin had become so thin that the pain and suffering of others penetrated my own blood and mingled with it and drove me to an agony of distraction that meant I had to act.

Fourteen years later I still believed in the need for change. I began to converse with all those radical spirits, comparing what I imagined they had gone through to what was happening to me. I thought, *If it isn't worse than this, I can manage it.* But then it got much worse.

Chapter 4

Conviction

OUR TRIAL, IN April to May of 1985, was a three-week accelerated collision between the prosecution and us. In the months leading up to the actual court proceeding, we remained housed in New York City. Every time we went to the federal court, in Newark, New Jersey, escorted in a high-security caravan that included helicopters and police of every type, the Holland Tunnel was closed down. If we were not already misunderstood or despised, our impact on thousands of harassed commuters would have been enough to spark an instant mass hatred. The outcome of the trial was a given even before the jury was selected. We did nothing but escalate it.

The security team responsible for us was assembled out of the Joint Terrorist Task Force, which included U.S. marshals, FBI agents, and local New York police. One member of the team was Bernard B. Kerik, who many years later would become New York City's police commissioner under Mayor Rudolph Giuliani, and later still go to jail on charges of tax fraud and perjury. The first time we were due in court for pretrial motions, we were taken to the underground garage of the detention center, where one of the waiting cars was a black Mercedes-Benz. A member of the security team told me to get in. I had over forty pounds of chains wrapped around me, which was standard transport attire. I looked at him and said, "I refuse to get into that Nazi car." The officers thought that was very funny. One retorted, "This is the car we use for officials; you don't know how lucky you are." Then, several of them picked me up and put me headfirst into the backseat. That was the end of the discussion.

Our trial was a venomous and hostile drama. The judge was Frederick B. Lacey. He had been a naval officer, and then the U.S. attorney for the district of New Jersey from 1969–71. He was appointed a U.S. district judge by President Richard Nixon, and his reputation was that he was tough. He was also a member of the Foreign Intelligence Surveillance Court. This was the court that heard FBI and CIA applications for international wiretaps in cases pertaining to national security. Judge Lacey was as highly politicized in his way as we were in ours. We tried to present a necessity defense, saying that the government was guilty of war crimes against people in the developing world and at home. We had lawyers who helped us research and prepare our brief. Judith Holmes, an attorney who had experience in defending other political activists, worked with us for weeks as we organized our own defense. We said that we were part of an organized illegal resistance movement and that we were acting out of conscience. We opposed the covert U.S. involvement in Central America, the government's backing of the Contras in Nicaragua, and the illegal sale of arms to the right-wing paramilitary groups throughout Latin America. We also opposed the racist regime in South Africa and wanted an end to apartheid. We argued that the United States had waged an illegal war via the FBI's COINTELPRO (Counter Intelligence Program) against the radical and progressive movements for freedom and liberation among black people, Native People, the people of

Puerto Rico, and other oppressed people, forces, and groups. We believed that as a result of COINTELPRO the civil liberties and human rights of thousands of citizens had been abrogated.

The prosecution, however, asserted that because we were apprehended with hundreds of pounds of explosives, numerous guns, and extensive amounts of false identification, we trafficked in violence (although they did not link any of the materials found to any actual activities) and therefore could not talk about politics. We were simply terrorists. It was their court and their outcome.

Our lawyers, Susan V. Tipograph and Mark Gombiner, both lawyers who were part of the legal community that fought to uphold constitutional rights and defend extremely unpopular defendants, believed that if we put on a necessity defense we would face the wrath of the court, and so we fired them the day our trial began in order to represent ourselves. Still, they sat with us and acted as our legal advisers, and when sentencing came, their hopes took over and they predicted that we would get fifteen years. But Tim and I knew differently—the lawyers had been right in the first place about the anger of the court and we expected stiffer sentences.

We were each convicted of eight counts of conspiracy to possess and transport explosives, guns, and false identification across state lines. We were each sentenced to fifty-eight years in federal prison for possession of weapons and explosives. It was the longest sentence ever given for a possession offense. Judge Lacey compared us to Russian spies during the cold war and instructed us to read *The God that Failed*, a classic collection of essays by six prominent thinkers who had become disillusioned with communism and through their ideological rebirths became militant anti-Communists.

About a week after our sentencing we were in the visiting room at the MCC. The rumor was that Tim was being shipped out any day. Every visit was charged with intense emotion because we did not know if it would be the last time we would see each other. We felt we had been living in hell since our arrest and it was almost impossible to deal with the idea that we would never meet again. There were several people visiting us that day. Our lawyers, who had heard the rumor, too, had come to say good-bye to Tim. They were joined by paralegals from various groups that had supported us during our trial.

Someone said that we needed to file a notice of appeal. There was a thirty-day deadline for filing from the time of sentencing, and the clock was ticking. Tim, at one end of the table, said no, he did not want to file anything, because there was no expectation of justice. Everyone at the table weighed in on this one way or the other and several people agreed with Tim. I looked around the table and thought, *Wow, these people don't have to do fifty-eight years. We do. I want options. We have to fight this sentence.* Our trial had been on many levels a farce, in part because of the drama we had chosen to create. I had begun to realize that the question of how to challenge the criminal justice system has almost as many answers as the number of people who are caught up in it. I said, "I want to file. I want to fight the sentence every way we can, through an appeal, through parole, through political pressure. Even though we said the system would not last as long as our sentence, I am not sure I believe that at all." Tim said nothing, and the appeal was filed.

Ironically, the charges related to the Brink's case that had sent me underground in the first place, were dropped by then U.S. Attorney Rudolph Giuliani. The U.S. attorney's office said they were dropped because I had such a long sentence from my conviction. But I and my lawyers believed that the charges had been dropped because of lack of evidence.

By 1985, there were many other people who had been arrested from various radical political movements. The list included sixteen

Puerto Ricans from an armed group called Los Macheteros[1]; the Ohio Seven[2], four men and three women from a clandestine collective against apartheid, racism, and economic injustice charged with the bombing of U.S. military and corporate targets; the New York Eight who included African American revolutionaries, who together had been targeted in the post-Brink's investigation and subpoenaed to a grand jury but had refused to testify; Joe Doherty, an Irish Republican Army member who had been involved in one of the most spectacular prison escapes in Northern Ireland, who had been caught in New York and was now being held on extradition charges to be returned to Ireland; and Marilyn Buck, a revolutionary who spent all of her adult life supporting the black liberation struggle and who had been in and out of prison as a result, and Linda Evans, a member of SDS, and later the Weathermen, women from the group with which Tim and I were involved. Marilyn was wanted on the Brink's charges, and Linda had been indicted for harboring Marilyn.

Almost forty political prisoners were being held in the MCC. It was a security nightmare for the authorities to have so many political prisoners together in one facility, but for us it was a moment of incredible solidarity. All the women, housed on the same floor, had daily access to one another.

In September 1985, we were facing our prison terms or future trials, and we all knew that the time we had together in detention was limited. I was twenty-nine years old. Each one of us had a story behind why we were there. We were a diverse group. We were activists and revolutionaries and all of us were motivated to act against the government because we thought it was our responsibility to right the injustices and wrongs as we saw them. I was one of the seventeen people who were wanted stemming from a federal indictment alleging association and conspiracy with the group that carried out the Brink's New York robbery. In 1981, the Black Liberation Army[3], a small outgrowth of the Black Panther Party, had carried out an armed robbery of a Brink's truck in Nyack, New York. Two police officers, Waverly Brown and Edward O'Grady and a Brink's guard, Peter Paige, were killed in the shootout that followed the robbery. Four people were arrested near the scene, one of them a good friend of mine. The Joint Terrorist Task Force, a group made up of members of the New York Police Department, the FBI, and other intelligence agencies, began an investigation that led to two major federal conspiracy trials and a New York State trial. Scores of people were imprisoned for refusing to testify and cooperate with grand juries, and anyone identified through political association with those arrested or named by the government investigation was targeted. It was a terrible and dark time and we felt as if we were living in a raging war. I had never experienced this kind of repression, and there was a dangerous escalation of the stakes and consequences, for all involved. It was frightening.

I knew and had worked with several people who were under investigation. My longtime teacher and friend Dr. Mutulu Shakur was wanted by the FBI and the New York Police Department, and I was fearful that his life and work would be snuffed out. He had been an organizer in the black community and a revolutionary his entire adult life. He was a health worker in the South Bronx at Lincoln Hospital, and he later became a doctor of traditional Chinese medicine and acupuncture as a way of fighting the terrible heroin epidemic that was ravaging his brothers and sisters in the community. His FBI file was already thousands of pages. Now he was followed and harassed by FBI agents who would walk up to him in the street and open their jackets to reveal their guns and imitating the shape of a gun with their empty hands, pretended to shoot him. People would drive by his mother's house in Queens and then run into the house and fire their weapons. His mother was blind and lived alone, so she could not identify the perpetrators. But there was nothing secret about the doings of the FBI. As their investigation grew and evolved, I became a target, too.

In 1977, I was working as a drug counselor at Lincoln Hospital. In high school, I had watched one of my best friends become a heroin addict and end up dying from an overdose. By the time I was working in the Bronx, the community had been plagued by a massive heroin addiction, which many people thought was government sponsored, at least in the sense that the police looked the other way and used the presence of drugs as an excuse to criminalize the entire community. I was not sure if that analysis was accurate but I certainly witnessed the devastation that drug use caused and saw that no one was doing anything about it. Wanting to stop the vicious cycle of poverty and drugs, I began to study acupuncture and Chinese medicine with other community-based health workers at the Lincoln Hospital Detox Center. Dr. Shakur was one of them. He had gone to China and seen how with the use of acupuncture millions of opium addicts were effectively treated. In 1980, after a three-year course, we passed our doctoral exams at the Montréal Institute of Chinese Medicine and moved our practice from the South Bronx to Harlem. We were part of the beginning of the New Age holistic health movement. We were led by former revolutionaries and activists from the late 1960s and 1970s, people of color from what had been the Black Panthers, the Young Lords, a U.S.-based Puerto Rican Independence and advocacy organization, and White Lightning, a poor people's community organizing project. We treated drug addiction, diabetes, asthma, and all the diseases afflicting the poorest of the poor. We called ourselves the "sneaker doctors" after the "barefoot doctors" movement in China, which had been a project that trained a quarter of a million Chinese people to learn acupuncture to detoxify several million opium addicts.

In March 1982, I was on my way to work. I rounded the corner on 147th Street and Eighth Avenue walking toward the Harlem Institute of Acupuncture. As I looked down the block I saw an Army tank coming toward me with a huge gun rolling down the one-way street in the wrong direction. I had never seen a tank except in the movies. It looked obscenely out of place on the quiet deserted residential street. I had no idea what would trigger the men inside to start shooting. I knew that they could not have driven it to this Harlem block for show. Then I looked up and saw flak-jacketed sharpshooters wearing face masks and lying down or crouching on all the rooftops of the buildings next to the clinic. There wasn't a soul out on the street. No one was standing on the corner. No little children were stepping off their stoops to go to the park or to school. There were no patients standing in front of our office, I realized thankfully. I was the only one, a white person out of place, amid all the cops with guns. I knew that they were there to search the clinic and I hoped they were not specifically looking for me. I did not feel that I merited a tank and certainly not sharpshooters. Not wanting to find out how far down the block I would get before someone either shot me or simply grabbed me, I about-faced and walked as fast as I could short of a breakneck run to the corner, then around it, and down into the subway. I did not start breathing freely again until I was miles away, standing in the subway, alternating between fury and fear.

The FBI did not find the person they were looking for that day. No one was killed or shot or even arrested. Instead, they had kicked in the front door of the clinic carrying blank grand jury subpoenas, filled out the names of the twenty staffers present, and then confiscated all of the clinic's records. This was one of several raids by the FBI against black-led community institutions that had associations with black revolutionaries.

In September 1982, six months after the FBI raid on the Harlem Institute of Acupuncture, I was in my car listening to WINS radio, when I heard that there had been a new and superseding indictment in the Brink's robbery. This meant that the grand jury had added new people to the indictment. The announcer read the list. There were over twenty names. I almost missed hearing my own. I drove around the Upper West Side where I lived and finally parked on Riverside Drive and sat in my car. I was certain I could not get a fair trial; I was afraid of going to prison, but also afraid to flee. I had no time in which to think through whether I should flee or go to jail. What about my family? My burgeoning career as an acupuncturist? What about my dog? What about my new car? I was twenty-six years old. I thought, *I'll fight the conspiracy, I'll turn myself in, and I'll get a lawyer.* I went back and forth in my mind, weighing my options as I sat in the car. I caressed the dashboard and smelled the newness of it. I listened to the recurring WINS report over and over again. I did not cry, but I was terribly sad. I felt I was being forced to abandon my life. Instead of returning home, I drove to my office. After circling the block twice to see if any police were there, I ran in and grabbed all of the money I could find and random bits and pieces of things that I thought would be valuable or that I could sell. Then I fled.

Two and a half years later at MCC with all the other political people in prison, we were now trying to help one another reinforce our identity as political prisoners. One afternoon we were sitting together, eating our government-issue lunch of cheese sandwiches and coffee and reading a news article about the Puerto Rican *independentistas* on trial in Hartford, Connecticut. The newest woman prisoner was Lucy Segarra, one of the Macheteros. She had been charged with participating in an action in which toys were distributed to poor children in Hartford on Three Kings Day. What made this illegal was that the money used to purchase the toys came, allegedly, from the $7 million Wells Fargo robbery carried out in 1983 by Los Macheteros in Hartford. Though that robbery was the single largest ever carried out in the United States, no one was injured and the money was never recovered.

When our talk shifted from the trial to the effects of a hurricane on New York, something in the discussion of a violent storm triggered a reaction in Lucy. Her eyes filled up with tears of anger, hatred, shame, and fear. In a soft, halting voice she told us how the Mexican authorities, in conjunction with the FBI, had beaten her (without leaving marks), threatened her by saying they would kill her children, and interrogated her in a locked cell for days while her children were held outside. Finally, they had transported her, placing a hood over her head so that she would not know her whereabouts. They told her that no one knew where she was, that no one would be able to help her, and that as far as the world was concerned she had disappeared. They said that they had killed and broken others in her group, and that still others were giving her up. She went on to describe the men and the place and her deep concern for her children. Always she came back to her children.

As I returned to my own cell, I realized that living in the midst of this prison madness can either take your soul or give it back to you. I resolved to take mine back.

Throughout the months of pre-trial detention and then awaiting sentencing, my parents came to visit. It was the beginning of rebuilding our relationship. My parents attended my trial, despite their profound disagreements with me and my friends. Meeting for the first time since my arrest, my mother was so angry that she could hardly speak. She sat in the visiting room, all dressed up and seething. My father cried. It would be a long rapprochement, but even then my parents met me halfway. They always met me halfway.

Later that same year, John Gotti was arrested. Finally, someone else's notoriety had eclipsed me and the other political prisoners. I was glad he was in the spotlight. Seeing him in jail, with his swagger, his cigar butt, and the terrible charisma he emitted regardless of his circumstances, I knew it to be true—he was the boss, the man, the Don. During what was described as the Pizza Connection trial, the MCC housed as many Mafia members as political prisoners. Unbelievably, we all mixed in the prison's attorney-client visiting room, they with their gold crucifixes and we with our revolutionary passions. Although the two groups could not have been more different, we had in common a strong code of principle—we would not snitch, not in our cases, in our lives, or inside the jail itself. In that respect, our honor united us. John Gotti had never witnessed such loyalty before in a group outside the mob. He liked me, and he liked Tim, too.

On my thirtieth birthday I had a visit with my attorney and was off the women's floor for several hours. When I returned and stood in the saliport, which separated the outside world from the secured area inside, the cop removing my handcuffs gave me a big smile. I responded with the convict glaze, being in no mood to smile. As the steel door popped open and I walked in, everyone on the floor started singing and I saw the banner they had hung across a set of bars: HAPPY BIRTHDAY, SUSAN. The party—complete with wine and scotch and a sumptuous Italian meal of eggplant, veal, and chicken—had been bought and paid for by John Gotti. It was one of the best birthdays I had ever had. And there wasn't a cop in sight. (Several months later, thirteen corrections officers were indicted on corruption charges for selling the food contract at the

MCC to a Mafia-run company and several administrators were charged with bribery and corruption.)

In October, ten days after my birthday, eleven months after my arrest, I was transferred without warning to Arizona. What had been a year of turmoil, heartbreak, resisting capture, trial and prosecution, changed instantly into "doing time."

Part Two

Tucson

Chapter 5

Transport

THE TWO-LANE highway was empty except for speeding trucks and an occasional car. It was a cold November. The ice was thick, and the sun glistened on the snow piled high on each embankment. The light, mixed with the freezing air, made the passing scene sharp and clear. We were driving through the Pennsylvania hills early in the morning. In the now-familiar black Mercedes-Benz it was a smooth ride, for sure. The windows were rolled up, the air heavy. Five hours passed in silence, and the tension rose. The driver, part of a new detail, kept watching me in the rearview mirror. The trooper in the front kept checking his revolver. The jangling of my waist chains and a sporadic cackle from the police radio were the only sounds. The phone rang and the driver picked it up. After some murmuring back and forth the driver accelerated. The helicopter overhead flew low and buzzed us. The driver said, "We're late, but they'll hold the plane." When we passed the road sign for Harrisburg, I knew we were approaching our destination. I knew because I had heard that this was the East Coast departure point for the federal prisoner transport.

I never knew until I was in prison that at most major airports, in the back or off to the side, there is a military section. It is for use by all branches of the Department of Defense in case of national emergencies, for private use by those with executive privilege, for civil defense maneuvers, and for the shipping and handling of federal prisoners. We drove to the back of the Harrisburg airport, where we were screened, checked, and waved through the gate. As we passed through the rows of fences and barbed wire I thought, *Dual function, to keep us in—and keep the rest out.* I was sad and afraid: this was my departure from the past, from the life I had known. I was leaving the East Coast, my family, my friends, my patients, my compatriots, everything that was familiar though now distorted by the extreme circumstances of my arrest and the turmoil of the trial. Going to what? To where? To be with whom? Serving fifty-eight years in prison was impossible to fathom. I wasn't fazed by the military presence and police intimidation; rather, what I feared was the unknowable future. The slow death that had been imposed on me by vindictive prosecution and over sentencing produced the deepest of aches. And what of the movement? I didn't know.

We drove onto the runway toward the plane. It was a standard-looking Boeing 707. The stairs were down; ice hung from the wings. Prison guards and U.S. marshals surrounded the plane. They all had shotguns or automatic weapons cradled in their arms. It occurred to me that many of these men, these police, had probably been in Vietnam. In that split instant of surveying the scene, the full military nature of the transport hit me. Should I have tried to escape, the sheer overkill of the firepower would have been directed at me.

Then I saw a line of about sixty men standing perpendicular to the tail of the plane. All of them were dressed in short-sleeved khaki shirts and pants and blue prison-issue slip-on sneakers. They were handcuffed and chained. It was below freezing. Many were stamping their feet, jumping up and down, and blowing air that formed frost. Almost all of them were young African Americans. They had been removed from the plane so that I could be put on.

Time stopped, and thoughts began to crowd my head as I looked at these black men standing in the cold, surrounded by white men with weapons. I remembered the first funeral of a black revolutionary that I had ever attended. In 1973, a former Black Panther turned Black Liberation Army member was in a shoot-out with the New York City police. Wanted for bank robbery, twenty-one-year-old Twyman Myers led a rooftop chase for many blocks before being brought down by eighty bullets. His funeral in Harlem had brought hundreds of mourners, including busloads of schoolchildren from a community center in Brooklyn that was then part of the Black United Front. In one life-altering moment I watched the children pile out of the buses and then I looked up to see flak-jacketed sharpshooters lying facedown on rooftops with their rifles trained on the children.

As my mind returned to the present, I felt a unity with the men, despite the divide between us. I peered into the distance to see their faces, understanding that their history as black people had placed them there. Their journey had begun with the "middle passage" four hundred years ago when they had been originally captured as slaves, and now, in their struggle to survive and live, they were waiting to enter the modern slave ship. Knowing that these men were standing and waiting for me brought my life into sharp relief. I remembered the words of John Brown—"America is birthed in the blood of slavery"—and all my sadness turned to fury. I went hot in the cold morning.

The marshals had surrounded me and hustled me out of the car, almost picking me up to get me to the stairs and onto the plane. For hours, through the entire drive, I had not said a word, not uttered a sound, but as I stood up from the car in anger, I found my voice. I yelled to the men standing there, "I am sorry these police made you wait in the cold, brothers! I'm sorry! They didn't need to do that!"

And for one short moment, the chains, the guns, the cold, the agony—all of it receded into the background. A man on the line yelled back: "Aren't you Susan? I was with Ray at MCC!"

"Yes!" I shouted. "I am!"

He turned to the others and said, "She is ours! She's Black Liberation Army!"

Another man called out: "Thank God for the BLA! Don't worry, baby! The more they fear you, the more they respect you!"

"We will win one day!" I yelled. "Maybe not now, but one day!"

A third man said, "I know about Assata! Don't worry!"

In the few seconds the exchange lasted, the guards turned their weapons first on me and then on the line of prisoners. The marshals began to drag me toward the plane. At the top of the stairs I turned to look once more at the dreary, bleak northeastern landscape. The cold wind hit my face hard as tears streamed down my cheeks.

The prison transport is like no other air travel. The plane is stripped down to the bone; there are no dividers between first class and coach, and there is no movie telling you where emergency exits are or how to use your seat as a flotation device in case of a water crash. In addition to my forty pounds of chains, I wore handcuffs encased in the dreaded "black box," a wooden box that closes over the few links between each cuff and is in turn shut with a padlock, completely immobilizing the hands. The black box is always the sign of a serious criminal. Back then very few prisoners were black-boxed, and the number of women even fewer.

The prisoners who had been waiting on the tarmac were moved

to their seats, and the plane took off. In the front row, directly behind the cockpit, I was surrounded by marshals whose duty it was
to ensure that no one communicated with me. Every few days the
transport moves hundreds of prisoners—men and women—from
one place to another, all over the country. There are many reasons
why a prisoner is moved. Most prisoners are moved several times
during the course of their sentence. Some are being sent from their
trials to their first prison, some are being sent by court order to
a specific prison, others are being shipped to prison hospitals or
mental units, and a few are being released.

Our first stop was in Ohio. A group of men entered the plane
and the vibes, which were already hostile, got worse. This group
looked like they had been through a shipwreck. Six of them were
chained together by twos, and they were dirty and disheveled. They
all appeared to be drugged. I heard one marshal call them the "psy-
cho crew." These men were going to the U.S. Medical Center for
Federal Prisoners in Springfield, Missouri, known back then as the
prison for the criminally insane. I could not stop turning around to
peer at them. One man looked like he had been locked up forever.
His beard was down to his chest, his face so chiseled that his skin
was translucent. I noticed that his glasses were held together with
paperclips on both sides, and so he became "Paperclip" to me. He
was very tall and painfully skinny. The marshals shoved him into
a window seat in the middle rows of the plane. The man next to
him, a small, dark Latino, was none too pleased. He kept shooting
glances at Paperclip and scowling. I thought to myself, *Chill, the
guy is sick. He can't help the way he looks.*

On this leg of the flight they fed us. Everyone was given a white
box, containing an ancient apple, some colored juice facsimile, and
a wrapped sandwich consisting of two pieces of white bread and a
slab of mystery meat. The rumble of complaints that went through

the passengers only got worse when the marshals pulled out their Big Macs and fries and munched in front of us.

We were to land in Indianapolis, where we would all be driven to the county jail to wait until the airlift took off again the next day. As the plane began its descent, the marshals removed our lunch boxes. Just as the pilot said, "Everyone, be seated," I felt the air pressure drop. My stomach went into my throat and turned over. The landing wheels engaged and, in the same instant, a scream of terror reverberated through the rush of air. Air released at ninety miles an hour is one of the loudest sounds imaginable, and yet that scream cut through it and reverberated.

I turned around so I could see the rest of the seats in back of me. I took in the scene behind me. The emergency window exit was gone and the Latino prisoner was in danger of being sucked out of the plane. He had looped his cuffs around the armrest, but his body was horizontal. Paperclip had gone through the window and was lying flattened against the wing, holding on to the edge. The plane had still not touched the ground.

For a moment, everyone on the plane was frozen in time. Then a tumult ensued. The head marshal grabbed the clinging Latino prisoner and threw him into the aisle in order to reach the window. The prisoners started yelling and cheering. One marshal ran to the front, where all the others had gathered around me, since I had been deemed the greatest security threat and "escape risk." (*Good,* I thought.) Then the marshal in charge started screaming at one of the younger ones. "Get out on that wing, get that motherfucker."

The man looked at him a moment before screaming back, "Fuck you! You go out there, you fat fuck." The chain of command instantly broke. This only incited the prisoners to yell even louder. Now everyone was standing up and almost chanting, "Go, man, go!"

The plane taxied to a stop and the marshals worked to retake control. Stun guns and batons came out. There was frantic running in and out of the cockpit, the copilot finally emerging with a pistol in his hand. The prisoners got quiet and sat back down. While the plane was still pulling into the gate, the marshals were giving each other orders to search the plane and all of us. As soon as the plane stopped, they were on the ground handing off the prisoners one at a time, shaking them down, and putting them on the buses.

The sirens outside the plane began to blast. Alarms were going off everywhere. Paperclip had vanished. A team from the Federal Bureau of Prisons came out to meet us in full riot gear, loaded, vested, and now reorganized for a hunt. The buses drove off as soon as they filled up.

I remained on the plane, watching it all happen, until they transferred me to a van that was serving as the communications post for the search. I sat in that van on the runway for hours and listened to all the radio communications, first from airport security, the Bureau of Prisons (BOP), the U.S. marshals, the Indiana State Police, the Indianapolis police, and finally from the FBI. After the first hour, two Jeeps drove up. A team of marshals emerged from the first Jeep holding a pair of handcuffs and a torn BOP uniform shirt. One held part of the plastic frame from a pair of standard BOP-issue eyeglasses. Out of the second Jeep came three men wearing FBI windbreakers. They were the forensics team. They took the items and drove off. While I watched, I kept thinking I would see bloodhounds. I had visions of Tony Curtis and Sydney Poitier, in the classic movie *The Defiant Ones,* dragging themselves through the swamps with the dogs at their backs. But in the midst of all this manpower and activity, it took many hours before the lieutenant manning the radios realized that they had forgotten the canine unit. By then, Paperclip was long gone.

The next day, I was taken on a small jet to my newest point of entry into the system. The Men's Federal Correctional Institution in Tucson, Arizona, had transformed a portion of its segregation unit into a detention center for women. There were over a thousand men housed there and only three women. I arrived in the middle of the night. I was bundled off the plane and into a waiting van, accompanied by dozens of cars with agents of all types. When we arrived at the entrance to the prison, there was a line of correctional officers standing at the front gate. Every one of them was armed. I was rushed past them and into the prison, behind the walls. It was now early morning and I knew that there were many more staff people than there would usually be at that hour. I hoped that they were not all there to receive me, but they were. Even still, no one made visual or verbal contact with me. I was "the package" and I was being "delivered." Even though I was surrounded by officers inside the prison building, which itself lay behind two barbed-wire fences, I was still not in a secure enough setting for them. I was still in my street clothes—a pair of jeans, leather shoes, and a purple long-sleeved shirt with a suit jacket over it. I was happy to be dressed in those clothes; they were mine and they fit, and although I was surrounded by people foreign to me and shackled to the hilt, I still felt familiar to myself. Still, I knew that the people around me would not be satisfied until I was in a jumpsuit and locked behind a foot-thick steel door.

I was escorted into a large room that looked like a storage room, but it was devoid of any equipment or supplies. The officers locked the door and left me standing there. I was alone for the first time since leaving New York two days earlier. The reality of my situation was settling in, and I did not like it. I had seen too many cowboy hats on the way in and had felt lots of hostility. I had to assume that my reputation preceded me and that I was in for a bad time.

The fact that so few other women were there would mean almost complete lockdown, and I knew that I might be in solitary confinement for a very long time.

As I was dwelling on all these thoughts, the door opened and five female COs walked in. One of them was carrying an armful of jumpsuits, and another had a stun gun in her hand. None of them moved very quickly to remove my chains, but I did not make a sound. I really was in unknown territory and I did not know what was going to happen. I was afraid. The COs all appeared to be in their late twenties (my age), and they looked well fed and fit. All of them were white. The one carrying the uniforms dropped them on the floor. For a while we just stood there staring at one another. Then I stuck out my chained hands and said, "Can we take these off now?" The CO with the most stripes on her shirt nodded to the other officers and they flew into action. One of them uncuffed my feet; another removed the black box. But then the handcuff key did not work. Each one took turns trying to turn the key, but to no avail. It was ludicrous, but I was not laughing because the thought of their having to use metal cutters to break the cuffs made me anxious.

The tension grew until one of the COs walked out and, after a few minutes, came back with several people in tow. One of them was the prison locksmith. He was a smiling, jovial fellow who thought the whole thing was funny. He was also the first person in Tucson who spoke to me.

"Hey, girl, we won't cut off your wrist," he said, laughing. He took out a ring of keys and soon the lock fell open.

When he was through I looked him in the eye and just said, "Thanks, man."

Once the cuffs were off, everything went into high gear. "Strip, bend, spread them, lift your tongue, lift your breasts, raise your arms, squat again." And I complied—I had decided when I left New York that as long as I wasn't having a cavity search I would comply. Finally, one of the COs picked up an orange-colored jumpsuit from the floor. It was enormous. I looked at it with disgust, particularly since the others were at that moment ripping up my own clothes and putting them into a plastic garbage bag.

"What size is that?" I asked.

"It's a size forty."

I just looked at them. I was a size six. At last I said, "No way, you have to get a smaller one."

One of the COs blurted out, "We thought you'd be a lot bigger."

It turned out to be a men's size forty. But there wasn't a smaller one in the pile. And so they dressed me in it, walked me from building to building through a maze of halls and passageways, all of which led to a single cell with a steel door, and there I began my federal sentence.

Chapter 6

Tucson Federal Prison

IT WAS NOT until dawn that I could look out the window of my cell and discern anything about my physical surroundings. In the morning light I could see past the wooden fence and through the wire up to the sky, and I got my first glimpse of the land.

In Tucson, the federal prison for men is located in a valley surrounded by four mountain ranges. The arid weather produces a dramatic sky and that first morning I saw it transform from a wash of indigo into streaks of glorious purple before the darkness was gone and the clear blue looked like the hottest part of the inner flame of the sun. On an average day the temperature would reach 110 degrees. I learned later that if you touched a piece of plastic you'd blister.

When my cell door popped open at 6:00 a.m., a small, thin, auburn-haired woman appeared before me. Her intense brown eyes checked me out from head to toe. "Susan?" she asked.

"Alejandrina?" I responded.

We both nodded and a thrilling current ran through me. Alejandrina Torres—Alex—and I had never met, yet we were comrades. She had known I was coming, and I in turn knew about her history. Seeing her was a relief beyond measure. I had been cast into a series of unknowns, handled by people who hated me without even knowing me, surrounded by men who emitted an ever-present threat of physical assault, and then dropped into a desert pit in the middle of the night. It had been a matter of honor, dignity, and integrity for me not to exhibit anything but strength so that now, in the midst of all that mental anguish, finding a comrade seemed like a miracle, an electrical jolt to the spirit and at the same time a soothing balm to the rage I felt.

In my mind Alex was a courageous Puerto Rican freedom fighter. I hoped that we would become friends but I didn't really know her. I knew that Alex was one of four people who had been arrested, tried, and convicted for seditious conspiracy against the U.S. government, in 1983. The four were part of a long history of resistance to domination and colonial occupation, a history that reached back to 1492 with the tragic arrival of Christopher Columbus in the New World. The most explosive expression of this resistance had come in the middle of the twentieth century with the rise of the Puerto Rican Nationalist Party under the leadership of Don Pedro Albizu Campos and Don Juan Antonio Corretjer. Then came the Fuerzas Armadas de Liberación Nacional (FALN). By 1985 twenty members of the Puerto Rican armed struggle had been locked up in the United States. They believed that their homeland was an illegal possession of the United States and that it was their right and duty to fight to free their island in a war for national liberation. Refusing to accept the authority of the U.S. government, they considered themselves prisoners of war. They were not criminals, not terrorists, but rather patriots and freedom fighters who saw their incarceration as another front in their anti-colonial resistance. They considered themselves counterparts of the Irish Republican Army in H-Block, or the South Africans on Robben

Island. Their captors didn't know what to make of them. They were collectively considered a grave threat to national security, and individually they were fierce. Alex was one of these *independentistas*.

I walked with Alex to her cell. She told me: "With you here, we're now four women in this desert prison with a thousand men. We're in a corridor of the segregation building, and in daylight we're allowed to move up and down the alleyway and to sit in a small day room with a TV attached to the wall. We're locked back down at eight p.m." She continued, "This is the place they will keep us until the experimental small group isolation unit is finished being built. They want to practice new techniques taken from the experts in England and Germany." She was very formal with me.

I said, "It seems like we're already in small-group isolation right here." She nodded.

I told her what I knew about the plans for us, information that my lawyers in New York had been able to obtain from the prison administration and the prosecution. Tucson was just a holding pen. Alex and I would both be sent to Lexington, Kentucky, as soon as the Federal Bureau of Prisons finished building a new basement prison there. We were the only two women up to that point who had been identified for transfer to Lexington.

We both knew that the BOP is part of the Department of Justice (DOJ), which has federal correctional institutions (FCIs), federal prison camps (FPCs), federal detention centers (FDCs), and administrative detention centers (ADXs). Within these, it has special housing units (SHUs) and high-security units (HSUs). The institutions are run by associate wardens (AWs), captains and lieutenants, physician assistants (PAs), and finally correctional officers (COs). Behind all the initials, the penological rationales and security designations are more than 110 forms of barbed wire, concrete, and watchtowers. At a cost of more than twenty billion dollars a year, the vast corrections network encompasses thousands of acres of land, employs thousands of people, and warehouses over 180,000 human beings. In 1985, there were just fewer than 5,000 women in federal prison and nine women on death row.

"The administration is awful and they hate women. They don't know what to do with us or how to deal with us." As Alex explained what it was like in Tucson, I slowly began to understand that I had experienced only the first level of a wasteland.

Suddenly a face peered around the cell door and I saw a woman holding a dog-eared Bible in one hand and a romance novel in the other. She stepped into the cell and out again as though she were dancing. Her energy was frenetic. It spread out scattershot like pellets bouncing off a bulletproof vest. Her eyes were bloodshot, and her long limbs swung with a contained rage that I felt could explode with a fist faster than a breath. She told me her name was Debra and that she was twenty-four years old. She had grown up in the Cabrini-Green housing project on the North Side of Chicago. A gap in her teeth flashed in what seemed to be a rare smile, when she said she had heard about me. After a few minutes she waved good-bye and retreated to her own cell, where she remained the rest of the day.

Over the next few days I learned Debra's story. She stood convicted of multiple murders committed during a rampage across four states. She and her boyfriend had gone on a robbery run that turned into a killing spree, taking the lives of two children and three adults. She had two death sentences, one in Ohio and the other in Indiana. In addition, she had a federal conviction for taking a kidnapping victim across state lines. The court had ordered her to serve the thirty-year federal sentence first and then to die by lethal injection in Ohio. Her boyfriend, in the Marion, Illinois, federal penitentiary, was also waiting for execution. First, though, they wanted to get married, and Debra wanted to get baptized.

I didn't know her or get any good feelings from her, but as I watched Debra I felt a kind of anguish that I had never experienced before. Once in a while she would put on lipstick and do her hair, and I could see her as she had once been in the world, acting the grown-up and hanging out with her crew. When she was feeling okay she would watch TV and laugh, and for a moment she would seem to forget where she was. But those moments were few and far between. For the most part, she lived in absolute internal agony that breathed through every pore. She was in Tucson because the BOP considered her a high security risk. We lived side by side for over a year.

The BOP bureaucrats claimed that they were not in the business of punishment; they were only doing what the courts ordered. Their quick answer to everything was, "We didn't sentence you; the judge did." In their official rhetoric, they were neutral toward prisoners. But I could see that with Debra "neutrality" took an odd form. It wasn't even subtle. They spat at her and threatened her, taunted her constantly about her impending death, and denied all of her requests (none of which was ever unreasonable, not one).

The daily exchanges between Debra and the associate warden, Gibson, were unbearable. Gibson was a career prison administrator with ambitions of becoming warden himself. He was the one who signed off on everything to do with any of us. But it was clear from the start that he hated us without knowing us, believed that we were our crimes and that we were the worst of the worst, and he treated us accordingly. When Debra would ask him to allow a minister to baptize her, Gibson would simply smile and shake his head, and then he'd let loose. "There's no God in this world who will forgive you," he'd say, or, "It's too late to save you. If you want to get clean, take a bath." Then Debra would get mad and start yelling at him, which only made him smile more.

He would remind her of the obvious—that he, too, was African American—and would taunt her unmercifully: "You being black makes me think black is ugly."

Sometimes in her frustration Debra would scream, "Send me to the death house!" Gibson's response was always, "Don't worry—we will when we're ready."

There was no relief from the monotony of the routine, or the small amount of space. There was nothing to do except sleep, get up, eat, read, watch TV, talk with the other prisoners, gaze out the window, and go back to sleep, day in, day out, every day. We were a bored and unhappy lot, and I soon grew tired of hearing myself repeat the same things over and over.

Eventually I realized that I needed to fight the numbing sameness and isolation. I asked for and, miraculously, got a phonebook. I looked up the addresses of all the bookstores, women's groups, and any other organizations that I thought would respond to a letter. I wrote to all of them, explaining why I was in prison, how it felt to be two thousand miles from home, and how much I needed books and friends.

I began a correspondence with Peggy Hutchison, who herself was then on trial for transporting and harboring fugitives, along with fifteen other sanctuary workers from the Southwest. They were all part of the sanctuary movement, a type of Underground Railroad that provided aid to people from Guatemala, El Salvador, Nicaragua, and other parts of Central America who were fleeing state-sponsored repression but had been refused refugee status and then entry into the United States. Connecting to her and her codefendants made me feel less like a stranger.

Peggy's letters made me realize how vital writing would be in helping me survive imprisonment both physically and mentally. I started to read, study, and write. I began with Thomas Merton, Jean-Paul Sartre, Hannah Arendt, and others who had created relationships and deep conversations through correspondence. It helped. Reading them opened up mental vistas about making change, the impact of violence, and being accountable.

Then I met a University of Arizona law professor named Jane Aiken who had worked with other political prisoners. She had been given my name by an attorney in New York with whom she had interned. The attorney had said, "Go visit, she will need it." Jane was my age and had been raised in the South. She was beautiful and smart. She had a large easy laugh and was one of the tallest women I had ever met. She matched the guard eye to eye as he escorted her to the visit. She was, as she put it, a former member of the Junior League who had rebelled and transformed herself right out of her past. As we sat across from each other at the table, I with my leg irons and she with her legal books, we tried to imagine each other's lives. For me, meeting Jane was a great relief. She was a new friend, not a fellow prisoner or former associate, and her support gave me hope that I could still communicate and grow. She visited when she could and tried at points to intervene on my behalf with the prison. She didn't say, "There but for the grace of God go I," a thing that many people said, trying to be helpful, but that wasn't always easy to hear. What I came to represent to Jane I am not sure, but I surely came to trust and love her. I would later realize that having relationships with people on the outside had its own particular type of intensity and high emotions. I understood how women who began to write to men doing life in prison could fall in love, despite the barriers and problems.

Things were not good among the four of us in the unit—me, Alex, Debra, and Rosita, a Mexicana who had been convicted on drug charges. We were all going stir-crazy and getting more and more uptight. We spent a lot of time bickering with the COs. Rosita, especially, was going off the rails. She had grown up in Los Angeles and had been dealing in drugs much of her life. She was quick-tempered and mean. She had earned her reputation by walking away from a minimum-security prison, so now the BOP was holding her indefinitely as an escape risk. The isolation of Tucson was new to her (before she had always been "in population"), and she sought release from the tension and boredom by flirting with the cops.

One day I woke up and looked out my cell window, which opened onto a ten-by-twenty-foot stone enclosure that doubled as our recreation yard. Rosita was wedged up against the fence with a CO, whose pants were down at his ankles. I shut my eyes, but when I opened them the picture was still the same. I shut my eyes again, not wanting to watch; when I looked once more, the CO had his pants back on and, smiling, was handing Rosita a small plastic bag. *Fuck, fuck, fuck*, I thought. *Cops all around us and snitches among us.* Alex had seen it, too, and we couldn't believe how blatant the whole thing was. Rosita having sex with the CO meant that she would tell him anything he asked her. We should have known, especially since the CO was in charge of our little unit that our having witnessed this exchange would put us in danger, but we didn't.

The next day Alex and I were ordered to share a cell. There was no reason for this, since there were plenty of empty cells, but we were given no choice. Several days later the prison SWAT team swooped in after lunch. Debra, Rosita, Alex, and I were all shoved into the day room. Alex and I noted that during the shakedown, the team stayed in our cell longer than in the others'. When at last one of the guards came out, he held in his gloved hand a knife from one of the lunch trays. The same CO was smiling.

"They had it stashed in their garbage can," he announced, gesturing at Alex and me.

"No we didn't," we said in unison.

What ensued was one of the stupidest and most devastating series of events during my year at Tucson. Alex and I were charged with the possession of "high contraband," immediately stripped of all our property, and placed in detention pending a disciplinary hearing. Detention meant a different cell, with no personal property, no visits, and no outdoor recreation. It meant being locked in an even smaller space. It was a bad set of circumstances. First, someone had set us up and we had no way to prove our innocence. Second, our being "convicted" of this charge would not only mean the loss of phone, mail, and visiting privileges, but also serve as a justification for further enhancing our security restrictions. This would conveniently make our transfer to high security in greater compliance with so-called policy.

We were ushered through a series of locked doors and put in strip cells in the men's segregation unit. All prisons are a series of increasingly smaller spaces engineered to achieve greater control over and punishment of the individual prisoner. A strip cell has nothing in it but a metal slab attached to the wall and a toilet of some variety. At first we were placed in cells facing each other, which allowed us to pass books back and forth. Alex, though inwardly furious, remained calm. Things like this were to be expected, she said, recalling how guards in Chicago had injured her shoulder to the point where she was left with limited use of one of her arms.

Still, she was unbroken. I heard Alex tell the captain that she might be under his control but that she recognized neither his authority nor that of the U.S. government. This captain was a squat, sandy-haired cowboy in his mid-thirties. I couldn't tell whether it was his drawl or his slowness of mind that made him take minutes to complete a sentence. He called us his "favorite little bitches" until the day Alex told him he was a mere peon and therefore irrelevant. Then it dawned on him that he had never run across prisoners like Alex and me. He began to get angry every time he saw us. He seized our pencils because they were more than three inches long and could therefore be used as weapons. He took away our toothbrushes for the same reason.

Although there was a special hearing officer just for institutional infractions, the captain himself usurped the job. Alex and I were chained and escorted to an office. We stood before the captain, who sat with his feet on the desk, chewing a cigar. His hat, tipped back, was held on by a strip of rawhide around his neck. I started by telling him that what Alex and I were being subjected to was pure political harassment, that everyone knew we had no reason to possess a knife, which was, anyway, a butter knife that had been brought to the unit on a food cart, and so on.

The captain laughed and kept repeating, "Horseshit." At one point, though, he got angry, pushed his chair away from the desk, and fell backward onto his head.

Alex and I tried to muffle our laughter, but we couldn't, even though we knew the whole procedure was not funny at all.

The captain jumped to his feet and said, "This is crap. You're guilty."

Our "conviction" carried a penalty of forty-five days in segregation. For the first ten days, we were placed in cells on the men's tier. I never actually saw the parade of men next to me, but I heard every word each one said in that excruciating week and a half, the most difficult period I had yet endured. The man housed right next to me cursed me and spent hours describing—in the minutest detail and at the top of his lungs—what he would do to me if he could.

I asked him to stop, but that only made it worse. I sat there with tears streaming down my face, unable to block out his screams. It was impossible to rest, eat, read, or think. The only relief came when they brought him his meds, which made him fall asleep for an hour or two. It was no consolation to know that farther down the tier Alex was getting similar treatment from other men.

We were allowed only one shower every third day. The first time, we assumed we would be taken to the women's unit, which was two doors away. But, instead, the guards paraded us past all the cells to the men's shower. We protested and argued with them the entire time, but to no avail. It was impossible to take a shower. The verbal abuse, aimed at our very sex by fellow prisoners who hadn't seen or been with women in who knew how long, pierced us like bullets. As we walked back, Alex whispered, "I'm going on strike—no showers, no food, no cooperation until they move us back to the other side."

The next day they took us outside to the recreation yard. It was a small dog run, but at least it was outside in a space bigger than any we had occupied since arriving in Tucson. We walked in a tight circle, almost march-stepping in our orange jumpsuits. I agreed to strike with Alex, to refuse showers, food, and even any further rec. The two of us then started singing as loud as we could: "La Borinqueña," "Gracias a la Vida," "This Land Is Your Land," songs by Woody Guthrie, and on and on until they came for us. Our strike lasted several days. Finally, they moved us back to isolated cells—"segregation"—on the women's side. This meant that we were no longer side by side with men in the next cell. They said it was because they needed the cells we were in.

Initially, the month spent in segregation after those horrendous days in the men's unit was a relief. It was possible in the quiet to think. But it was in that month that the full and terrible meaning of doing time hit me. It hit me so hard that I, in turn, fractured my hand banging on the cell door.

Daily life was a kind of nothingness alternating with verbal abuse. There was absolutely nowhere to go; it felt like death. All that lay in front of me were the ruins of my life. I was losing everything—my dreams, visions, and hopes, my routine and my family, and even my favorite color, favorite food, and favorite season. I began to understand that the very small things, the details that are different for every individual, that make up the identity of each person, but that I had paid little attention to on the outside, get stripped away in prison until the days seem like hours and years like days.

One day a guard walked by my cell wearing some new brand of cologne that I did not recognize. It assaulted my nose and reminded me of a smell that I had once enjoyed. That one small whiff sent me back through a tunnel of memories, lined with images, but I could not recall the name of the cologne or the place I first found it or what it cost or who else told me they liked it. I began to panic— my heart beat faster, I started to sweat and shake, and I could not stop. There was nowhere to go, nowhere to move except within the box in which I had already counted every step back and forth ten thousand times, and nowhere to look because I already knew every single inch of every single surface, every single crack in the concrete. This panic, this terror, this unbelievably painful feeling that ran from the top of my head to the soles of my feet, from my inner being to the hair on my arms, had all been caused by a man walking past my cell. It was then that I knew that pieces of me were melting away; I was losing some things that I would never get back. I realized I was doing time, and it was endless.

Then I adopted what is known as the thousand-yard stare, the convict glaze, or the impenetrable face. When in the presence of any official, show nothing, feel nothing, and try to ignore the broken shards of yourself that are falling at your feet. But when I was alone, I railed against my fate and beat at the bars, smashed my head and hands against the stones, to release the horror. Nothing worked, and I could only lament, *What have I done?* I wept until, finally, I lay curled up on the bunk, replaying the grief of being there, until sleep overtook me.

When Alex and I got out of solitary confinement and went back to the unit, we resumed the routines of prison life, but things weren't the same. We were angrier, and both of us were viewed as more dangerous and more hostile than before. The COs rarely spoke to us. The two other women were less friendly and less inclined to talk with us. I stayed to myself, read and wrote and inspected my garbage every day to prevent another setup. I waited for visits from friends and lawyers. I had a bleak feeling about the future.

Visits from lawyers were important. One lawyer in particular, Mary O'Melveny, had been among the first lawyers to litigate Freedom of Information Act suits against the FBI and had been instrumental in exposing the FBI's Counter Intelligence Program. Mary had represented the Harlem Acupuncture Clinic when it had been under attack by the government and had agreed to do my appeal, although she had not been my lawyer at trial. (I had asked her to represent me when I was first arrested; her answer, however, had been an emphatic no. She said she knew I would not abide by her strategy and she did not want to be involved in a legal fiasco. She was right about that.) I was so happy that Mary had agreed to appeal my sentence and work on my case now, because I had great respect for her and knew I needed someone with fighting capabilities. Mary was a litigator and therefore a great advocate, but she also had a passion that always seemed to light her from within. She surpassed all the male lawyers that she was surrounded by because of her brains and her looks. Being in Mary's company was always a great relief because she helped to shoulder the suffering. When she came to Tucson, she was shocked at both the conditions she saw and the stories she heard. I had been there only seven months, but the reflection in Mary's eyes let me know that I looked terrible. Her visit helped, all her visits helped, and over time they became a lifeline—they meant that I was still in the world in some way—but in the end my appeal was denied.

One day Debra, Alex, Rosita, and I were sitting in the outdoor recreation area the guards had made for us. Alex and I sat at one table and Debra and Rosita at the other. We called it our "patio," because that was about how big it was. It was a fenced-off enclosure that ran the length of four cells along the side of the building. The chain fencing that formed the roof had a partial wooden covering and was surrounded by barbed wire. A wooden fence outside the chain-link blocked our view of the rest of the prison, but it also prevented the men out on the compound from seeing us. Still, our view of the sky was quite complete and magnificent. It was a sweltering day. The air was filled with the buzzing drone that comes when heat reverberates off asphalt.

I heard it before I saw it: *tse tse tse*. Then in the corner where the fence connected to the building I saw a large coiled rattlesnake, its head moving off the ground, its rattle shaking. It was about five feet from me. Very softly, almost whispering, I said, "Nobody freak out, nobody yell, but there is a rattlesnake by the wall." Unbelievably, the other women did not scream, but glided quietly inside. I measured the distance between the door and me. There really was no decision to make, though. I had read somewhere that they don't bother you unless you bother them. I made it inside and stood with everyone else at the window, watching the snake. It was not moving. About three minutes later the cellblock door swung open and a group of heavily suited COs burst in. They looked like astronauts, down to the visors covering their faces. One of them had a large paddle. They pushed their way onto the patio and stomped the snake to death. They battered its head so hard that even from where we stood we could see how broken it was. One of the COs took off his helmet and held the snake up, shouting, "Victory!"

Another officer took his helmet off and, with sweat pouring off his head, grinned at us. "Rattlers are our mascot," he said, and he was serious. It was then I learned that every prison has its own animal, almost like a totem.

Passover was approaching. After many lawsuits over prisoners' religious rights, the BOP had agreed to allow every prisoner one ceremonial meal a year—Passover for Jews, Ramadan for Muslims, Vesak for Buddhists, and Christmas for Christians. I had been a "once a year celebrate" kind of Jew before I had come to prison, but as I spent more time inside I realized that fighting for my right to practice Judaism was a way to fortify my identity. I wanted to have a seder, but I could not do it alone. Knowing that there were several Jewish men in the institution, I made my request to the associate warden, who came to our unit every other day. He rejected it. I argued that there was a precedent (I had been allowed to attend a seder at the New York Metropolitan Correctional Center the previous year), it was my right, and so on. He merely ridiculed me, saying my request was a ploy to see the men, that I wasn't a real Jew. As we stood face to face at my cell door time was running out.

In jail there is an understanding that there are three things you never talk about: sex, politics, and religion. Those things are considered personal, and one's beliefs about them worthy of respect, at least by old convicts and smart administrators. But the reality is that Christianity dominates what religious life there is within the BOP. Even if there are no other books to be had, there is always a Bible at hand. Even if the policy prohibits volunteers, they can get in if they are Christians. Other religions are seen exactly as that— other. In Tucson, there were not many Jews. In fact, Jews were more alien to the administration than other minorities. That's why I was stunned on the eve of Passover to see the associate warden who had fought with me so viciously show up with two COs to escort me (though still in handcuffs and leg chains) to the Passover seder.

The ceremony was being conducted in the visiting room. When I walked in, the twenty-two men sitting around the table stood up and started clapping. They made room for me at the table. As I sat down one man immediately said, "Hey, Susan, good Pesach." It was Harv, whom I knew from the New York MCC. He was a short, burly man with an unkempt beard, intricate tattoos from head to toe, and an enormous smile. I liked him. A former head of the Connecticut Hells Angels, he had been convicted of con-spiracy, bribery, and extortion under the Racketeer Influenced and Corrupt Organizations (RICO) Act, but I didn't know the details. He moved to sit next to me.

He said to the CO standing watch, "Take off her cuffs."

"No, orders are not to."

"That's bullshit—this is a religious service," Harv continued. "I want to see the associate warden."

Several other voices chimed in and I had visions of this small incident ruining the dinner. Harv whispered to me that he and the other men had been demanding for weeks that I be allowed to at-tend this meal. The men had not seen a woman prisoner be treated with such harshness before and they didn't like it. I was surprised; the associate warden had certainly said nothing about it.

"Thanks a lot," I said, "but I don't want to be the cause of ending it."

He gave me a look. "What? Are you crazy, girl? This whole ceremony is about fucking freedom—you are not sitting here in cuffs. Besides, you're a girl and we need one."

I smiled. "Okay, whatever happens will happen."

One of the men who was standing seemed to have an air of authority. He said his name was Levi and he was conducting the seder, because there was no rabbi. He added that he had to agree with Harv. I turned to a CO and said he had to call the lieutenant, the captain, the associate warden, or the duty officer—anyone who had not gone home.

Levi, it turned out, was a devout Orthodox Jew from Brooklyn, doing time for diamond theft. He said, "We will not have a seder with anyone in chains. It's sacrilegious and we'll sue for violation of our religious rights."

That got a response. Several minutes later the captain, my old nemesis, walked in, acting as if he had just ridden up and needed to leave to relieve himself or feed his horse. He looked at me with the same degree of hatred I felt toward him and said, "Rosenberg, you are one pain in the ass."

I responded, "Captain, take off the cuffs and chains. It's ridiculous, and even you know it." The captain was my personal Pharaoh at that moment.

He removed my handcuffs but, as someone who always had to have the last word, refused to remove the restraints around my legs. Then, as abruptly as he came, he was gone.

I told the men to let it go at that—time was running out, and we had to begin our service. We did, and throughout the meal Harv held my hand under the table; he would not let go. When we got to the part about fleeing from Egypt, every one of us felt a surreal edge to the whole thing. I told the men about being in segregation and asked them to spread the word so we women would not be hurt, so that other people would know just how difficult things were for us. Harv promised. We ate everything in sight, including all the ceremonial elements. It was a great seder and an experience, for me, of unexpected solidarity. While I doubted that any of my Jewish compatriots would have agreed with my views of the world, under those circumstances nothing mattered except our Judaism and us.

In September 1986, nearly a year after my arrival in Tucson, Alex and I heard rumors that the Lexington High Security Unit was almost finished. We had been wondering why the construction was taking so long since the HSU was in the basement of an already existing prison. Now the tension of our transfer grew with each day. Every time the doors opened unexpectedly I jumped, thinking we were on the verge of leaving. Even though I had visitors whom I had come to care for deeply, Jane, and friends from California, and my parents who had traveled to see me, where we sat and actually laughed at our situation and shared a great time, I desperately wanted to get out of Tucson. I had a feeling of foreboding there that cast a pall over everything, and the constant and intense contempt directed at both Alex and me was increasingly hard to deal with. I realized that the consequences of my life choices and my incarceration had only just begun, and I wanted to move on with things, as though I had a date with my own destiny, even if it meant worse conditions.

The morning they came for me was like every other morning except that the COs would not let me out of my cell until I had put my arms through the food slot backward so that they could attach the handcuffs securely. I knew the time had come. They would not let me pack my legal papers, books, or photos, much less the few personal items I had been able to keep. "Step out" was all they said. There were several women COs standing in the hall. Alex stepped out of her cell—handcuffed, as well—and I knew we were both going. They walked us through the doors into the men's segregation intake room. It was five in the morning and very quiet. We yelled good-bye and heard Rosita's and Debra's good-byes echoing down the corridor. We walked out of the building and down a path that led toward the receiving and discharge room, but the COs turned and hustled us into the medical building. Right then I knew they were going to pay us back for being who we were.

I started talking. "Why are we here? What's going on?"

One woman CO with whom I'd had some conversations throughout the year said, "We have to search you." She wouldn't meet my look.

"Search us? Oh no."

We were all standing in the hall and then the captain and the associate warden showed up. The captain had papers in his hand; he shoved them at us. I saw the heading "Permission/Notification for High Security Contraband Search" and the boxes with writing next to them. The first box that was checked was "cavity search," the second was "rectal." They wanted us to sign the forms.

Alex said, "You can do an X-ray instead."

The captain laughed. "No, we don't have to and we won't. You are going to a control unit and it's our call on this. We have the right to do it."

My voice was pitched. "You don't have to do this."

The captain looked at the associate warden; the warden looked at us, and nodded. Then he walked out of the building. I started to curse, but the next thing I knew the COs had surrounded both of us. Some of them took Alex down the hall and into a room; others held me in the hall. The physician's assistant appeared, snapping his surgical gloves, and entered the room where Alex was. Within minutes there came a long, loud scream—"Nooooo!"—and I tried, without success, to get away from the COs and go to Alex's aid. Then there was silence.

Five COs pushed me into an examining room. The physician's assistant came in and said, "We can do this easy or hard. It's up to you."

I went crazy. I started hitting and kicking with every ounce of my being. I might have to do it, but I would not do it easy. They overpowered me, pushed my head down onto the examining table, pinned me there, and pulled down my pants. I kept kicking backward until they held my legs. I was cursing and yelling. "This is rape. You're fucking raping me! You could do an X-ray. You know we don't have contraband!"

The physician's assistant took his fist and rammed it up my anus, and then he took it out and did the same thing up my vagina. He didn't "look" for anything. The woman officer who had talked to me had to leave the room. That it was too much for her was merely an irrelevant triumph for me, but I was glad just the same. I was shocked, in pain, and so angry that I would have strangled one of them if I could. They all had to hold me to get my pants up and to cuff my legs. They half carried, half walked me down the hall out of the building into receiving and discharge. Alex was sitting on the floor against a wall. She was shackled with full chains. I sat down next to her. We didn't speak. What was there to say? When the marshals came to transport us and I stood up, there was blood on the floor. They wouldn't let me change my uniform or get medical attention. It was just policy. We left Tucson covered with the stench of hate.

Part Three

Lexington

Chapter 7

Lexington High Security Unit

I HAD ALWAYS loved old cemeteries, especially in the crisp, blustery New England fall. I especially enjoyed the quiet. But my love for such things was ended that October day in 1987 when I descended the flight of those narrow steel stairs into the basement of the High Security Unit of the federal prison in Lexington. The space was cold and small, airless and frightening. Alex and I were going to our own burial with that downward walk, only we were still alive. I would never find a cemetery compelling again.

I looked around and was overcome by the sheer whiteness of the space. It was a bright, gleaming, artificial white, the kind of white that with any lengthy exposure could almost sear your eyeballs. It was the kind of white that can make you go mad. Lexington was over fifty years old. It had been built in the 1930s as an insane asylum, and then it became a federal drug treatment center and later a women's prison. Billie Holiday had detoxed in this facility.

The basement, however, was new. They had gutted everything and constructed it all over again. It was lifeless. The only sounds were the rattling and clanking of our own chains and the barely audible buzz of the rotating surveillance cameras mounted on every wall and at every crevice. At the entrance to the tier were eight metal doors on each side. They, too, were white except for their steel handles. All the cells were locked. It was colder in the hall than outside. The air-conditioning was on full blast and there was no natural light to provide warmth anywhere. The space resembled the refrigerator in a morgue. Nothing living had yet left an imprint.

After being herded by several officers through the set of steel doors leading ever deeper underground, we were put in an airless room containing only a standing scale in one corner. A sign over the scale read MEDICAL ROOM. The men accompanying us stepped outside and several women COs filed in. They did not look at us or speak. Neither Alex nor I tried to tell what had happened that morning in Tucson. They unchained us, strip-searched us, and left us naked. As one of them went off to find uniforms, another examined our bloody underwear and remained stone-faced. Still, no one spoke. Once we suited up in large blue jumpsuits, several men returned to escort us to yet another small room where we found our "property" sitting in opened boxes. It had arrived before we had, and had been searched and secured. The COs had inventoried all of it: photos, earrings, underwear, a favorite pen, our legal papers and books.

Mr. Ogden, the unit manager who would oversee us, secure us, and implement our psychological program, was waiting. He was a big, rambling man in his early forties, with lank dark hair that fell across his receding hairline. An American flag was pinned to his lapel. He spoke in drawn-out, excessively enunciated words as if he were speaking to someone hearing impaired.

"Well-ll, girls-s-s, welcome to your new home." We looked at him. "We've spent a lot of money on this place, just for you. I hope you can ap-pre-cia-te that.

"Now, all that property you have there"—he pointed to the

boxes—"you can't have most of it." He pulled out a photo album filled with fifty or so pictures of Alex's family. Sitting down on a metal folding chair, crossing his legs, he started flipping through the pages. "Nice kid. Whose is it?" he asked as we stood there watching him. "Mrs. Torres, you can have five of these. Pick the top five."

"You have got to be kidding," Alex said.

"Nope. We'll send the rest home at our expense," he said.

"We're allowed a photo album," I said. "You sell them in the commissary."

"Not here, not in this unit. We have our own rules. Pick five; that's it."

And so it went with everything: no shoes, no underwear, no jewelry, no religious medallions, nothing personal. We really argued about the book limit. The rule was five, like the pictures. Except, we realized, he was making up the rules as he went along. When we asked to see a copy of the regulations, we were told that Washington, D.C., was still working on them. It was clear that he was playing with us.

Finally Alex said, "Take it all, and send it all out. I don't want any of it."

Mr. Ogden demurred, stating that he wanted us to choose in front of him the one or two items of most importance to us. Right then, in our first hour after the morning in Tucson and the entrance to Lexington, it became clear to me that this was an initial attempt to make us dependent on the prison. More important, it was the opening salvo (albeit small) in what would become a war between two distinct sides, one of which had overwhelming power and force while the other—our side, my side—had only beliefs and a view of the world to hang on to. Alex and I would have to divest ourselves of all material ties to our world, to our past lives. We had to begin to acclimate and internalize the idea that less is more, that everything important in our lives, the things that bound us, would go on only in our heads and hearts, with nothing tangible to stir the memory. We decided in that very first hour to hang our sanity on our identity. We would not comply with our jailer's command to choose. He seemed disappointed.

We were then handcuffed and walked through the unit, back to the cells. At the last electronic gate we were surrounded by a group of officers and officials. In the silence and whiteness even they were slightly dumbstruck. Alex and I looked at each other. We knew we were entering a tomb. I whispered out of the side of my mouth, "Nazis." She nodded and whispered back, "A white sepulcher."

As I looked down the hallway, my mind filled up with images of other places that were centers of human suffering: death rows in Huntsville, Angola, and Comstock; white cells and dead wings[1] in Germany where captured enemies of the state experience the severest effects of isolation; the torture center on Robben Island in South Africa and La Libertad in Uruguay. As these images rose and fell, my ideas and goals—my whole life—passed before me, I began to disassociate from myself.

But freeze the frame, pull the camera back: there are only two calm, small, battered women standing there, waiting. The prison camera swiveled in a 360-degree turn and a bark sounded over the intercom: "R-two gate, R-two gate, we don't see you."

A CO standing next to me said, "Move! Get in line with the camera—you can see where it is."

He shoved me and I pulled away, inadvertently stepping into direct view. "Fine," said the disembodied voice. There was a loud electronic click, but instead of the gate swinging open, the fire alarms went off. All the men jumped. Alex and I looked at each other and started laughing.

Eventually, the alarms died down and we got through the gate. The door swung shut and Mr. Ogden stood on the outside, staring at me through the small glass windows in the full metal front door. He smiled, gave me a one-handed wave, and disappeared from view.

The first three months, Alex and I were the only two prisoners at the HSU. Every day was filled with confrontations between us and the COs over every human need: getting hot water for a cup of instant coffee, taking a shower, going outside, getting medical attention, getting a book. We were allowed to come out of our cells and talk with each other but stayed locked on the tier, not allowed beyond the gates. There was a camera at each end of the tier and three gates between the end of the tier and a hall that led to the rest of the unit. Our cells had windows we could see out of only by standing on tiptoe on the bed; the view was of shrubs at ground level in the main inner courtyard of the prison. We really were in the basement, and the side we were on received no natural light. In each cell there was a nineteen-inch TV mounted on the wall. There were no books. We were allowed no physical activity inside, no communication with anyone other than the Bureau of Prisons, and no educational or other programs. But there was that omnipresent TV. That TV came to justify and answer all charges of abuse and deprivation.

We were told by Mr. Ogden that we could submit a list of fifteen people, and only those who were approved by him would be able to correspond with us. Those same people were the ones we could telephone during our one ten-minute phone call a week, and if they submitted to fingerprinting and strip searches they could visit. He went on further to explain that the same conditions would apply to our lawyers. Alex would always ask "by whose authority" was this being said or done to us. His answer was always "ours." Our reaction was to tell our families, friends, and supporters not to visit and we refused to submit a list.

We felt that the BOP was not only burying us alive under layer upon layer of lies and doublespeak, but also trying to construct extreme and unnecessary conditions designed to intimidate everyone connected to us. We felt that if we participated in their effort to define our lawyers as security threats, this would be tantamount to accepting the government's view of us as "terrorists." Alex especially did not want to play into their attempts to criminalize the Puerto Rican independence movement. At that time, fingerprinting lawyers was unprecedented, and clearly designed to have a chilling effect.

Every day got harder and harder. I had been incarcerated for more than two years and Alex more than three. While each prison had been difficult, the HSU brought new heights of control, harassment, denial of basic human rights, attacks on our gender, and terrible cruelty.

One day we could go outside to our tiny dog run for recreation ("rec"), and the next day it "violated policy." One day we could take rec together, and the next we had to go separately. One day they would bring us hot food, and in the following days the food would be ice cold. But always there were verbal harangues.

When Chaplain Bits came one day to "counsel" us, he wouldn't open the cell doors. He stood outside, staring through the window at me as if I had two heads. He was a short, red-faced, balding man with stains on his collar. His thin mouth was pursed in a sanctimonious way bred by years of misusing the power of the cloth. I remember answering his stare with "What's the matter? Never seen a Jewish woman prisoner before?"

He finally spoke. "I have never met a woman with such a long sentence. You know, you are going to die here."

When I said that I wanted to see a rabbi, he said no. Then he moved down the tier to the next cell. Alex's husband was a minister in the United Church of Christ, and minister to one of the largest Methodist congregations in the Chicago neighborhood of West Town. Alex is a devout and dedicated Christian. She can quote from the Bible chapter and verse like no one else I know. I stood at my door trying, unsuccessfully, to hear their conversation. Later Alex told me that all she wanted from him was permission to have and wear a cross. To which he replied, "Not when you live by the sword, you die by it. You hardly need a cross." An argument about peace and rebellion ensued. His utter lack of compassion was evidenced when I heard him mutter "that bitch" as he quickly walked down the tier past my cell.

So it went, until one day Mr. Ogden took us into the day room and sat us down. "There is a way out," he said with a deadly seriousness, nothing jovial about him at that moment.

We sat silently.

"You can be transferred out of here if you renounce your associations, affiliations, and your . . . uh, err, uh . . . views. You can have the privilege of living out your sentence in general population."

"On whose authority?" We both asked in unison.

This time he said, "Take my word for it."

He can't be saying this, I thought. *I have the right to my beliefs, to free association. I'm an American.* Then I had to smile, even laugh at myself. The idea of this country and its glorious democracy still held sway in my thinking. I still cried whenever I heard Dr. Martin Luther King Jr., even though I was an "enemy of the state." Then I realized that if we could somehow convince him to put what he had just said in writing, we could expose the HSU for what it was—the first official prison for women political prisoners in

America. We knew where we were, and we knew that the BOP was concealing its real mission behind exaggerated distortions of our "dangerousness." Its officials were trying to justify the dehumanizing conditions they had put us in by slapping a label on us (and on top of that claming the conditions were not inhuman because we had TVs). I was very happy that this had just happened. I felt that he had just given us the tool to fight back with. We told Mr. Ogden that we knew what they wanted us to do, and that he could forget it. He smiled, as though to say that time was in his favor. He let us walk unchained back to our cells.

Later that same day, we were escorted through two gates and placed behind the locked gate at the entrance to the shower stalls. A voice said, "Jim, move—you're blocking the view." My eyes searched the walls until they found the camera down the hall, facing the shower entrance. It was trained on the two-foot-wide space between the shower stalls and the wall, the space where Alex and I stood to take our clothes off before stepping into the shower.

"You're all sick," I shouted. "Watching us in the shower is perverted. What do you think we are going to do in the shower?" I shouted furiously.

After that, we refused our shower privileges until we figured out that we could wear layers of clothes to the shower and hang the outer layer on the bars to block their view.

The only visitor I saw was the rabbi: under BOP contract. I assumed that the officials allowed him in to see me because they felt that violating prisoners' religious rights was one of the few places that they were still vulnerable to a legal challenge in the federal courts. He was the head rabbi of the Lubavitch community in Cincinnati and he drove once a week, every week, year in and year out, to meet with the twenty or so Jewish women in the general population of the more than twelve hundred women at Lexington.

Rabbi Josephson had been ministering to Jewish male felons there for more than twelve years, before the prison had been turned into a place for women, in 1984.

That first time we met, he was accompanied into the basement by Chaplain Bits and two lieutenants. Rabbi Josephson was in his forties, with black curly hair and black clothes. He was a burly man who fit my exact preconceived notion of an Orthodox rabbi. Even though he was sweating and seemed nervous, his eyes were direct and searing. I have no idea how he perceived that first meeting, but I committed the first infraction right then by trying to shake his hand while introducing myself. Of course he wouldn't take it, and at first I thought it was because he was afraid of me. Then I realized that he wouldn't shake a woman's hand. My heart sank, and I thought, *I've been struggling all my life against this type of backwardness.*

But he smiled and said, "Let's sit."

We were standing in the day room with cameras whirring, COs watching us through a window, and the chaplain and the lieutenants hovering nearby. I said, "I want privacy. How can we talk with all these people?"

"Let's sit and talk. Forget about them."

I began to object, but he moved to the corner of the room, pulled up two chairs, put his back to the men, and pointed for me to sit. I sat. Very softly he whispered, "I've never seen anything like this, in all my years, never. They didn't want me to see you. I've been trying for weeks to get down here."

I said, "Thank you for coming, and making it happen."

"Ms. Rosenberg, Susan, what did you do? Why all this hatred?"

I whispered back, "Whatever they told you, it is a lie. I am not a terrorist, nor am I dangerous."

And then his face split into an enormous grin. "That I can see."

Chaplain Bits and the others were talking among themselves and laughing loudly. Again, I wanted to tell them to leave us alone. The rabbi said, "I have only five minutes now, but I promise I will be back. What do you want from me? How can I help?"

I was taken up short. I had been arguing with the COs for a long time about my right to see a rabbi, but now that he was here I didn't really have an answer. I realized that I had gotten caught up in "my rights" without having a deeper reason. I felt embarrassed at that. "They're torturing us down here. You can see we're buried alive. And every day it gets worse and worse," I said. "Regardless of my conviction, I think I should be able to celebrate my religion, and practice it. I want to go to the Jewish Passover with the other Jews here. I want to explain to you why I am here."

The rabbi said, "In all my years here I have never been escorted anywhere, even to segregation. Upstairs we study, we pray, and we practice together. I oversee the holidays and the kosher kitchen; I teach and give solace and ensure that the religious rights of Jews here are upheld."

"I don't want to study. I am not a Jew who believes in that way, but I am proud to be a Jew and these people won't ever stop me from being one. The COs read their Bibles out loud over the intercom going directly to our cells. Hellfire and damnation are the order of the day, every day. It's driving us crazy, Jews and non-Jews alike," I continued.

He sagged at my words. He didn't say anything, but I could see that he believed me.

"It's Stammheim[2] down here. You know what that is?" I asked. He shook his head, so I kept talking, rushing to get as much out as possible, with my eye on the clock. "It's the prison in Germany designed to hold political prisoners and modeled after the Third Reich's penology. Attorney General Edward Meese, the current

German government, and others have agreed to build these prisons in all the Western countries."

His eyes said, *You go too far, this can't be right.*

I knew I was losing him. "No, really, it's modern and new. It's small-group isolation in what are called 'dead wings,' with the goal of identity destruction."

Before I could get another verifiable detail out of my mouth, Chaplain Bits broke in. "That's it. We are leaving, now!"

The rabbi stood up rapidly, and I could see that he was more than ready to go. "Susan, where are you from?"

"New York, New York City," I answered.

The rabbi's face lightened ever so slightly. "Me, too; Brooklyn." As the COs hustled him off, he called back over his shoulder, "I'll bring a study book next time." Then the elevator doors closed and he was gone, and all the men with him.

As soon as Rabbi Josephson left, several COs came in. They were bruising for a fight and their hostility was palpable. "Rosenberg, get in that room. We're doing a strip search," the head CO, Ms. Marshall, barked.

I had known ever since my arrival that I was part of an experiment in dehumanization and that no one involved in it could risk any empathy. Their role was to transform me into the "other." In spite of this knowledge, when I got back to my cell after the strip search I couldn't help falling into a deep sadness. I thought, *Rabbi Josephson thought I was crazy, a paranoid, crazy woman.* I berated myself for hours for not being calmer, or more thoughtful, for not making a plan prior to talking with him, and for not putting on my neater and cleaner uniform. And then I wished he had been a Reform rabbi and not Orthodox, which made the terrain of our Jewishness so wide. Yet despite my self-doubt, and my fear that I was losing my grip on reality, I knew I felt better simply from the familiarity of his New York self. It was only later that I realized that his very orthodoxy was what drove his commitment to me and the other prisoners; it was his mitzvah (good deed) which had enabled him to listen and understand me. His open-heartedness and his willingness even within the confines of the extreme security measures to risk engaging with me challenged my own rigidity. This challenge made me see beyond my own stereotypes.

After the rabbi's visit, something extraordinary happened. My food tray changed. The rabbi had put me on a kosher diet. He had told the food line that it was a religious necessity for me (although we hadn't discussed it). The food was infinitely superior to the standard fare, and it came in huge servings. It was prepared separately from the rest of the food, for a small segment of the population and in small batches with better ingredients. It was cooked in a pork-free kitchen by both Jewish and Muslim prisoners. This was the result of several lawsuits that had been won over the previous decades that upheld a prisoner's right of religion.

At a time when the regular food trays for everyone in the HSU were filled with heaps of processed American cheese, tiny bits of lettuce, and ketchup (then deemed a vegetable by President Reagan), three times a day for weeks on end, Rabbi Josephson's small act of solidarity saved all of us from nearly starving. I shared my better fare with everyone in the basement. Later, I learned that one of the Muslim cooks was a woman named Apple. She was a good friend of Laura's, my dear friend and political associate of over a decade. Laura Whitehorn, who had been arrested in Baltimore, MD in 1985 and been held in preventive detention ever since, detained in the women's prison in Alderson, West Virginia, awaiting trial on politically motivated charges of weapons possession and bombing. Apple was responsible for the enormity of the portions. There was an informal grapevine and network in prisons all over the federal prison system. The grapevine was used by both prisoners and officials. For prisoners, it was a way to get information about people and where they were and how they were, and for officials it was a way to hold people in line with what they wanted prisoners to know. Apple had been in prison with Laura in West Virginia, and had heard all about me from Laura, so when she got to Lexington she did what she could to help me. She succeeded beyond measure.

I was never allowed to see the other Jewish prisoners. They wanted me to participate in their services, and I wanted to, as well, but my basement status overrode religious rights. In April 1987, after I had been in Lexington six months, I asked the rabbi to bring a message to the Passover service. I wrote:

> I wish to share my spirit and love with you tonight. I wish that I could be there with you, but for obvious reasons, not of my choosing, I cannot. Tonight as you celebrate the Passover and remember the struggle for liberation and freedom, I will also. Coming to prison has taught me much about anti-Semitism in America, and as a result I have come to better terms with my own history and the most positive and progressive aspects of our traditions. I long for peace between Israel and Palestine. I will drink from Elijah's cup. In solidarity, Susan.

It was in that basement where I began a study of Jewish history and thinking. I had consciously rejected the Holocaust as a frame of reference when I had been in previous prisons as too extreme and not accurately comparable. I did not want to overstate the conditions that I was experiencing, yet I found reading about it crucial to my mental framework and my very survival. I felt encompassed at Lexington by an ideologically driven evil, beyond anything I had yet experienced, and I desperately needed a frame of reference to understand it. I read modern European history, German history, Antonio Gramsci, the great Italian Communist and writer who wrote *Prison Notebooks,* and one history of the Jewish people after another. I followed the path of repression over the twentieth century through a circuitous route that led from the "disappeared" in Argentina, to the work of Auschwitz survivor Primo Levi, to the poet-philosophers like Elie Wiesel and Tadeusz Borowski, a Polish poet and writer also imprisoned in Auschwitz, who had survived the concentration camps of Nazi Germany. Primo Levi more than other survivors showed me a way to give meaning to my suffering and to try and give voice to the others who were suffering alongside me. I found a purpose in the anguish, if not the philosophical and moral explanation I was looking for. I would bear witness. I would render from the isolation and repression and torture a record. Finding this purpose, grasping this idea and making it my task changed my life, my thinking, and ultimately my view of the world. And on a more internal level (before I learned that all my poet heroes— Levi, Borowski, Paul Celan, and others—had committed suicide), I found a new way to survive by reading and writing and thinking with purpose.

I had help in this realization, help and support. It was during this time that Mary, my lawyer, had really become my lifeline to the outside, to a semblance of sanity, to a human and loving connection, which all took place through weekly twenty-minute phone calls. I think Mary understood the limits of what she could do to help me and at the same time understood that her work in relation to me and her communication with me was the most vital in staving off madness from the conditions. Mary knew that the tenuous thread connecting me to the outside—maintaining my strength and sense of humor—was critical to surviving. We developed an ongoing private joke that served to underscore the battle we were in. I would tell her about one horrendous violation after another and she would say, "Write it down, *for the record.*" I half believed that keeping a record was a futile effort, and she half believed it would be of use in fighting for justice, but that sentence became a signal between us, a way to reference acts of violence too difficult to discuss.

"Write it down," Mary said on a phone call that I was allowed to make after several weeks of concerted sleep deprivation. Hysteria was rising in me as I recounted the past nights of forced waking, and I could hear the tears in Mary's voice acknowledging my pain. I knew she believed me, yet neither of us could express our outrage directly (over a surveilled phone). "Write it down, for the record" was Mary's way of helping me see the means I had in front of me. She never grew inured to my suffering. She felt it as her own.

Primo Levi wrote that the best historians of the concentration camps were political prisoners. Because the camps were fundamentally a political phenomenon, he said, it was the ex-combatants and anti-fascist fighters who had the background to interpret the events. They realized that recording their testimony was an act of resistance. I started to write.

Alex and I had successfully resisted our jailers' attempts to fingerprint all our visitors. We felt that underneath the policy of fingerprinting them was an assumption of guilt by association. We believed that if the authorities succeeded in implementing it at the HSU, they would then make it national policy. It would be a step toward criminalizing people as a preventive measure. For the first several months we simply refused visits. Eventually, with the legal community on the outside publicizing the HSU's violations of constitutional due process, the prison authorities backed down.

Mary's first visit brought me great joy and relief. She had come to see me and Alex, and to see the unit for herself. With her dark blond hair, her vibrancy, and her warmth, she looked so normal that the sadness mixed with fury that emanated from her was astounding and beautiful.

Alex and I had been there for three months. By then we had already begun to look sick. We were thin, pale, drawn, unkempt (haircuts had been out of the question). Our beige uniforms were the same color as the walls in the visiting booth. We were beginning to blend into the concrete.

"What is it like?" Mary wanted to know. "Tell me. How is it different from the other places?"

To see a friend, to see someone who was not an agent of the government, brought out the emotions I had been suppressing. "It's got eleven surveillance cameras. There are no visible cameras in our cells, but the surveillance extends into the area of the showers. There is a little room on the tier with the cells called the multi-purpose room, and we are allowed in there. We eat in that room. It is about the size of a cell, six by eight. To get off our tier, we have to go through two electronic gates. We are always accompanied by an officer. It is controlled movement." Without pausing for breath I kept on. "We have no contact with anyone outside of the staff, yet we are subject to strip searches anytime. We are constantly patted down by men, and our cells are shaken down every day. It is utter craziness! No one comes here, and no one could get us any contraband unless they were an alien with magic powers."

Mary was writing as I was talking. She didn't look up, but she kept asking questions. "Go on," she said. She knew I needed to tell her the details. Somehow she knew that I had been humiliated beyond imagination and that maybe recounting it all would help me.

I wanted her to believe me, to know that I wasn't exaggerating. "We see no natural light, we breathe no natural air, and we eat no food that hasn't been microwaved. We see nothing but white color. Our social contact is with a television. Our mail and our reading material are either withheld completely or censored. We don't get outdoor recreation, we can't take showers except when the COs say, and they always tell us to shower when men are on duty."

I finished this description by telling her about my cell. The thing I wanted Mary to understand was that we were being subjected to an orchestrated psychological program. I told her that Alex and I had cells on the "dark side" of the tier, the internal side of the building. I described our high-up windows and limited view of the courtyard. On the "light side," the windows, at normal height, looked out onto a fenced-in field that was part of the prison grounds. We had been told by Mr. Ogden that the light side was the privileged side. When we heard that, we laughed.

I don't know what Mary made of my account. I know that I felt embarrassed at my appearance and at what a mess I was, and how I sounded, even to myself. I remembered her from the days when I had been free and we'd both been political activists. Now I felt awful and sad that she was seeing me like this. But there was no way to talk about that, to even get close to those kinds of feelings, because they took energy and energy was diminishing with each passing day.

Mary brought up the subject of my parents visiting me. I didn't want them to come; I didn't want them to see the prison, or me in it. They had visited me regularly in New York and in Tucson, and the connection between us was growing, not diminishing. But I felt that it would be too hard here. Mary told me that it wasn't my decision to make, that they were my parents and they needed to see what was happening. We argued, but in the end I knew I couldn't stop the visit. She then told me about other friends on the outside and people I had come to know on the inside. Just watching her sitting across the table from me was a calming experience.

Then she began to talk about the beginning of the campaign to get Alex and me out of Lexington. There were groups and organizations on the outside that would not let us be disappeared. The Puerto Rican independence movement and, more specifically, the National Committee to Free the Puerto Rican Prisoners of War were not going to let Alejandrina Torres languish in a basement. She was considered to be one of fourteen Puerto Rican prisoners of war in U.S. prisons having been convicted of seditious conspiracy. The Movimiento de Liberación Nacional (MLN) and other independence organizations had launched a campaign to free them, defend them, and link their continuing resistance in prison to an anti-colonial campaign against the U.S. government. They were planning to engage the progressive churches and get them to examine and monitor the conditions at the HSU.

The United Church of Christ, the Episcopal Church, and other religious denominations had also heard of our plight and were just beginning their support work. There were people from the left who were organizing and supporting us. A small number of women lawyers and students from Lexington and Louisville had begun a group to protest the conditions at the HSU and had organized several small demonstrations outside the prison. The committee to shut down the Lexington High Security Unit had been formed, and people were working to defend us.

I knew that we were not forgotten, but the isolation was profound and on some levels effective. So while Mary's words made me happy, their meaning didn't really penetrate. Then Mary said,

"You know, Susan, you have to explain what this place and the conditions here represent because there are other people living in conditions that are just as bad. Laura is in Alderson in the hole; Tim and Alan [Berkman] are at Marion, and you know Marion is in a twenty-three-hour lockdown."

"Mary, a hole is a hole for sure. It may vary in size and temperature, but its purpose is always to further punish and control the prisoner's behavior and access. No doubt, most county jails are filthy, unsanitary, with horrible food, and no physical activity. I know because I have been in some while in transit from one prison to another. I've been in Oklahoma, in Dallas, in Birmingham. But this place has to be viewed in its political context. We have to look at how it developed, what counter-insurgency techniques are being used, how the Bureau of Prisons created new classifications for women, the psychological conditions, and, most important, who is in it! There is room here for sixteen, but there are only two of us." I was on a roll now. "Prisoners, especially political or militant people, spend years in holes. Martin Sostre, Geronimo Pratt—both spent seven years in the hole. And there are many others. But here, the authorities are saying, 'Because you are political, you will spend *your entire sentence* under these conditions unless you renounce your beliefs.' And it is *written* in the coming regulations about this place, and that is what makes it different. Supposedly, we in America don't have political prisons, and we don't use torture to coerce people to renounce their beliefs." I sat back exhausted. I could see from Mary's eyes that she thought that getting that kind of analysis out into the public arena would be difficult. She wanted to see the regulations in writing herself. But I could also see that she agreed with me. Mary would organize as much as she could, to the best of her ability.

After every visit the COs retaliated against us for breaking their control over every aspect of our lives. The strip searches increased.

By the spring of 1987, there were five of us. When Silvia Baraldini was brought to Lexington in the late winter of 1987, Alex and I had been there for four months. Silvia had been quietly living in general population in California for four years. She had a record of clear conduct and despite her forty-year sentence had managed to create a life inside. She had been the prison librarian; she had visits from her sister Marina and her mother, both of whom lived in Italy. She was reconnecting with her past—friends from her days with the Students for a Democratic Society in Madison, Wisconsin; friends from her defense work for the Black Panthers; friends from her years in the women's movement. Silvia had created a network of support and survival. But when she refused to talk to the FBI agents who came to question her about other people, the very next day she was transferred to the HSU at Lexington. Silvia was the only one of us who knew what life in general population was like. Because she knew that general population in prison was less restrictive, she had something to compare our conditions to. Having that knowledge made doing time harder for her.

I knew Silvia well. We had worked in political organizations together for more than a decade. We had been in a leadership body of the May 19 Communist organization, an outgrowth of the Prairie Fire Organizing Committee, which had been a support organization for the Weather Underground. We had both been indicted in the New York federal conspiracy case. Silvia had been convicted of conspiracy, the same conspiracy that included the prison break of Assata Shakur and several bank robberies. We had been partners, but I hadn't seen her for five years, and we hadn't been on the best terms when we had seen each other last. But Silvia and I made an agreement on the very first day to build our unity in that basement, and we wouldn't let them divide us.

I had my parents. My mother and father may at one time have been left-leaning liberal, secular Jews from the Upper West Side, but they had moved far beyond that stereotype to become dedicated advocates for my human rights and freedom. I saw this at Lexington and watching their transformation was fantastic. They embraced Silvia, Alex, Tim, Marilyn, Mutulu Shakur, and many other political prisoners. They refused to be intimidated by all the forces that the government unleashed against them directly and through its attacks on me. When in 1982, the FBI threatened my mother with prison if she didn't testify in front of a grand jury, she immediately got a lawyer and said, "Try it." When the FBI went to my father's dental office and warned him that they could hurt his practice, he threw them out.

At the start, my folks had been furious with me. They said that I had brought my punishment on myself, that I was wrong to choose political violence over pacifism. But as they involved themselves in my defense, they came to believe that those of us involved in the "struggle" were moral and that our political principles were motivated out of concern, not out of hatred. I don't know exactly how their views began to change, but I know that after they visited Lexington they were with me with a fierce and undying love.

My desire not to have them visit, which had sparked my argument with Mary, was partly due to my own arrogance: I was afraid they wouldn't be able to deal with it. Up until then, in all our visits we had been able to maintain at least the pretense of well-being, a semblance of normalcy. Alex's husband, the Reverend Jose Torres, had visited at Tucson the same time as my parents, and we had all spent time together. Somehow we laughed, and ate, and carried on as families do, even if we also wept. Those were good visits. But the HSU was a living tomb, and I knew it would break my parents' hearts.

I spent hours preparing for the visit. I thought about all the best things to say, how to be positive, what we could talk about that would not be too painful. Mainly I tried to be calm and appear okay. I wanted to protect them and to manage our emotions. Knowing that the visiting room was filmed and taped, I felt it was important to keep control. I was even then losing the ability to distinguish between the repression that was directed against me in the HSU experiment and the wall of ice I was building between me and feeling anything at all. I was clamping down on my own self and my own feelings in order to repress myself rather than succumb to the BOP's repressive tactics.

I waited in the visiting room for my folks to be processed. When the CO escorted them in, they bounded toward me, enveloping me in an embrace of love and support that was like a laser cutting through ice. We hugged as tightly as possible until the CO watching us rapped on the glass window and said, "No more contact. You can only have contact at the beginning." I turned to say something, and my father put his hand on my arm to tell me not to waste time on them.

We sat cramped in this ridiculously tiny room, happy for the tight quarters that allowed our knees to touch and our energy to envelop us. My father's eyes filled with tears. "This is unbelievable," he whispered.

"Let's not cry," I said, barely managing to keep my voice from cracking.

"No, we won't cry, we'll just be quiet for a while," my mother replied.

After we all pulled ourselves together, we began to talk as if our lives depended on it. All my careful thinking, all my preparations, evaporated and I told them as much as I could about my life in that basement. They told me about all the people they were meeting and learning about who were sympathetic. The words poured out of our mouths.

When we stopped to catch our breath, I asked about my father's side of the family. None of my uncles, aunts, or cousins shared my parents' liberal sympathies. My father had taken a different path. He had been the only son of his Polish-Latvian immigrant family to go to college and then on to dental school. He had veered from their rigid and narrow immigrant community during World War II when he had met Communists and radicals in his Army unit in the Pacific. His vision and politics was a mix of humanism and socialism (although he voted Democrat) for the rest of his life.

My father married my mother when they were in their thirties, and it took a long time before his family accepted her. To them, she was an exotic, bohemian beauty whose experience surpassed their understanding. The daughter of a Hungarian immigrant and factory worker, my mother had come from Detroit, Michigan, by way of Hollywood, California, where she had become a film editor and movie producer, a radical and an organizer. Most problematic, though, was that she was divorced.

Over time, however, everyone mended the rifts and coexisted in the way that dysfunctional families do—that is, until 1965, when they all argued over the Vietnam War. I remember visiting at an uncle's house when the subject of the war came up and the screaming started. It didn't take long for the differences and then the old prejudices to spill out.

My uncle told my father, "It's my country, right or wrong. You love it or leave it, you unpatriotic bastard."

My father turned so red with anger that I thought he was going to have a heart attack. Then my aunt said something about my mother that I couldn't quite hear. My father grabbed me and herded us out of the house. We never went back.

Forgiveness had come twenty years later, but now, when I asked how each one was by name—Uncle Jack, Aunt Ruth, and on and on—I felt the hesitation and a discordant energy.

"Did someone die?" I quietly asked. "Who is it?" When you are in prison, you always think about people dying; it is what time and hostile surroundings do to your mind. But this time I knew. "Is it Neil?"

Now there was total silence in the room. Neil was my favorite cousin. Only a few years older than I, he was a painter, an artist, a fellow tortured soul who had for much of his life been in and out of mental institutions with schizophrenia. Neil's father had died when he was little, and my father had filled in. They loved each other. My parents had tried to help Neil throughout his childhood and had encouraged him to study at the Art Students League. They visited him in the various hospitals and homes that he bounced in and out of. They introduced him to other artists; they tried to sell his work.

Neil lived with us for short periods when I was growing up and I loved him. Everyone said that we looked alike, more like brother and sister than cousins. I was an only child and Neil was a middle child, the problem child. He was odd, and I felt odd, and we had an uncanny affinity. I hadn't seen Neil in over five years.

"Please tell me," I asked.

"Susie," my mother said, "Neil is dead."

"He died of a heroin overdose," my father added.

"Heroin?" I asked, surprised. I hadn't known he was a junkie. I wasn't shocked to hear he was dead, just terribly sad.

And then my father said, "He died the night you got arrested."

"What? What do you mean? That's over three years ago. How could no one tell me?" Now I was shocked.

"We didn't want to tell you when it first happened, when we first saw you in New York. We thought it would be too much, and then it never seemed to be the right time, and you didn't ask about him. Then it got harder and harder to figure out how to tell you," my mother said, searching me inside with her eyes.

I began to cry. I don't know if it was about Neil, about their not telling me, or about the idea that I could be so isolated from my past life that a favorite person could be gone for three years without my knowing it. "This is cosmic, this is too much. The same day— me and Neil on the same day," I said.

I looked at my parents sitting across from me and I realized that we were alike in many ways. The three of us were always trying to parcel out our pain in limited quantities, to protect ourselves. I knew they had withheld the news about Neil to protect me, just as I had tried to plan our visit in order to protect them. Yet I was angry, too. I felt they should have told me about Neil a lot sooner. That they didn't made me feel excluded from our family. Sitting there, I couldn't sort out my emotions. I had thought my parents would be devastated at seeing Lexington, but death had intervened and made the HSU recede.

Our visit was terminated arbitrarily by the guard, lest we forget for one second where we were. I was left with only a promise of more talk the next day.

I went back to my cell exhausted. That day more than any other, I hoped there were no cameras in the cell. I lay there weeping and raging. I chain-smoked until my fingers were brown. I paced back and forth, and could barely keep from banging, pounding, and punching the cement walls. I felt a terrible, heavy sadness as I thought of the consequences that we were all living through. All

these unintended consequences were from actions of my own doing. I raged against myself and against my captors until I finally
fell asleep.

I woke with a start. Both Silvia and Alex were yelling through
the food slots in their doors. "Susan, Susan, turn on your TV!" I
hopped up and flipped the switch. There on the local NBC news
were my parents, surrounded by the women from the local Lexington support group, made up of a few women human rights activists. They were holding a press conference right outside the front
gates of the prison. My mother had fire in her eyes as she defied
the small jam of reporters to contradict her. "This place is a prison
within a prison. No one deserves this. I don't agree with what my
daughter did, but she's a human being, not an animal." She was
furious. Then my father read from a written statement.

About this same time I filed a Rule 35 motion. This is a "safety
valve" in federal sentencing that allows prisoners to appeal to
the sentencing judge for a reduction of sentence. There are many
grounds upon which to file such a motion. It is predicated on the
idea of compassion in sentencing, or if not outright compassion,
then a consideration of extenuating circumstances. Those can include family hardship, acceptance of responsibility, new evidence,
or a willingness to comply with requests from the prosecution.
Such compliance could mean cooperating in an investigation or
testifying in another trial. After initial sentencing and the comple-
tion of all appeals, the clock starts running and the convicted person has 365 days to file a Rule 35 motion. Everyone files it. For the
most part, it is an exercise in futility, but once in a while a judge
will grant the motion and the lucky convict will get a time cut or
will be released with time served.

I had no appeals left. During sentencing, I had scoffed at my sentence. I had thought that the system itself wouldn't last fifty-eight years. In giving me the maximum time allowable under the law, Judge Lacey had said that he was not sentencing me for anything other than what I was convicted of in his courtroom, which was a possessory offense. He had said that he was not in any way swayed by any other charges that I was facing, and that they played no role in his sentence. He was referring to the charges stemming from the federal conspiracy case that included the attempt to free Assata Shakur from prison and the Brink's robbery. Although it was certainly not his intention, his making that assertion would help me years later. Then he was ensuring that there would be no constitutional challenge brought on the basis of bias or prejudice on his part. He didn't know that the Southern District of New York would drop the Brink's charges and refuse to take me to trial.

Now it was 1987 and time to file the Rule 35. What made it even a consideration was that Judge Lacey had retired from the bench. I could bring the motion in front of an entirely different set of judicial eyes. Three years after passions had cooled and the prosecuting attorney had also retired and moved on, none of the original players would be there except for me. Mary wanted to file. I did, too. But I was in Lexington and it was taking every ounce of strength for me to manage there. Mary told me that because such a motion had to be premised on remorse or "changed circumstances" (such as a major witness recanting in a trial), there was no point in filing unless I had something new to say. I had no new circumstances, so I was left with remorse.

Remorse is a complicated thing. In this case, it didn't mean simply taking responsibility in front of the court—saying, "Yes, judge, I did it"—but also apologizing for endangering people and a lot more. I *was* sorry that I had endangered people by moving hundreds of pounds of explosives without numerous precautions in place. I had spent a lot of time thinking about it, and thinking how fortunate it was that no one had been injured. But, still, I wasn't thinking that it was wrong to have done it at all, wrong to have resorted to the use of arms; not yet, anyway. At the time, remorse to me meant apologizing for my politics, and *that* I wasn't prepared to do. I felt that I had taken responsibility for my actions. I felt that by saying that my government was responsible for war crimes and genocide, and that in all good conscience I could do nothing less than oppose it, was equivalent to saying I had "done it." But the meaning of "it" was the issue. To me, "it" stood for revolutionary opposition to my government up to and including the right to use arms. To the court, "it" stood for a violent criminal intention to murder innocent people.

The new judge in New Jersey was Marion Trump-Barry. All I knew about her was that she was Donald Trump's sister, and hardly a liberal. When Mary, my parents, my supporters, and several hundred friends went to court to argue the motion, all Judge Barry wanted to know was what I had been intending to do with the explosives—what I had been planning to blow up—and who else was involved. Mary answered that, to her knowledge, there had been no specific plans and that the court knew that everyone else involved had been arrested. She further argued the disproportion and disparity of the sentence, citing cases in which KKK members and anti-abortion clinic bombers had been sentenced to five years or less for similar charges.

It took the judge less than an hour to deny the motion. A year of work, of emotional investment and energy on the part of so many, was gone in a matter of minutes. Mary and everyone else who had worked on the appeal were crushed at the ease with which the decision was rendered and knew that there were very few mechanisms left to use to change the sentence. My mother wept in the courtroom as the judge announced the decision. I heard about it over the phone in a monitored legal call. The guard who was listening laughed and rushed away to inform the other cops on duty in the unit. They had a small party in their office.

My heart hardened, even though my rational mind had expected the outcome. There was no end in sight, and I remembered a quote from Franz Kafka: "There is hope, but not for us." Still, the magic elixir of hope and possibility had taken hold even in that stone-cold concrete box. From that process, I had learned that fighting for freedom is a constant and that in the fighting itself comes the energy and will to carry on. I learned that freedom has many meanings and levels to it, and that I could be chained to ideas as tightly as to any cell. And I learned that hope is a fantastic dream in its most shining beauty and its profound dangerousness. Hope can pump blood through frozen veins. Hope can stir the near dead.

But all of life cannot be lived on hope. So amid the turmoil of this defeat, I again turned to think about what I did and didn't believe. I had to ask the question: "Why am I here?" "What is my worldview?" For the first time since I had been arrested, I began to reassess my own views and most deeply held beliefs. Then, over a period of many months, all long in the making, a series of earth-shattering events took place, one after another. Though external, they penetrated even our prison within a prison. The Berlin Wall fell and the Velvet Revolution brought new governments to Czechoslovakia, Poland, and Hungary. At the same time, the winds of *glasnost* carried in *perestroika* and shook the foundations of the Soviet Union. The revolutionaries in Central America, in El Salvador and Guatemala, laid down their arms and began peace negotiations. Peace processes began in Northern Ireland, in South Africa, and even in the Middle East.

I watched it all on CNN World News, a weekly two-hour show that used international news service feeds and that was my primary connection to the outside world. I was watching people assert themselves in many different ways to fill their long-unmet needs. I was witnessing the victory of the United States in the fifty-year-long cold war. I was seeing revolutionaries who were my contemporaries recognize the stalemate that their national liberation processes had led them to. I saw them choose to stop the death of innocent people by entering negotiations and renouncing political violence.

I sat in that basement heartbroken because I could see even from that isolated basement, the idea of an alternative world based on socialism and the collective was slipping away, and at the same time I was in awe. Socialism and revolution had failed, but millions of people were demanding—and gaining—greater freedoms, economic and political justice, and above all peace.

I was not awed by the power of my own government's role in all of this, though I understood it to be crucial. As an avid student of history and current affairs, I knew all about which corporations controlled which policies and which financiers were profiting from war, and the military industrial complex. Rather, I was awed by the very simple idea that people do make history and that the old saying was still true—that the power of the people is the force of life. And I remembered what it had felt like in the late 1960s and 1970s to be a part of that power. It was a far cry from the isolation of the Lexington High Security Unit. Now I began in earnest to rethink not only my beliefs, but also my whole ideology, the very framework that had driven me to act all through my adult life.

Chapter 8

Litigation

ALEX, SILVIA, AND I understood what was happening to us. We understood that sensory deprivation and isolation were harming us. We knew that we had to resist if we were going to emerge out of there with our minds and bodies intact. This was getting harder every day. A 1979 study done by Amnesty International on German political prisoners found small-group isolation to be "cruel, inhuman, and degrading." It was also found to be in violation of Article 5 of the United Nations' Declaration of Human Rights. After lengthy stays in conditions similar to ours, people had killed themselves.

The local COs were trained never to speak to us and to deny every request we made. The guards for the most part had been so successfully brainwashed about us that there was no communication. A German prisoner had described her experience in similar conditions as one of constant confrontation. It was true. The remedy was to ask for less. After weeks of asking for hot water and always getting the same "not now" as an answer, I simply stopped asking.

Because the HSU was brand new, the BOP showed it off to everyone they could. There were weekly tours of judges, police agents, state troopers, and correctional officers. As each tour passed, we would hold up handwritten signs saying, "This place violates human rights," "We are women, not animals," and "We are political prisoners." The visitors didn't know how to react. All they knew was what they had been told—that we were terrorists, dangerous and crazy, and that the place was clean, quiet, and white. It was unlike any prison they had seen before. People trained in prisons might reference Marion Federal Penitentiary, the all-male, super-max prison, where a sentence could last years and years with no human contact except with fully loaded security personnel. Once in a while when a visitor was touring, they would say, "It's a control unit, isn't it?" But the staff was instructed only to mouth certain answers and would always say, "No, it is just high security."

One day in the early spring of 1987, Silvia and I were in the day room. We were drawing the watchful eye of the ever-vigilant head CO, Ms. Marshall. She was watching us through the glass view. The other prisoners of the HSU were in their cells. We heard the elevator and then the gates pop open. Lieutenants and a visitor were talking as they got out of the elevator. We heard a voice with a thick Irish accent. The men went in the other direction and their voices receded. After about fifteen minutes, they returned to the front and we heard a lieutenant explaining the features of the cameras. As the group passed through the gate into the day room, the visitor said, "This looks just like the dead wings."

Silvia said, "It certainly is. We call it 'the tomb.'"

The visitor, a small wiry blond, was dressed casually and held a cap in his hand. He nodded. He asked if he could talk with us. It took a few minutes for a decision, but then the lieutenant looked at his watch and said, "Fine, a few minutes. I'll be back." He left us alone.

Then the visitor did something we were no longer used to: he pulled up a chair and sat down with us. I stood up, watching him. He said, "Sit down, sit down, it's fine. There is no problem."

Silvia asked, "Where are you from?"

"Derry, I'm from Derry, in Ireland."

"Yes, I know Derry is in Ireland. I've been there, to Derry," I said.

"Really?" he said.

"Yes, I did a bike tour there years ago. It is very beautiful." I sat back down.

"What are you here for?" Silvia asked.

"I'm a recreation specialist, you see."

We didn't see. "A prison rec specialist?" I said.

He nodded. "I see you're recreating." He pointed to the drawings. We all laughed. It seemed so stupid, the two of us drawing.

"This is a control unit, you know—there is no outdoor recreation. Did you ask to see the outdoors?" Silvia continued.

"I work in the Maze prison. I'm doing a tour to get ideas for our program there. But then I heard about this unit and requested a look-see."

We just sat there and said nothing at this news. The Maze was infamous for holding the IRA prisoners. It was where Bobby Sands and numerous others had died on hunger strikes for political recognition. "So you recreate the IRA, do you?" I said.

"You know about the Maze, do you?"

"Of course we do," I said.

"And you're Irish. How can you do it?" Silvia asked quietly.

The rec specialist went into a long explanation about how his job was to foster peace between the Provos and the Ulster boys so they could get out and live together. He had them playing soccer, and that was better than fighting. Didn't we agree?

We didn't argue with him. Somehow both of us felt that we

would rather talk to him than have him leave. He commented that the unit looked like a part of the Maze. He called it small-group isolation. As we were talking, several officers had congregated at the window and were watching us. They looked surprised that we were all sitting and talking. The lieutenant came back and the fellow got up and shook our hands and thanked us.

Everyone was taken aback. As they walked out, one of the guards said, "You talked to them."

"Of course," the Irish visitor answered. "The politicos are the easiest to talk to."

Silvia and I looked at each other and laughed. It was a sad comment on how devastated and lonely we were that we had enjoyed talking to him, but what was sadder still was that we could never have had a similar conversation with any of the guards or officials responsible for us. We were from a different planet. Still, that conversation made us less crazy.

We knew that we had to bring a lawsuit against the BOP if we were going to close the unit down. We also knew that we had a lot of different issues to resolve, and steps to take in order to even get the argument right. The first question was: Who would bring the action? Filing a lawsuit challenging prison conditions always faces enormous legal hurdles. Yet Alex maintained that she was a prisoner of war and didn't accept the jurisdiction of the U.S. government, so she wouldn't be a hypocrite and sue in a U.S. court.

That left just Silvia Baraldini and me. For the most part, Silvia had the best case. She had been convicted of conspiracy in New York in the black liberation movement case that included the freeing of Assata Shakur and the Brink's robbery. The circumstances of her transfer from the California prison to the HSU supported the argument that Silvia was with us at Lexington because of her political beliefs.

The next problem was how to frame the suit. We knew that because the HSU was clean and looked brand spanking new—and because it contained a miniature facsimile of things other prisons had, such as a Ping-Pong table and of course the TVs—it would be difficult to get the courts to agree that the treatment was cruel and unusual and therefore a violation of our Eighth Amendment rights. We had to show that the rules, policies, and practices as designed and carried out amounted to psychological torture. We had to convince some prisoners' rights organization that we were worthy of their intervention. We had to convince them that this was the beginning of a whole new and heightened level of politically motivated and unconstitutional punishment. Above all, somehow we had to break through the layers of government propaganda that defined us as the "most dangerous."

In truth, the three of us had not killed anyone through our own acts. Silvia, in fact, had been acquitted of participation in any violent acts (except the freeing of Assata Shakur, during which not a shot was fired). But all of us had supported and engaged in activities that used political violence and armed struggle. I believed that guerrilla movements that came out of national liberation struggles were legitimate and just. I believed that the right to self-determination of oppressed people included the right to armed self-defense and the right to use arms to gain liberation. I believed that the U.S. government was both directly and indirectly responsible for global violence in the form of military intervention, control, and manipulation of other governments for U.S. corporate influence and profit. I believed that as an American citizen, I had a responsibility to oppose all those things. Further, I believed that the only way the endemic white supremacy and four-hundred-year legacy of racism could be changed was for a black revolution to lead a challenge against the U.S. government's power.

And so, in keeping with all my beliefs, I pursued a path that seemed to me a logical step beyond legal protest: the use of political violence. Did that make me a terrorist? In my mind, then and now, the answer is no. I say this because no act in which I was involved ever had violence against persons as its object or consequence. The point was not to kill or maim innocent people, nor was it to create fear and terror. It was to underscore the demands of people in motion who were organizing against the system. It was to attack the structures of power that contributed to the death and destruction of people resisting U.S. intervention. It was to stop the U.S. war machine. I believed that legal protest alone could not always confront power.

Because I believed all that, did it make me a terrorist who could not be controlled even in prison? Would we be able to make a nuanced argument to the court that our beliefs and convictions in the courts were not equivalent to each other and in fact, there was no danger of our using violence against our captors? Should we be kept in experimental small-group isolation for things that we *might* do while living in prison? Did we have any rights of due process left or, because of the government label, did it not matter how we were treated?

Up until that point within the U.S. prison system, prisoners were put in indefinite lockdown (segregation or isolation) only if they committed infractions while in prison. Those who committed serious infractions also had to go through a behavior modification program (the most well-known and active program was then at the maximum-security penitentiary in Marion, Illinois). Through good behavior, prisoners could work their way out of isolation, back into general population. While Silvia and I were trying to talk all this out, people on the outside were way ahead of us.

In March, *The Nation* did a cover story about the High Security Unit at Lexington. At the same time, the General Board of the Global Ministries of the United Methodist Church began inquiries and requested a tour of the unit. The National Prison Project of the American Civil Liberties Union also wanted a tour. Congressman Robert Kastenmeier, then chairman of the House Subcommittee on Courts, Civil Liberties, and the Administration of Justice, and Congressman Ron Dellums wrote to BOP director J. Michael Quinlan, asking why there was such punitive treatment of us. In May, Amnesty International wrote a letter of inquiry to the BOP about the reported conditions in the HSU, asking for an explanation of the conditions there. The BOP denied the entire set of questions that Amnesty posed. Amnesty's main contention was that there was no basis for our being kept in the HSU other than our beliefs. The BOP's response was that Alex, Silvia, and I were there because outside groups might try to free us. They had not a shred of proof that such an action was probable or even likely, but they held to this as their rationale.

One day in July 1987, a SWAT team of ten men charged through the gates of the tier. A BOP SWAT team is made up of the biggest guys on staff, all of whom are armed with plastic shields and clubs. They usually are dressed all in black with helmets and high combat boots. This SWAT team was no different. They did a shakedown like none before. They progressed cell by cell, throwing things into the hall and searching the walls with metal detectors. Finding nothing, they confiscated a lipstick that one of us had gotten through the commissary. Then they came back with wooden bulletin boards measuring about a square foot and told us to put them up on our "desks"—the metal shelf that was attached to the wall and served as desk, table, eating place, and so on. Then they wanted us to put up family pictures on the bulletin boards. They had forgotten that we didn't have any.

That night I found a line from a poem that I had copied from somewhere and stuffed inside my legal papers. It was by Nazim Hikmet, the unofficial poet laureate of Turkey who had been imprisoned for seventeen years for being a Communist. It was the last line of the poem: "Capture is beside the point, the point is to never surrender." I put it on my bulletin board.

The next day, Alex's lawyer and longtime advocate, Jan Susler, a passionate and committed supporter of Puerto Rican independence, a calm, clear-thinking, and warm woman, and a member of the People's Law Office in Chicago, was scheduled to come to see her. Jan was one of the lawyers with Mary and others to challenge the BOP and our treatment. She also represented other prisoners of war in other prisons. Jan had become a de facto advocate for us all.

But the cells weren't opened in the morning, and no one came to get Alex for her visit with Jan. Hours went by, and we yelled and banged with no response. Then our new unit manager (the replacement for Mr. Ogden, who had done such a good job with us that he had been promoted to run witness protection programs) walked down the tier, accompanied by the unit guard. We had names for them both: the manager, R. Sigman, was "Sig," and the guard was "Lurch" (named for the Addams family butler). Lurch was tall and dark, his prognathic lower jaw protruded in front of his face. He unlocked our cells and we charged out, yelling about being locked down for no reason, wanting to know where Alex's visitor was, and complaining to him about the SWAT team's abusive search from the day before.

Sig stood there with his tie askew and his jacket open over his large belly. He was beginning to look like a sausage whose skin was about to burst at the seams. When he had taken over "managing" us a few months earlier, he'd been just a stocky man who still had that ex-military look of thickening middle age. He had served in the Marines and had retired to the BOP. Every other sentence he uttered was a variation on the theme of how much easier it had been for him when he was working with men: "Men don't argue. They may try to bust your face, but they don't argue." We always told him not to worry, that even he would get a promotion from all this; after all, everyone else had—it was considered "hazardous duty." He was implementing the program, but we were driving him to massive anxiety-induced overeating.

"You're having visitors, all of you," he shouted over our noise. "Your side is coming."

"Who?"

"I want to see that you have your bulletin boards up, and are dressed in uniform." That meant in khaki skirts and shirts, which we never wore as part of our general protest. Instead, we wore gray sweatpants and T-shirts, or blue hospital pants.

"Who's coming?" we wanted to know.

"The American Civil Liberties Union." He said it as sarcastically as he could muster. "They're going to walk through, they can enter your cells, and then they'll talk to each of you individually."

At last, I thought. "Praises be," someone said.

We had known that they had been trying to get in, but we had not heard that they had succeeded. Sig and Lurch left us all standing on the tier. As I waited for them to arrive, I thought, *We can win, somehow we can make them see what's really going on. They've got to believe us.* The next thing I knew, the gates popped open and they were walking down the tier. They were the first civilians outside of BOP and law enforcement to see our cells. I felt like crying, because to have resisted enough to force the administration to let observers into the prison was in and of itself a victory. There were two of them, and they were surrounded by a gaggle of public relations and administrative BOPers. The smell of Brut was strong as the prison administrators tried to funnel the ACLU representatives through.

I heard Adjoa Aiyetoro's voice before I saw her. "Mr. Sig, uh, uh, Sig . . . there's no curtain between the camera and the shower area. How is that possible?"

Yes, I thought. Her tone conveyed her utter outrage, yet she had a power that she conveyed even in the quiet of her voice. *Yes.* I stood in the doorway of the cell, watching them approach. Adjoa Aiyetoro was the lead litigator for the National Prison Project. She had been a prisoners' rights advocate for several years, and her reputation was one of fierceness, stubbornness, and meticulous preparation. She was a very thin, high-energy African American woman. Her appearance that day emphasized the African, which I thought she had done partly for our benefit. She was wearing what looked like an African textile shirt, and her hair was held back by a bright kente cloth head wrap. Seeing her that first time, I felt that I was being liberated right then and there, if not in body, then certainly in spirit. Her physical contrast to all the white men in their tight-fitting polyester suits and dark ties was a beautiful thing to behold. Following close behind her was a big, full-bearded man wearing a worn worsted-tweed suit. He looked professorial in that leather-patch-on-the-elbow kind of way, except that in his hand he was holding a large leather safari hat. Under his arm he had a leather-encased pad. He was in full scowl as he listened to Mr. Sam Smith, the warden's representative.

"The prison psychologist monitors them? I would like to speak to him. I would like to see his files."

"I doubt that will be possible. They haven't signed releases for that," Smith said.

The bearded man saw me in the door and smiled. He stuck his hand out. "Dr. Korn, Dr. Dick Korn." He pumped my hand. "May I?" He pointed to the cell.

I said yes.

"You're Susan, right?"

I nodded. He and I were standing alone in the cell. He had partially closed the door. I felt so strange, embarrassed that this was where I lived, shy that he was actually standing in my cell, happy that a real person and not a corrections officer was seeing it. He walked up to the bulletin board and read the poem pinned to it. His whole face split into a grin. "Oh my, oh my, he is my favorite poet. Do you know him?"

"Yes, that's why I have his poem."

"You've read his poetry?" Dr. Korn asked.

"Yes, I have read his epic poetry and prison poetry," I answered.

"I wouldn't call it prison poetry, I'd call it his prison period. He wrote for years after he got out." Dr. Korn was now staring at me. I may have shrugged, not at all sure what to say. "He really is my favorite poet."

I did not say, "Mine, too." I did not know what to do. I could not really chat anymore. It was beyond my capacity. "Ask them why we can't live on the other side of the tier; ask to see one of the cells that gets sunlight," I said.

At that point Ms. Aiyetoro came into my cell. "I just realized you all are on the same side, the interior side," she said. She turned to Smith. "I want to see all the cells, every one of them, occupied or not." They walked out. At that moment, I felt elated by her attitude.

They interviewed all of us. We had thirty minutes each. I went first, and when I was finished I hoped that everyone else had been more detailed in their descriptions, as I didn't think I had been clear enough. The ACLU team had been sympathetic, but the problem of my "terrorist jacket" seemed to be a big concern. They asked me question after question about my record. Dr. Korn said that it was clear to him that the unit had a specific intent. He said that by limiting the overt physical brutality of the living conditions, coupled with the creation of such a highly controlled group that was at its core hostile, the BOP was ensuring that we would internalize the control and the rage, allowing it to intensify until someone snapped. What he meant was until someone could not control their rage any longer and would have to express it. They asked Silvia about the difference between general population and the HSU. They talked to Alex about her medical condition. They talked to Sylvia Brown and Debra Brown about how they felt.

After the ACLU tour, things got more hostile and intense than they had ever been. A constant in all prisons is that when the prisoners fight for their rights or dignity, the authorities retaliate—and retaliate they did, in every way they could. First, they went on a campaign of sleep deprivation, waking us every fifteen minutes night after night. This drove all of us so close to the edge that we knew it was dangerous. We had until now succeeded in keeping our unity, but they began a divide-and-conquer strategy that involved trying to turn Sylvia and Debra, the two social prisoners, against Alex, Silvia, and me. Still, we kept our sense of humor, slim though it was. There was no further disciplinary measure they could take, except to remove our TVs, which they did. They gave us write-ups upon write-ups. But if they wrote us up for having six books instead of five, we would laugh: "What are you going to do to us? Go ahead, take us to segregation." They would not let us near the rest of the population, not even in segregation.

We went on a protest in response. We refused to go to "recreation" and we went on a work strike. The only work was cleaning and folding men's underwear in a closet that had been deemed the UNICOR satellite factory (UNICOR is the prison industry system). Not working was not very difficult.

Dr. Korn's report deconstructed the unit in every way and condemned it from every penological and psychological point of view. It said, "Taken in its totality, the HSU seeks to reduce prisoners to a state of submission essential for their ideological conversion. That failing, the next objective is to reduce them to a state of psychological incompetence sufficient to neutralize them as efficient self-directing antagonists. That failing, the only alternative is to destroy them, preferably by making them desperate enough to destroy themselves." After the report was released, there was a growing demand to inspect the unit from other groups, including the General Board of Global Ministries of the Methodist Church and Amnesty International.

One day that summer the SWAT team came again. My cell was closest to the entrance, so they began with me. They were yelling, "Move it, move it!" The SWAT team often used screaming and group grunting to pump themselves up, to intimidate us and to make themselves believe that they were in combat. The uncertainty of what was happening and why, coupled with the threat of imminent violence, made my heart pound so hard I thought my ribs would crack. Then Sig, the unit manager, appeared and everything got quiet. He ceremoniously removed a ring of keys from beneath his fat gut and opened the cell door directly opposite mine. Without any acknowledgment, he said, "Put your stuff in here." It was a cell on the light side.

I thought, *Why me?* But I did not dare ask aloud. I did manage to ask, "Is everyone moving?"

"None of your business. Get in there," he ordered.

They pushed me into the cell and shoved in all of my belongings, including the mattress, the bedding, and my bulletin board. They slammed the door and locked it. I bent down to peer through the food slot to see what they were doing. In those moments, I realized that they were trying to divide me from Alex and Silvia. Then I got mad. It was, admittedly, a delayed reaction and it replaced the heart-pounding fear. I yelled through the slot, "You don't have to do this. You don't have to treat us this way!" Then the other women started yelling, asking me what was going on. I yelled back, saying I had been moved to the other side. Then they went to Alex and moved her.

They continued down the line until they stopped at Silvia's cell. Silvia was in another part of the unit on a legal call. When she came back to the tier, accompanied by two COs, Alex and I started talking through our doors. Silvia wanted to know why she had not been moved. She needed daylight as much as anyone else. The cops refused to speak with her, and locked her in. We proceeded to have hours of discussion and debate at mega-volume through the vents. We finally agreed to lock in and refuse to come out of our cells until they moved Silvia. Everyone was upset and exhausted. It seemed like such a minor thing, yet we knew it was enormous and terrible. In Spanish there is an expression: *Qué lástima*. It means, "Woe is me," "This is the ultimate," "This is the worst of all ends." We had not been in the HSU a year yet, but our world had been so successfully narrowed that we no longer could keep perspective. *Qué lástima.*

That night in the new cell was bad. The three-foot-square window was at waist height and the floor of the cell was level with the ground outside. The window was covered with a thick, steel-mesh gate that made it impossible to see anything directly. The only way to see the outside was to eyeball the small holes in the mesh. They blacked out the green rolling hills of Kentucky, but they did not block the spotlights that ran adjacent to the razor-wire fence that surrounded the building. It was that fence's inescapable shadows the spotlights cast onto the walls of my cell.

That night my despair was the worst I had ever felt. I was consumed by the shadows. Having lived for so long on the cavelike dark side, I now found that the light drove me crazy and left me absolutely sleepless. Worse still, the wire shadow that hung on my wall seemed to cut into me. I kept muttering to myself, "Now I am in a concentration camp." I had the first of several panic attacks that night. I could not control the terrible anxiety that caused me to shake and then alternate between feeling cold and then hot. I felt I was breaking.

In the morning I went to Alex and Silvia and told them about the panic attack. They were very kind, and I am sure upset for me and for us all. They calmed me down and told me to come to them if I felt it coming again. Later, the COs moved Silvia to the light side. Later still, the prison psychologist, whose nickname was "Call Me Mark" (because no matter how many times he appeared at each cell door, his first words were always "call me Mark") came to ask each of us how we were doing. We all told him to go to hell.

Night after night, I tried to cover the window. The only thing that worked was stuffing a sheet through the mesh holes with a pencil, but at each hourly count the CO would stand at the door and scream at me to take it down until I did. I finally made peace with the cell one night when I was peering out and looked up to see the full moon. I hadn't seen the moon, in any of its phases, for almost a year. It made me very happy. I shouted to the others, "Check out the moon! You can see the moon—it's full!" I was entranced by the beauty of it. The mystical energy of its glow penetrated into me and forced me to move. At first I paced around, but as I basked in the moon I began to dance. And then I saw my own shadow over the wire moving through it, around it, and in between all those jagged edges. I realized that I had actually forgotten the moon. I hadn't thought about the moon for months, not once. I thought, *Never again, never can I forget the moon.*

The Methodist delegation toured the unit. One of the members was the Reverend Ben Chavis. I was so excited—almost delirious— that he was there walking around, asking questions. He had been a political prisoner himself as part of the Wilmington Ten[1] case. The Wilmington Ten conspiracy case began during the racial rioting that occurred in February 1971 when Wilmington, North Carolina's, African American students announced a boycott of the city's schools. Reverend Chavis, along with nine others, was arrested during the aftermath of the rioting. The Wilmington Ten case aroused national and international outrage. In 1978, Amnesty International cited the Wilmington Ten as the first official case of political prisoners in the United States. On December 4, 1980, the U.S. Fourth Circuit Court of Appeals overturned the convictions, exonerating the Wilmington Ten.

I knew that if anyone would grasp the implications of our conditions, it would be Ben Chavis. We were given five minutes to talk with his delegation. One of the women on the tour knew a woman who had worked with Silvia in Zimbabwe, when she had been invited to be an international observer of the first democratic elections in Rhodesia in 1980. We could tell that our visitors were angered by the prison. Reverend Chavis told us, "Hang on, people know, hang on." After each interaction with people who were not our captors, we always felt better. Their words fueled our ability to resist.

A writer from *The Nation* came to interview us. Mr. William

A. Reuben was a longtime progressive journalist and he talked to us with a depth of understanding that helped us articulate our own reactions. He was very sympathetic and kind to us. He had interviewed Morton Sobell at Alcatraz in the early 1960s. Morton Sobell had been one of the coaccused in the 1950 Rosenberg trial that had convicted and sentenced Ethel and Julius Rosenberg to death for being Soviet spies. Morton Sobell was convicted of "conspiracy to commit espionage" in 1951 and served more than eighteen years in prison. His experience writing about other politically motivated prison treatment gave him greater understanding of our conditions. The article that resulted from his interview with us broke the silence in which we had been shrouded. One thing followed another, and then NBC news—led by Danny Schechter (an old acquaintance of Silvia from her SDS days) in conjunction with the documentary filmmaker Nina Rosenblum—was given permission by the BOP to do an on-camera interview with all of us. I could not believe that they were going to allow the interview to take place. The BOP believed that it would be our undoing, that we would appear as insane and paranoid individuals. They always underestimated us and the support we had outside. They believed that their total control over us meant that they had full authority. It was an important distinction in the war of wills in which we were engaged. They had control, but we resisted as best we could by not accepting their authority. They hated us for that more than our politics.

While the story was getting out into the public, the ACLU was in discussions with the BOP. We were never privy to those conversations, but we heard the end result: the ACLU told our lawyers that they would not take our case because the BOP was planning to close the HSU and transfer us to a new maximum-security women's prison in Northwest Florida. They estimated that it would take a year or two to build the new prison. The BOP said that the closing was an administrative decision and not the result of outside pressure—they simply needed more space for maximum-security women. We thought that rationale was funny because there were many empty cells in our basement. There were sixteen cells and only five of us.

Initially, we were happy. When the warden came and walked through the unit, I could not contain myself. I said, "We know all about closing the HSU. Your experiment failed."

"Your opinion and your words, not mine," he retorted.

"Yes, those are my words. All you do is lie about your abuses."

"Your opinion, not mine," he said again.

"Fortunately for us, human rights activists agree with us and not you. That's why we are leaving this nightmare. We shut it down, no matter what you tell the press."

But I spoke too soon. As the days turned into weeks, the five of us on the unit realized that "a year or two" was more like "three or more," and conditions were not changing for the better; things were getting worse.

The BOP had admitted to the ACLU that while we had been housed in the HSU, there had been no threats by outside forces to either retaliate against the BOP or to free us and that our placement there was simply a matter of the "justice community's" decision. We believed that if we relied on the BOP's answer, we would never get into general population and never get rid of the "terrorist jacket." They would construct a larger version of what we were in, with all the necessary controls in it. We further believed that our psychological files needed to be released to prove that the HSU was an experiment in psychological torture. We were deeply concerned that if we did not expose the program now, the BOP would institutionalize psychological maltreatment and manipulation as a form of behavior modification and mind control for all the political women prisoners. Work began on a lawsuit by the ACLU and our lawyers and other progressive organizations.

Our suspicions were right: nothing came of the BOP's pronouncement. Life continued. One morning, Mr. Dozier, the head CO, came charging onto the tier, yelling as he approached, "Get up! Attention! I have orders for you, direct orders!"

Mr. Dozier seemed like he was a man who was stuck in his life, as though he had put a foot down into the mud and couldn't lift it up. He was in his mid-forties and had a glistening buzz cut (but, we were told, no wife). Unlike so many others of our jailers, however, he was still fit. He had worked in a Kentucky men's maximum-security mental institution for years, and when he transferred to the federal system there were promises of opportunities to use his skills and of promotions. But he had not made it past CO, because working in a mental institution hadn't required any special skills. He was angry, all of the time.

"Your orders are to clean the unit," he bellowed. He wanted it spotless and shining. By then, however, we were through with cooperating or listening to orders; we were no longer complying. No one moved, no one stood, and no one even came to a cell door to look at him.

He went ballistic. He began screaming at the camera to whoever was watching in the video control room. "These fucking bitches, these lazy fucking bitches! That's it!" He left the tier. An hour later, he was back with two lieutenants and two other COs. We had expected him to return, so we stayed in our individual cells. They locked us in and then slid pink slips, the disciplinary write-ups we called "shots," under our doors. We were all charged with refusing to work, disobeying a direct order, and slothfulness. I didn't care. I don't think anyone did. Someone down the hall said, "Take the fucking TV." Later that same day, Sig came and unlocked us and asked us to clean the unit. He was being polite. We thought that maybe he had seen the tape and knew how crazy and hostile Dozier had been. He ripped up the shots. But again, we said no. That night officers came and cleaned, a sight I had never seen before. They were mopping and buffing the already gleaming floors. Their glares were filled with hatred for us.

The next morning, Silvia had a visit with her lawyer, Elizabeth Fink—Liz—a longtime radical who had fought numerous political cases and won many of them. Among many cases, Liz had been the attorney for the Attica brothers in the case stemming from the Attica prison rebellion in the 1970s, and worked unceasingly on the brothers' behalf. Because we were jointly working on the lawsuit against the BOP to close down the HSU, I was allowed to visit with Liz and Silvia. We were in the midst of explaining to her why we had to sue and not accept the BOP status quo. I looked up and, out of the day room window, I saw the director of the Bureau of Prisons, J. Michael Quinlan. He was walking past us down the hallway, flanked by numerous "men in suits." Men in suits, as opposed to men in uniform, were always a signal that higher-level administrators were walking the unit. The director was one of the shortest and slightest and mousiest men I had ever seen. "It's Quinlan. It's fucking Quinlan," I said.

The three of us stood up all at once, getting ready for battle. Liz stepped out into the hall. "Mr. Quinlan," she absolutely roared, "we'd like to speak with you." Because the men had to wait for an electronic gate to open for them, they were trapped with us in the hall. Quinlan turned and trained on us a look that was both contemptuous and hesitant, as though he expected us to rush his party and physically attack them in the hall. "Mr. Quinlan, we must talk to you," Liz intoned again.

As she started moving up the hall, Quinlan apparently decided that it would be safer to talk to us in the tiny legal visiting room. He turned and approached us. I was seething. I simply could not believe that this was the man responsible for our condition, this small, ugly, nondescript man. Liz is a big woman, physically intimidating, a woman who can command a chaotic courtroom into utter quiet. She used that skill now. Standing as close as she could possibly get without stepping on the man, she said, "This unit is an abomination. It is the most repulsive and degrading place I've ever seen, and I've seen a lot."

"I'm sure you have, Ms. Fink." Quinlan did not blink. "It looks very good to me," he went on, "but we are, as your clients know, opening a bigger unit and they'll be sent there soon."

"It will be just like this. You know we should be in population," Silvia broke in, with such anger in her that tears spilled out of her eyes.

"I don't think so, Ms. Baraldini," he replied, eyeing Silvia.

"And where is this new control unit prison? And when is it opening?" Liz demanded.

"In Florida, within a year or so." And with that, his security guards hustled him through the gate.

Later, after Liz had left and we were put back in our cells, Quinlan took another tour of our tier. When he walked past Alex's cell, she told him that he would need to build many units because they couldn't build enough prisons to contain the Puerto Rican independence movement.

We were terribly demoralized by what we felt was the inactivity of our supporters. We thought that they were acquiescing to the

BOP's newest statement that they were closing the HSU. We felt that believing anything they said was a grave mistake. We needed to use whatever mechanism we could in order to resist. We needed something to struggle for. Without it, we felt increasingly stifled. It was during this lull that I developed my suicide plan. Until that point in my sentence, I had not seriously thought of suicide as an option. But now planning one's own death seemed like the ultimate exertion of power over one's own life. It was my back-door escape plan if all else failed. I revised it over and over again. I felt that if my mind turned to mush, or they succeeded in breaking my spirit and mental capacities, then death would be the most honorable end. It was not romantic or hysterical; it simply was an option that, given my circumstances, I believed I had to consider. And once my plan was complete, I felt a great relief, as though I had liberated myself from the fear of being destroyed. The final act of control over myself would then be mine to determine.

My plan was very simple. I would hang myself with a sheet. There was a water pipe that ran across the ceiling of my cell, and it was high enough off the ground to do the trick. I asked myself if I would know when the time came. I worried that I would decide on the moment but then be too screwed up to be capable of actually doing it. For months, I practiced yoga and meditation to strengthen my mind so that I would know when the right time came. And as I prepared my plan to die, I thought about how much I would miss the moon, and Aretha Franklin, and my family and friends, and Chinese food, which I could hardly remember. I thought about everyone on death row, and of Debra only two cells down the tier, fighting to live. And I thought how awful it would be not to know how things turned out.

On the unit, we never discussed suicide among ourselves. But we were getting sicker. Alex had a heart condition, a mitrovalve prolapse. Every day we asked the COs to take her to a doctor, and every day we were told only, "The PA is coming." Each day, Alex got worse. The COs accused her of hunger striking and used that as the explanation for increased physical weakness.

It took a week for the physician's assistant to come to the unit. He wouldn't go through the electronic gate. He called down the tier, "Mrs. Torres, Mrs. Torres, I'm the PA."

Alex came out of her cell and walked to the gate. The PA said, "Come here, come closer."

As she approached, he picked up his stethoscope, which was hanging around his neck. "Unbutton your shirt," he said.

Alex looked at him in utter disbelief as he put the stethoscope through the bars. "You have got to be kidding."

All of us were standing at our cell doors on the tier watching this. "Come on, Mrs. Torres; let me have your heart."

"Forget it," Alex said as she walked back to her cell.

"She's refusing medical care—see, its all bullshit; she's lying," the voice from the control room yelled through the intercom under the surveillance camera.

The PA said, "She's refusing," as he walked down the hall out of our vision.

We were so stunned by what had just happened that we did not protest. We all looked at one another with a combination of fury and grief. Silvia said, "That's it. I'm going on a work strike until Alex gets to see a doctor. Can you beat that shit?"

I said, "Me, too." Both Debra Brown and Sylvia Brown also wanted to strike. Witnessing the prison's version of medical care fortified our resolve to do whatever we had to do.

Functionally, going on strike meant that we would all be locked in our own cells all day instead of being allowed out on the tier. It meant that no one would clean or go outside. It meant that we would get a write-up and have our TVs taken away. Sig, who by now was ready to take early retirement, came and talked to us. His conversation with Silvia went like this:

"I can't understand how you would jeopardize your status over what you call this thing, this ridiculous thing you call solidarity. I mean, throwing out your record for someone else."

"Come on, Sig, you were in the Navy or the Marines or some military. You know it's like the esprit de corps, or going down for your buddy, that kind of thing," Silvia said.

"Yeah, okay, I understand that, but I only stand by my buddy if he's right, not if he's wrong."

"Well, we think we're right. You should give proper medical treatment to Alex, and until you do, that's the way it is."

"I'm trying to informally resolve this. I'm offering you a way out of lockdown." He was pleading.

"Look, this isn't going to work. We have been cooperative, we asked, explained, even pleaded, and all you people have done is thrown shit in our face. We've utilized every possible informal channel and you know it." Silvia's voice was rising with exasperation.

"I don't understand you people," Sig said.

"We know," Silvia replied and turned her back on him.

He moved down the tier and took Alex out of her cell through the gate and into the officers' station.

Alex started, "My attorney told me that you told her that you don't think I like you, and that fact concerns you. Frankly, Mr. Sigman, that has absolutely nothing to do with this conflict we are in. We know that decisions about us are made from Washington—

you've certainly told us that often enough—so really, you are just an errand boy for them. Like and dislike are not relevant."

"I don't like you? Uh, uh, no, no. I didn't say that. I like you. You don't like me." He was stymied.

"Mr. Sigman, I know that we have not been communicating, and it seems as if we talk at cross-purposes, and that you don't listen to me, and I don't listen to you. So let me try to explain it again." Alex was calm.

He interrupted, "You have to admit that the last time we talked you screamed at me. You said, 'Go ahead, do the courageous thing, lock me up. Don't be a coward. Do what you all wanted from the day we got here.'"

"No," Alex said, "I said lock me up anytime you want, whenever you feel like it, because you don't use your own procedures, and I won't be played with. I refuse to play the little power games, and so lock me up so that we don't play this anymore. That is what I said."

"But Alex, you were screaming at me, and someone in my position isn't used to being screamed at by people."

"You mean by a prisoner. That is the way I talk when I am angry. I raise my voice; it's the way I am."

"Well, I have three medical people who tell me you are fit to work, that you're just malingering. It is a medical department decision. It's out of my hands, except, you see, I'm in charge of the work assignments."

"I am trying to tell you how I feel. I feel very bad. I am not talking about a PA who refused to examine me or a doctor who reads an old chart. I'm talking about what my body is telling me, and it is not well." Alex kept going. "Can't we come to some agreement or understanding about this?"

"Well, we'll discuss all this with your attorney." He didn't bother to escort Alex back. He nodded to a CO, who accompanied her the two hundred feet she had to walk.

The next day the lieutenants came with the COs and handed out shots. We were locked in. Sig came to my cell and spoke to me through the window in the door. "Too bad you're not Catholic."

"What?" I said.

"Now that you're in the hole, it could be penance to sacrifice, you know, to avoid purgatory to get to heaven quicker."

"Every day here is penance," I answered, "and believe me, I am going straight to paradise as quickly as possible."

Part Four

Washington, D.C.

Chapter 9

D.C. County Jail

I HEARD ABOUT our indictment over the phone. I was standing in the medical room with two COs standing next to me. Mary had gotten a call through to me, and as soon as I picked up the receiver, she said, "Are you sitting down?"

I knew it wasn't good news. "Yes," I lied.

"A secret indictment against you and Alan, Laura and Linda, Tim and Marilyn was unsealed this morning in Washington, D.C. You are charged with conspiracy to bomb the U.S. Capitol and other government buildings."

I sat down.

Mary went on, "You are being brought to D.C. in the next few days where all of you will be arraigned."

"But what about the lawsuit against this place?" I asked.

"It will happen," Mary said. I could hear the fury in Mary's voice through the thousand miles of wire.

I tried to keep mine out of my voice. "Will you come for the arraignment?" I asked.

"You know I will," she answered.

The COs at my back sneered as the conversation continued.

Whether or not they had known before I did about the new indictment didn't matter; they were just pleased that I would be put on trial again. They were pleased because they thought my leaving the HSU would help the BOP win the lawsuit. I had been in prison for three and a half years, and almost all that time had been spent in either segregation or one form of isolation or another.

Three days later, I was airlifted to Washington in a BOP Learjet along with Linda Evans. It had been two years since I had seen Linda. The sequence of events that had occurred after my arrest had led not only to Linda's arrest, but also to the arrest of Marilyn Buck, Dr. Alan Berkman, and Laura Whitehorn. They were the people I was with while I was underground. When Tim and I were arrested, the FBI had been able to trace the evidence from us to Alan, and from him to Marilyn and Linda, and finally to a house in Baltimore where they had arrested Laura.

All of them were longtime political radicals. Together, we had gone underground to organize an invisible component of what was then called the anti-imperialist left. Marilyn, and I had been charged with participation in the federal conspiracy case stemming from the Brink's robbery investigation in 1982. Alan had been charged with treating and then not reporting medical care to a person who had been shot. By that day in May 1987, Alan had been convicted of possession of weapons, Linda had been convicted and sentenced to forty years for harboring Marilyn and purchasing four guns illegally, and Marilyn had been convicted of the conspiracy case and sentenced to sixty years in prison. Laura was the only one who had no previous federal sentence.

Linda and I were the only two passengers on that little plane in the security detail. The plane's previous flight had held a congressional delegation, and their leftover food was given to us. There was spectacular fruit, which neither of us had eaten in a very long time. We laughed as we ate it with our hands cuffed. We were thrilled to see each other, and loving the moments of contact. But, at the same time, we were angry at the indictment and that we were now facing this new trial. Both of us had been doing our time; now we were facing life in prison.

We arrived at the jail with a cavalcade of security the likes of which I hadn't seen before. We were accompanied by a phalanx of police cars and there were several helicopters following us overhead. The District of Columbia had taken the occasion to parade us through the streets. Linda and I went through receiving together. The jail's procedures included fingerprinting, a strip search, an interview, and a chemical hosedown. We protested the spray; we were coming from other prisons, not from the street. They sprayed us anyway, taking pains to cover every inch. We were the only women prisoners in the area, so just before Linda was escorted away, we agreed to demand to be housed in the same unit. Then, several lieutenants and COs came for me. Everyone we had seen up to that point was African American, including this group. Handcuffed, waist-chained, and dressed in an extra-large orange jumpsuit, I was moved upstairs. I had been in many holding cells and several prisons by then, but when I got to the floor and was let into the block, my heart did a flip and every muscle went into flight mode. The block was one long tier with open-barred cells on each side. There was no solid door or wall at the front end. That meant zero privacy and no safe space, not even an inch.

They put me in the last cell and then took the chains off through an opening in the bars. I wanted my phone call, which I had started telling them from the moment we walked in. No answer. I kept asking questions: Where am I? What unit is this? What is it called?

Finally, as the COs were leaving, one of them said, "Intake. You'll get a call when someone has time."

Linda was nowhere in sight, but out of desperation I started shouting her name as the COs retreated. They were laughing as they walked away.

My cell was all white. The cell across from mine was all white. It wasn't a Lexington blinding white (there were no fluorescent lights), but a filthy white. It wasn't a strip cell exactly, but it was bare and sterile. Everything metal was bolted to the wall or the floor. I had no sheets or towels; otherwise, I would have hung them on the bars. No one was across the tier from me. I was isolated within the isolation. I began to pace. I examined the space; I looked up and down the tier with my face pressed to the bars. I realized after a few minutes that it was really silent. I had seen women in the cells as we walked past, but they had all been lying down.

I did my ritual meditation: *If it doesn't get worse than this, I can find a way to get through it.* Except this time I knew I couldn't kid myself. I thought, *I can't do this. I cannot live in an open cell.* And then I thought that maybe the segregation unit would have closed-front cells. But I couldn't demand to be put in segregation. I couldn't demand that because it was the same as demanding protective custody, and only snitches got protective custody, snitches and ex-cops. I got more and more agitated as all my mental tricks and racing thoughts led me back to exactly where I was. And just when I had bottomed out, several women down the tier started talking and then yelling. And then one voice rose above the rest and formed itself into a howl, and then another woman, and then another, and another, began to howl until the noise was a collective roar. As I stood at the bars to see what had caused this down the tier, I saw something fly through a set of bars. My mind didn't compute what I had seen until another voice said, "There she goes again, the shitter." The same voice then called out, "Shelia, stop. Don't throw that. They'll be back. You don't have to do that garbage." It was shit that Shelia was throwing. Whoever Shelia was.

Speechless, I stepped back and sat down. This was beyond my capacity to handle. The yelling kept up, and I tried to count the number of voices. If I had been less flipped out I would have tried to talk to someone, but I couldn't stand up. I don't know how long this went on, but eventually the door popped open and there were COs on the tier. One of them started yelling, "Shut up, everyone shut up, or you won't get your shit!" Slowly the roar was reduced to a din and I stood at the bars. There were two women COs pushing a med cart, stopping at each cell, They were handing little plastic cups to the women, all of whom were now docilely standing at their bars.

They stopped short of my cell, but didn't even look my way. I yelled, "I want my phone call!" No response. They just wheeled their cart off the floor. It got quiet. I realized then that I was on the psychiatric ward. I started to cry.

When the cops came back, I was ready. They were there to do "feeding." A different set of COs was putting plastic trays on the shelf outside each cell. I stood facing them. "I demand my phone call. I am not supposed to be on this unit. Why am I on the psych unit? I demand to see the captain." Again, they would not acknowledge me. "I am a political prisoner, and I want to see someone in authority. This isn't Russia; we don't put political prisoners in psychiatric units. Where are my codefendants?" Now I was raging. The cops thought this was funny, but they refused to speak. I knew they had been instructed not to talk to me. I told them, "I'm not eating until someone comes and speaks to me. Not until that or I get my phone call. You want to be responsible for that?"

How many hours later the captain finally appeared, I don't

know. By then I was disoriented and beyond angry. The captain, again with multiple lieutenants, chained me up and escorted me down the tier and out into the hall. A pay phone that I had not noticed on the way in stood glistening, like a mirage. Flooded with relief, I asked, "What time is it?"

The captain scowled. "It's eleven thirty. Hurry up—it's shift change."

I called a number I knew by heart and got hold of Susie Ways-dorf, a paralegal who had moved to Washington, D.C., to work on the Lexington HSU lawsuit. She was also an old friend. "Hello," I whispered not wanting the captain to hear me.

"Susan?" my friend said. "Where are you?"

"I'm on some psych unit in the D.C. jail. Please get me out of here. I got here with Linda, but she's somewhere else."

"We've been trying to find you all day." Susie sounded upset. "The jail refused to tell us if you'd arrived or where you were. The BOP wouldn't tell us, either."

I realized then that Linda hadn't been able to make a call, either. "Please get me out of here. I don't want psych added to my jacket. This is the worst. This is worse than the HSU," I said.

"You're being arraigned tomorrow. We'll get you moved then."

It was not what I wanted to hear. I wanted out of there that second. My skin was crawling. "Are Alan and Marilyn and Laura here in D.C.?" I wanted to know.

"We think so," Susie said. "We'll see you tomorrow."

A few hours later, another captain, a woman named Swanson, showed up with two lieutenants. They took me to another unit to take a shower. The captain and I stood in front of that shower while she uncuffed one hand. I took off my jumpsuit, stepped into the stall, and stuck my cuffed hand out. The captain said, "Give me your other wrist. I have to cuff you back up."

I couldn't believe it. Showering cuffed was new even to me. I told her no way, it's impossible. How can you get clean with cuffs on?

She told me that it was policy, that my being on three-man hold made it mandatory. Three-man hold means accompaniment with no less than three officers whenever I was out of the cell. Again I told her no way. Her answer was, "Susan, if you don't let me cuff you, I will call the lieutenants over here to remove you, naked or not, and you'll go to court without a shower."

As I gave her my wrist, I berated myself for being a coward and not fighting it out, even if I couldn't win. The only relief in the experience of that first particular humiliation was that I could control the temperature of the water, even with cuffs on. And then as I soaped up and the captain turned her back on me, I slipped one hand out of the cuff, put it back, and then slipped the other hand out. My revenge, as I thought of it, made me feel a shred better. This was the first of six months of these showers. This was the only woman captain, and the only high-ranking officer who was ordered to "shower" me. Needless to say, I didn't get more than the legally allotted three showers a week.

Laura, Alan, Tim, Linda, and I were all taken to court separately, but we met in the courtroom in our orange prison suits and bracelets. We were angry, and I know I at least was shell-shocked. Seeing everyone there in the courtroom was exciting. We were without counsel and several of us had not even read the indictment. There were cops of every stripe all over the courtroom. We were fortunate when William Kunstler, Ron Kuby, Mary O'Melveny, Susan Tipograph—all lawyers from New York—walked in. All the lawyers were among the most progressive and powerful civil rights lawyers in the U.S. The judge was Harold Greene, a long-standing liberal who everyone said was a fair judge. What to do? Obviously, we would plead not guilty. If this was courtroom drama and spectacle for the Reagan administration's anti-terrorism policy, if this was designed by the government to counter the Iran-Contra hearings and the indictments of Oliver North and company, then we had to resist in kind. But having gone through one trial in which I had used the courtroom as a platform to argue my beliefs—throwing legal consequences to the wind, and then living with the consequences for three years—I did not want to do it again.

Our first joint discussion, right there in the courtroom, which continued throughout the next two and a half years in countless forms, centered on whether we should say we were revolutionaries or political prisoners in our not-guilty plea. Should we say only that we were "not guilty" or that we were "not guilty of crimes." To others it might sound as if we were splitting hairs, but the distinctions were important to us. We were revolutionaries, but all of us had already been in prison for years and had been fighting our struggles as prisoners. We had all broken the law. Yet, like political prisoners all over the world, we did not see ourselves as criminals and felt it imperative to oppose the government's attempt to label us as such. And that is what William Kunstler told Judge Harold Greene: We were political prisoners, not guilty of crimes.

No one could go head to head with authority better than Bill Kunstler. And that day, when the gavel fell and the judge was "doing housekeeping"—legal jargon for scheduling witnesses, paying the lawyers, unshackling the accused to allow them to prepare for trial—the discussion of my housing on the psychiatric ward took place. Mary and Bill wanted Judge Greene to court-order me off the unit and into population. They argued that we do not imprison political prisoners on psych wards in the United States. They further argued that I had no history of psychological disorder.

The judge grew angry. His bald, high forehead turned red.

"How dare you compare this great democracy with the Communist regime in Russia!" he yelled. "These defendants are not political prisoners; they are anything but that," he went on.

He knew this would be one hell of a trial, and he was not going to allow the rules and definitions to get reinterpreted. But, despite his angry outburst, Judge Greene ordered me moved. His decision was reasoned: I had no history of psychiatric disorders, I was not a danger to myself or others, and the only reason I had been placed on the psych unit in D.C. was that I had been transferred there from a psychological experimentation unit. And so began our legal case.

From May, 1988, until November, 1989, the biggest challenge for me and my fellow defendants was the set of conditions under which we were imprisoned. The FBI's Joint Terrorist Task Force, which led the training sessions for a security team of our D.C. jailers, classified us as "special handling." This meant we were locked down, shackled even in legal meetings, denied recreation, kept under special surveillance, and constantly harassed, with an underlying threat of physical assault. It also meant that anytime any one of us was let out of his or her cell, all other prisoners had to be locked in. This alone created conflicts between us and the rest of the population. The top of the administration's agenda was to instill fear in the rest of the population so that no one would support us or help us. Each of us was housed on a different block at the jail. There were over three thousand prisoners, 99 percent of whom were young black men and women predominantly from the southeastern part of Washington, D.C. Most were caught in the revolving door of poverty, drugs, gangs, low-level crime, and jail. Most of the women were drug addicts and needed medical treatment more than anything else.

The cell blocks were old, dark, and dirty. There were eighty cells in a block, all of which held short-term-sentenced women. Each cell had a forty-watt lightbulb, a metal bunk, a toilet, a sink, and a metal desk and stool attached to the wall. My cell was the first one on the bottom tier; it was under the COs' station, an enclosed Plexiglas control room known as the "bubble," where the COs sat and operated the doors. Perpendicular to my block was another, so this bubble controlled the movement of 160 women.

The cell door was solid steel with a vertical window cut out of the steel, one foot high and six inches wide. The window had no covering, which meant that anyone walking by could throw something inside. It also meant that every sound could be heard. In those first days, I stood at the window watching everything. Several of the women had duties as kitchen workers, hospital workers, and orderlies in other parts of the jail, so there was a lot of movement in and out of the block. I had not seen this many people in one place for several years. Fascinated, I observed all the women and their comings and goings.

After a few days, the sergeants started giving disciplinary write-ups to prisoners who tried to stop at my cell door and talk to me or even just look at me. But, as usually happens when you tell a group of people not to do something (especially if you say the restriction is for their own good), eventually curiosity gets the better of them and they question the order. In fact, they disobey the order. Slowly, one by one, every woman on my block came to check me out. Some spoke and some did not. They all peered in and made their own assessment.

The first woman to break the rule was named Donna Nelson. She was someone who had grown up in D.C. and in the jail. She was short and stocky, weathered but young. She had one big gold loop in her ear, a missing front tooth, and a short red-blond Afro on which she had perched a knitted skullcap. She was vigorously chewing gum. "You a terrorist?" she asked.

"Nope," I answered.

"You a white supremacist?"

"Nope, just the opposite. That's why I'm locked up." I stared into her eyes. I liked her immediately.

"You pretty skinny to be so dangerous."

I laughed. "I'm not dangerous. All this is to make you think I am, me and the other folks in my case."

She nodded and sauntered away. Five minutes later she was back. She tossed me an orange and a Snickers bar, and kept walking.

Someone had seen her do it. The next morning I woke up to a lot of yelling. There were sergeants and a lieutenant on the block; the prisoners had been herded out of their cells and into the TV area. I heard the sergeant talking. She was giving a speech: "These people are racists. They are in the KKK, they are charged with bombing Jesse Jackson, and they have tried to blow up the jail. They are cold-blooded killers who want to kill your children."

I screamed at the top of my lungs, "That's a lie, that's a damn lie! We hate the KKK. We're here because we support the Black Liberation Army. We would never bomb you, your kids, the jail, Jesse Jackson, or anyone else. Don't believe this bullshit!"

A lieutenant ran toward my cell, shouting, "Shut up, bitch!"

I expected a beating. Everyone stood frozen, and I guess the lieutenant realized that he did not want so many witnesses. He stopped in his tracks and turned, facing all the women. "This terrorist is lying. Don't believe her. And do not talk to her. You will be punished." They ordered everyone to work or back to their cells and then locked the block down.

I was livid. I paced and raged, and desperately wanted to

tell someone the jailers were setting up me and the others to be killed.

A few hours later, Donna appeared at the window. "Don't worry—no one believes their shit." She was gone before I could stand up. This would not be the last time Donna Nelson would come to my aid.

As the afternoon wore on, first a candy bar was thrown in my cell, then a cigarette, then a book of matches, then a piece of fruit. All the most precious commodities. No one else talked to me that day, but I knew the jailers had just lost their first battle in their propaganda war against us. This happened on every block where the "codefendants" of the Resistance Conspiracy case (as we became known) were housed.

The D.C. jail is just blocks from the U.S. Capitol. A hair's breadth from the center of U.S. power, it seems to have been designed to keep the poor black community out of sight and out of mind. But the people who run the jail are from the same community as the prisoners. It is as Malcolm X might have put it: the field and the big house rolled into one big auction block. In the late 1980s, two epidemics hit urban centers all over America: crack and AIDS. And, since life in every city jail contains all the same social problems that exist in the larger society, crack and AIDS hit the D.C. jail with force.

I had never seen crack and knew little about HIV. For the first several months, I just watched the women and noted two distinct types of energy. One was a laid-back, almost relaxed kind of fluidity. The other was a loud, frenetic, jerky, hostile energy. Finally, I realized that the differences were chemical: the first type of energy came from heroin, and the second from crack. Crack was even worse than heroin, if that was possible. In 1989, forty-five people were violently killed in D.C., and every single one of them was crack related. By the time people came to my block, they had been detoxed with the help of methadone, but crack, heroin, grass, speed, downers, and psychotrops were all easily "purchased." Usually turning one trick was enough. Trading sex for drugs was the number one commodity. The COs made a little on the side with the drug trade.

One night in the late fall of our first year, I was awake battling the cold. Steel and concrete were the only surfaces in the seven-by-four-foot box in which I lived. I was sitting on the bunk wrapped in every item of fabric I had. I was trying to breathe deeply and not succumb to the chattering that was rising in my chest. My light was out. All the lights were out. Everyone was quiet and the COs were asleep in the bubble. I heard the cell door next to mine pop open. I knew it was next door because by then I knew the origin of every sound in the place. I did not get up. Then the block door popped open and I went to the slot, standing to the side so that no one would see me. Several cops were half carrying and half pulling a woman down the stairs. She was flailing against them, but to no effect. They dumped her next door and nodded to the bubble cops, and the door slid shut. They walked off. Then it was quiet again.

I whispered through the slot, "Hello, hello, hey there."

No answer. I went back to my cold self. Then the moaning began. It started low and in short spurts. Then I heard rustling. Maybe the woman had gotten off the bunk or stood up from the floor. Then I heard the sound of crying, interspersed with deeper groaning.

"What's going on? What's wrong? Are you sick?" Stupid questions, but I didn't know what to do, or what else to say.

Then she started retching as violently as I have ever heard anyone retch. It made me nauseous to listen. What could I do? I went to the door and started yelling at the bubble. There was no one in it. "This woman is sick, she needs assistance," I called.

Someone at the far end of the block said, "Good luck."

She threw up long after a body should, long after whatever poisons were in her had been expelled. And all the while I stood watch, waiting for one of the guards. Finally, it got quiet and she stopped. I sat down exhausted, freezing, and freaked out. I dozed off. I jerked up with a start as I realized that a rhythmic knocking had been coming from next door for what seemed like a long time. I couldn't integrate the sound at first, but then I knew what it was. She was banging her head against the wall.

I ran to the window. "Oh, honey, stop that. Stop it. We'll get you help—don't do that. Stop!" I begged. The thudding kept going. In the midst of that frozen night I started to sweat. She was killing herself and no one was going to do anything about it. I lost it. I started banging and hollering and cursing and throwing whatever I could to get someone's attention (preferably someone with a key), to get the woman to hear me, to break the cycle, whatever. A few other women down the tier started yelling, too. And then a few others yelled to shut up. But no one in authority came. I slid down and sat with my back to the cell door and wept. The pounding kept on until it finally simply stopped dead.

Later a CO came to do a routine count. It was close to 5:00 a.m. I sat there until he came to count me. I didn't know him, but I started yelling, "You're responsible for the woman next door. She's dead! Where the fuck have you all been?"

The CO looked in the cell and, without a word, ran out of the unit. A few minutes later, a group of lieutenants and COs showed up. I was standing at my door talking in their general direction. Crazy, I was absolutely crazy. One rookie looked into the woman's cell, turned, and stuttered, "Oh, sh-shit."

The lieutenant came right up to my face and said, "Shut up, bitch"—one of the officers' favorite sayings—"she's not dead." He said that several times at a loud volume.

They got a stretcher and went in. They carried her out with a blanket draped over her. I couldn't see her at all. Then they broke from normal procedure and cleaned the cell themselves. Everyone stayed locked down. Had she died? Yes. Who was she? I never knew. The prison was responsible. Not that the administration ever acknowledged it.

I told my codefendants about this as soon as I could, and I told my lawyers and friends. They could not find anything out. It was as though it hadn't happened. There were no records. No one came forward to find a missing person. No one inside knew who she was.

Later, a woman on my block, in response to my attempt to protest the woman's death, said, "Shit, Susan, she OD'd on PCP and crack. It happens all the time."

For the next year, we tried every way we could to keep body and soul together. We eventually were among the longest-held prisoners in the jail. But the extreme and excessive security conditions had been lessened. After eleven months of total lockdown, we had been released into general population and were allowed to meet together daily. This in effect put us smack in the middle of the life of the jail. We were given a large room and lockers for our papers. We were ultimately allowed to meet together without lawyers or paralegals and with guards posted outside the room.

It was our most productive and most difficult time. We had worked in various organizations with each other for over fifteen years. We had all been great friends and at different times in leadership. We had worked together, organized together, lived together, loved one another, and fought with one another. We were all inspired by a vision of a just and radical society. We had all been willing to give our lives in pursuit of that vision. We believed that we were justified in attempting to build a revolutionary underground, to actively oppose our government's aggression and racism in all its manifestations, and to make women and gay people equal and free. But we had all experienced our arrests, trials, and imprisonments alone, for the past three years. And we had all drawn our own conclusions from those experiences. Regardless of our differences and changes, we knew we needed unity more than we ever did before if we were going to survive and win now.

While all this was going on, the legal motions in our case were progressing through the courts. We were charged with a conspiracy to use violent and illegal means to protest and change U.S. foreign and domestic policy. The indictment read, "Charged in a conspiracy to influence, change, and protest policies and practices of the United States government concerning various international and domestic matters through the use of violent and illegal means." The indictment also charged us with aiding and abetting nine bombings of military and governmental buildings—resulting in property damage. The U.S. Capitol bombing in 1983 was the most significant. But there had been other bombings against the United States to protest its policies and practices in Central America, its support of the Contras in Nicaragua, the U.S.-led invasion of Grenada, the establishment of dictatorships in El Salvador, Guatemala, Honduras, and Chile, and the continuing disappearances of people in the region.

During this same period, the Iran-Contra hearings produced indictments against Oliver North and Elliott Abrams. The Iran-Contra scheme had begun in 1983 and was a plan to provide funds to the Nicaraguan Contra rebels from profits gained by selling arms to Iran. The Iran-Contra scandal was the product of two separate initiatives during Ronald Reagan's presidency. The first was a commitment to aid the Contras, who were conducting a guerrilla war against the leftist Sandinista government of Nicaragua. The second was to placate "moderates" within the Iranian government in order to secure the release of American hostages held by pro-Iranian groups in Lebanon and to influence Iranian foreign policy in a pro-American direction. Despite the strong opposition of the Reagan administration, the Democratic-controlled Congress enacted legislation, known as the Boland amendments, that prohibited the Defense Department, the Central Intelligence Agency, or any other government agency from providing military aid to the Contras from December 1983 to September 1985. The Reagan administration circumvented these limitations by using the National Security Council (NSC), which was not explicitly covered by the law, to supervise covert military aid to the Contras. Under Robert McFarlane (1983–85) and John Poindexter (1985–86), the NSC raised private and foreign funds for the Contras. This operation was directed by NSC staffer Marine Lieutenant Colonel Oliver North. The indictment of government officials was a political blow to the administration and they wanted to recoup their losses.

We believed the prosecution's plan was to use our trial and the attendant publicity to counter the congressional revelations and indictments surrounding Iran-Contra. Our case was to be a "show trial" of Americans citizens who, with the use of armed propaganda, opposed and showed the vulnerability of the Reagan administration's entire Central American strategy and all of its foreign policy. It was intended to have a chilling effect on activism and they hoped it would divert attention from the Oliver North and John Poindexter hearings going on down the hall from our own trial.

When we counted all the previous trials that we had gone through either individually or in various permutations, they totaled fourteen prosecutions. We had all been incarcerated for three or more years and all had lengthy sentences, with the exception of Laura Whitehorn, who had yet to be brought to trial but had been held in preventive detention for three years. When we realized that the government was stacking the charges, meaning that they were using the same acts to try us over and over again, we thought that we had found the flaw in the government's case against us. They already had convicted us in all cases. On top of that and most importantly, Tim and I had already been convicted of conspiracy, as had Alan, in our first trials. The government was using the same conspiracy and the same evidence from our New Jersey case to try us again in Washington, D.C. In January 1989, as part of an agreed-to strategy, Tim, Alan and I filed to have our cases severed from those of Linda, Laura, and Marilyn. In April, Judge Greene dismissed the charges against the three of us. He had agreed that the government was committing double jeopardy. The government appealed and we remained in the D.C. jail.

Throughout this time, the Lexington HSU legal case was running on a parallel track. The political struggles around it were evolving. It was independent of the Resistance Conspiracy case, but the two cases intersected through me. While at the jail, I had been called to testify in Judge Barrington Parker's courtroom. The idea of testifying in the case, of being able to tell the judge in an open courtroom how the Bureau of Prisons was treating us, to tell him how I actually felt, was overwhelming. It would be the first time I had been in public, not in a prison, in over five years. It was bad luck, coincidence, or destiny that I was even there in Washington to be able to testify. It was only because of the Resistance Conspiracy indictment that the judge agreed to have me in his courtroom. The BOP had opposed my testifying, had opposed anyone from our side giving evidence. Their grounds had been that we were too dangerous to be allowed into an open court, with a secondary argument that it would be too expensive to secure the proceeding. But Judge Parker overruled them. The BOP's next motion was to move the hearing to the special anti-terrorist courtroom where they had built a Plexiglas wall between the well of the court and the rows for the public observers. The government's argument was that I was too dangerous to be in open court, and that the public needed protection from me. Judge Parker was in a wheelchair and had a special ramp built between his chambers and the bench, which allowed him to enter the courtroom without assistance. He would not move to another courtroom under any circumstances. He again overruled the government.

On the day of the hearing, the U.S. marshals, D.C. police, and FBI agents in a ten-car caravan with sirens blaring and helicopters swarming above escorted me to the empty holding cells in the basement of the federal courthouse. I was nervous; I felt so much was at stake. I had to be clear and articulate and not be afraid, and I had to represent the other women who were still being held at Lexington. I was out of practice speaking publicly and I had never taken the stand in a courtroom before. I needed a haircut and my clothes didn't fit. I weighed about one hundred pounds.

While in the holding cell, Mary and Susie came downstairs to help me prepare. They stood on one side of the bars and I paced back and forth close to the bars on the inside. Mary was giving me strength; I could feel it through the bars. She said, "Just tell the truth. That will be enough to make the case." Susie was trying to pat my arm by reaching her own arm through the bars. "It will be great," she said reassuringly. Then they went upstairs and I kept pacing, practicing what I would say out loud to the empty space.

Two marshals came into the room and one of them, without uttering a word, held out a pair of handcuffs. I, equally silent, put my hands through a section of the bars and they cuffed me. We walked into a small, old-fashioned elevator with a manual handle. We stopped and they opened the door and we stepped out into a very small room. It was wood paneled and airless. It was the witness room connected to Judge Parker's courtroom. The court was in session; I could hear murmuring through the door. One of the marshals had a radio transmitter in his ear and he was intently listening to whatever was being said on the other end. I felt I was suffocating in that room with them, as though my spirit and personality and very being were tamped down, waiting to explode.

The taller marshal nodded to his partner and the next thing I knew, they were literally carrying me into the courtroom, holding me up by my arms with my feet off the floor. The rush of seeing all these people sitting in front of me, the judge on the bench to the side of me, and the many cops standing and ringing the back of the courtroom was electric to me, causing a huge adrenaline rush. They sat me down at our side's table. It was all women attorneys and paralegals sitting in a row. They were all in colorful ensembles, Adjoa most strikingly wearing an African fabric of many shades of yellow, gold, and blue. I looked at the government's table and it was all men in gray and blue suits. It was a fantastic contrast, and at that moment it gave me a visual cue that built my confidence. Our side was beautiful. Then I turned and looked at the public spectators' rows. I saw my parents. Before I could take it all in, I was called to take the witness stand. The proceedings had been in full swing when I had walked into the room. The marshals wanted to keep the cuffs on me but Judge Parker thundered from the bench, "Not in this courtroom," and ordered them to take the cuffs off. He was staring at me from the moment that I had been carried into the room.

I walked unencumbered to the witness stand. My body recouped from the anxiety that my mind was feeling and my legs carried. It was the first time in a long time that I was not chained and surrounded by hostile men. I took the stand and put my hand on the Bible as the clerk asked me to swear. I couldn't help turning my head and looking at the judge, trying to size him up, but at the same time afraid of really meeting his stare. The U.S. attorney representing the BOP stood up and began. He asked me my name, which I answered. Then he asked me to explain why I was in prison. He asked me to clarify a point I said about being in prison for possession of explosives. He wanted me to describe the explosives. He was aggressive in his tone and his demeanor. I answered him back rather quietly, at which point the judge started to ask me questions directly. He told the U.S. attorney to sit down. Judge Parker asked me to describe the Lexington High Security Unit. He asked me to supply details. Then he had me stand up and go to a blackboard and draw where the cameras were located in the showers. As I stood up and got off the stand and walked into the well of the courtroom, I realized that the whole scene was pretty incredible. The marshals and the different police agents scattered around the courtroom where on full alert as I walked back and forth to the blackboard, explaining to the judge my answers to his questions. After he questioned me for forty-five minutes, he then asked me what I thought the effect of the Unit was on me. At that moment, there was complete silence in the courtroom. I answered, "I feel that my humanity is diminished." I was crying, because all of this was so difficult, and I was ashamed at my reduced capacity to act as a full human being. I was whisked from the courtroom by the marshals as soon as I stepped off the stand and taken back downstairs to the holding pen.

In his decision to immediately close the HSU, Judge Parker said that the conditions there bordered on human indecency and that our First Amendment rights had been violated by our being placed in these onerous conditions, with no due process and no remedy.

We had won our lawsuit. Amnesty International had conducted its first investigation of a U.S. prison-conditions complaint and found the United States in violation of international law on torture. Nina Rosenblum's documentary about the HSU had been completed and had aired on PBS. It went on to win international film festival awards and was nominated for an Academy Award. When Silvia Baraldini and Alejandrina Torres were transferred to other prisons, Alejandrina was diagnosed as having had a heart attack at the HSU and Silvia as having a rare form of uterine cancer. When I had arrived at the D.C. jail, I was suffering from severe post-traumatic stress disorder (PTSD). I weighed one hundred and four pounds.

Chapter 10

AIDS Epidemic

DURING 1988–89, seven women prisoners at the Washington, D.C., jail died of AIDS. The epidemic hit the population head-on like a speeding truck. While thousands of gay men had been dealing with AIDS since 1983, it was still early in the epidemic and little was known about the disease. There were few preventive treatments for opportunistic infections, and the drug AZT was still in clinical trials. President Reagan had gone through his first term without ever once mentioning AIDS. The medical establishment still believed that women couldn't get infected by HIV and that they could only transmit it. Most people had no idea what "casual contact" (contact without any exchange of body fluids) meant or how the virus was passed. At the jail, the small number of people who had been tested positive or had started to get sick were further sickened and ultimately destroyed by fear, stigma, and stupidity. HIV-positive prisoners were fed in separate Styrofoam trays by gloved workers.

The anguish from AIDS was compounded by the general state of conditions in the jail. A young black man died after his intestines burst and he was refused medical treatment. There was an outbreak of dysentery and all the kitchen workers were tested. People were sick on every unit, with high fevers and diarrhea. The size of the population, over two thousand, had exceeded the court-ordered limit; not one bed in the entire jail was empty. The count did not clear for three days; this meant that no one could leave their cells and guards came and counted and recounted and counted again and still couldn't get the number of prisoners in the jail to match the number that they had on paper. So, for four nights in a row, dinner consisted of a piece of American cheese, a slice of white bread, and a few peas. The noise was so bad it was impossible to use the phone. There were fights over food, the phone, medication—and battles with the COs. Once done weekly, the tier and cell shakedowns were now done daily.

And then physical assaults started on HIV-positive prisoners. On my unit, one woman shared a cigarette with another woman. After lunch, when the cigarette owner realized (because of the Styrofoam lunch tray) that the other woman was HIV-positive, she broke every finger of the woman's hand. "She won't smoke with that hand," the cigarette owner said as she walked away.

My codefendants and I had been discussing AIDS among ourselves since we arrived at the jail. Now we began to study the virus and discuss the public health implications for people in prison. Alan Berkman, a doctor who had worked in poor communities and hospitals, had been actively involved in public health for decades. He understood both the medical and public health aspects of the epidemic. We asked our outside supporters to send us information about HIV/AIDS and we began to study the virus, the immune system, biochemistry, testing, transmission, and treatment. We wanted to develop a survey so that we could get some honest idea of the depth of the infection rates and correspondingly a definition of infected prisoners' needs. We wanted to develop HIV education and prevention programs for prisoners, and we wanted decent care for HIV-positive people who were not yet sick and for those who were. We organized inside with prisoners, and we petitioned the administration. We wrote request after request to the head of the jail and asked him to meet with us to talk about the HIV epidemic. We asked our friends on the outside to help, and we worked with the jail chaplains and psychologists, who all recognized the need for a response to the epidemic. After months of asking, and then demanding, we succeeded in launching a prisoner-based peer education program with the help of the Whitman Walker Clinic, a D.C. clinic devoted exclusively to serving HIV/AIDS patients in poor neighborhoods. It was one of the first programs of its kind in the country in a city jail. The HIV/AIDS work that we began in prison gave me a means to my own salvation. It helped me put into context the worst of conditions and gave me something very meaningful to do. What made it happen was meeting the extraordinary women who, in the face of all the outrageously horrible conditions, stood up and struggled for their dignity.

Despite this initial effort, people continued to die all around us. On my block, one of many skirmishes in what by then we were calling the AIDS war was playing out most excruciatingly. Every day I would hear Theresa call out at the top of her voice, "Rider, Rider, where are you?" Rider, a friend of mine, one of the coolest and hardest-looking women I had met at the D.C. jail, would answer, "Okay, baby, I'm coming, hang on." Rider would glide down the stairs to the bottom of the tier and slide into Theresa's cell, and they would talk. Then she would slide out and go on about her work on the unit as an orderly.

One day when I was on the phone, I looked into the cell that Theresa and Rider shared. Rider was sitting on their trunk with her back against the wall and looking at the bed, where Theresa was sitting, knees-up. The intensity and intimacy they shared was as clear as a day after rain. Rider was cool, and she had years and years of practice at showing nothing. She lived behind a mask of nonreaction. She never lost at poker or spades, never. But this feeling she had, this love for her partner, she could not hide. The outer corners of her forty-five-year-old eyes began to turn upward, and the squint lines slowly became laugh lines. Their love affair affected anyone who acknowledged it. They navigated through the jailhouse rules and prohibitions with practiced grace and ease. The police knew the deal and let them cell together.

One night Rider came to my cell and said, "Theresa is sick. She is really sick. Do you understand?"

"Yes, Rider, I think I understand."

For five months Theresa hid herself, hoping it would undo her sickness. She wasted away in silence. She shielded herself against the rumors, the cruelty of other people's speculation, and the pain of her mental and physical suffering. She never was counseled; if the medical care was inadequate, the social neglect was criminal. Theresa lied to keep her secret, to deny her reality. But Rider knew, and I knew. And then Theresa was too sick to stay in the cell block.

After Theresa was sent to the prison ward of the D.C. General Hospital, nothing could take away the stricken look of anguish from Rider's eyes. Rider was powerless. The fact that she and Theresa had been lovers for nine years, both in and out of prison, did not count to the officials. It mattered nothing to them that Rider loved Theresa more than anything or anyone, that she took care of her in sickness, that she wanted to spend her life with her, or lie down and die with her. There was no compassionate release in the District then.

Theresa was initially admitted to the intensive care unit in a Code Blue state. Her heart had stopped due to complications from pneumocystis pneumonia associated with the final stages of AIDS. She was revived and placed on a respirator. In the following days, she went into Code Blue again, almost died, and was revived, but finally failed to respond to drug therapy. Theresa had been serving a nine-month sentence on a parole violation. She had been scheduled for release in two months. Nine days after Theresa left the cell block, and four days after her thirty-third birthday, Theresa died while shackled to the bed.

The following day, Rider was at my door, telling me that the funeral was Friday. She asked me whether she should try to go— could she go, would it be possible for her to go as her husband, or her wife, or anything? "After all," she said, "I was real family. If I had been free, I'd have been with her every minute."

If you are in prison and a family member dies, you generally are not allowed to attend the funeral. It is a question of security, not humanity. But if a "grief furlough" is approved, you go in chains, accompanied by armed marshals to the funeral home, where you are allowed merely a few moments to view the body alone.

Rider decided not to fight it out, not to go. Then she held out a plastic bag filled with jail-issued medications. Cream, pills, and suppositories. She said, "Can you explain all this stuff to me?" The question of what had happened to Theresa was only partially answerable. But now Rider had to know. With their specific instructions, the pills and cream made it clear. AZT, acyclovir, and steroid cream were the only approved medications for prisoners with AIDS. They had been dispensed irregularly and with no monitoring. I explained each medication and its use.

As Rider stood at my door with tears streaming down her face, she said, "I knew she was sick, but I didn't know for sure she would die." And then the pitch in her voice dropped to a whisper. "You know, I am a very open-minded person. I would never have left someone sick, not ever, and never her. She was, well, you know, I love her."

If Theresa had lived longer, Rider would have tried for a hospital visit, to take her in her arms one more time, tell her it was all okay and say good-bye. Instead, we called a friend of mine and asked them to send her roses. The note Rider included was "To Theresa, My love always, Rider." We heard that Theresa's pimp was not happy, but kept the flowers anyway.

One night after many days of overcrowding and out-of-control tempers, there was a shakedown. We heard the COs, all twenty of them, marching down the hall leading to the block. Of all the conditions in the jail, the shakedowns were the most invasive, the most enraging, and the most irrational. Of course, there were drugs. Dope hit the unit every week. Of course, people made weapons. Of course, there was contraband food from the kitchen. We saw the cops sell dope, and a weapon could be fashioned from an aluminum can from the commissary. The COs would come suited up in combat gear. Each cell was hit one by one, and mine was always first. Having heard them well in advance of their actual arrival, I had already flushed my contraband coffee grinds—my big illegal item.

"Step out," they ordered. I was handcuffed and told, "Spread." This meant facing the wall and stretching out my arms and legs. I was patted down and told to stand next to the door. Four of them went in. They searched every single thing. They unscrewed the lightbulb, they climbed on the top bunk and looked at the windowsill, and they went through every legal and personal paper one by one. They dragged the mattress onto the tier. They took shampoo and talcum powder and poured them out onto the mattress. They took scooped peanut butter from an old jar and smeared it on my personal photographs. They uncuffed me, put me back inside, shut the door, and repeated the process in every cell down the line.

Everyone was yelling. In the cells that hadn't been hit yet, women were standing and watching. The violence seemed to increase with each cell. And then they got to the last three cells. They popped open the door and one of them roared, "Step out!" The woman inside was brushing her teeth. One of them stepped in and grabbed her. She spit out her mouthful of toothpaste and saliva on him. If they had waited ten seconds she would have stepped out on her own. But she was disobeying an order, so four of them began to beat her up, with all the rest of us watching.

This small woman fought back. Everyone was hollering and throwing things out of their windows. An egg went flying and hit one of the guards. Four of them dragged the woman up the stairs and into the entrance to the block. The cops had bloodlust in their eyes. In the hall they couldn't get the cuffs onto her. Her fury matched theirs. Eventually they overpowered her and carried her off. I had never before seen that level of brutality directed against a woman. We were all crying from anger, frustration, and fear. And yet in the D.C. jail, it was almost normal. It was not extreme—a little more brutal than usual, but only a little. To administer by fear and control by terror was a tactic that was understood by the prisoners; it was a natural way of life, inside or outside. I cried because I didn't know how to resist that level of dehumanization.

Amid the wreckage of my cell, I spotted a book of poetry on the floor. I found the well-known poem by Langston Hughes, "Harlem," the one that begins "What happens to a dream deferred?" I stood at my window and in the pulsating silence, in the aftermath of what we had just been through, I read it at the top of my lungs. No one said anything. Then a single voice started singing "Amazing Grace," and then another and another until there were many

voices. Everyone knew the words. It was a most beautiful rendi-
tion, the richest I had ever heard. And as the sound rose and fell I
remembered hearing somewhere that that song had been written
by a slaver, a ship captain who experienced a dramatic conversion
and later spoke out strongly against slavery. "I once was lost, but
now am found."

What I was learning in those endless days at the jail was the
relentlessness of prison and oppression and the constant abuse of
authority as a way of life. To lessen one's expectations about the
quality and content of life is a terrible thing. In prison one faces
a direct attempt to destroy the human spirit. More than anything
else, life in the D.C. jail was designed to dehumanize us in order
to enslave us.

> No nation can enslave a group of people for hundreds of
> years, set them free—bedraggled and penniless—pit them,
> without assistance, in a hostile environment against privi-
> leged victimizers, and then reasonably expect the gap be-
> tween the heirs of the two groups to narrow. Lines begun
> parallel and left alone can never touch.[1]

Living inside the community that has developed on that un-
equal parallel line transformed my eyesight, my heart, and my sensibilities. Living amid the suffering, the violence, and the beauty of
black people, experiencing their genius in multiple acts of compassion and tradition, and witnessing the physical and psychological
damage that results from racist oppression changed my entire life.
For the most part, the men and women in that jail were effectively
"disappeared." They were exiled from the free world, with little
chance of making their way back. The jail was a warehouse, as
most prisons are. When life is lived where human emotions are

always right on the very surface, and where any provocation can set off an explosive event, the tension and pain are never ending. There are moments when it feels like you have been hurled at a brick wall and all your bones are broken. At those times you can only pray to whatever you pray to, and hope that your bones knit so that you can go on another day.

My associates and I were not similarly ground down and thrown out, in part because we were a political group and because we were of the white middle class—and even in those most profoundly appalling and anguished conditions, that made a difference. We had come from a movement; we had family and friends. We were connected to others around the world in similar circumstances, and we built upon those connections. Without them we surely would not have survived.

There were political prisoners all over the world struggling for recognition, for freedom, and for justice. In South Africa, the seventy-five years of the African independence movement and the forty-year struggle against apartheid were coming to fruition. All throughout 1989, the Botha government was confronted with worldwide condemnation. The prisoners in Robben Island and all the other jails in South Africa were organizing. The mass demonstrations of millions in Africa and around the world were slicing through the steel girders of the most vicious and racist system in the world. There were rumors of Nelson Mandela's release.

In January 1990, the Velvet Revolution released thousands of prisoners all over Eastern Europe. In Czechoslovakia thirty thousand, in East Germany and Hungary twenty-two thousand each—all were freed by governmental amnesties. The European Parliament banned the death penalty, and the UN passed the "Basic Principles for the Treatment of Prisoners." The crumbling of various social systems, the protest against others, the ending of civil wars in Central America—these events were facts. We were entering a different world. It was a world of post-national liberation, a post–cold war world, and a world turning into . . . what? We would soon see. Yet the oppression in our own country continued. The gap between our narrow four-walled world and the heaving of change outside at most moments seemed unbridgeable. And then on February 11, 1990, Nelson Mandela, the single most important political prisoner in the world, walked arm in arm with his wife, Winnie Mandela, across a prison yard into a waiting Mercedes, drove to Cape Town, and addressed hundreds of thousands of South African people, an event twenty-seven years in the making.

At that moment, the chains fell away from every prisoner around the world. His freedom was ours, his victory ours. The project of human liberation that was repressed, no matter where in the world, breathed free in that instant. On my block, we watched his walk to freedom on television. The jubilation was extraordinary. A friend of mine named Celeste sat next to me. Celeste was a brilliant and thoughtful woman, and a twenty-year dope fiend. Her influences and the people she talked about were blues singer Billie Holiday, the jazz musician Charlie "Byrd" Parker, and the playwright LeRoi Jones (whom she refused to call Amiri Baraka). With tears streaming down her face, she said, "Thank God somewhere in this world there is an African who makes one want to live, who gives our children a model." Her wet ashen cheeks made her blackness blacker. "I lived to see this, thank God." Then she turned, facing me, and said, "I have AIDS." She whispered it. I hadn't known.

Later, I thought how Celeste had waited for the right moment to tell me. And I thought that there are some events in the course of one's life where everything one desires is crystallized into pure joy—a joy that reaffirms the spirit and potential and holds out the reality that this world can be wondrous, and just. And I thought about how these events are often brought about by the collective work of the known and unknown, of thousands, even millions commingling their efforts. Nelson Mandela's walk to freedom was one of those.

Chapter 11

Cancer

ONE MONTH LATER, in April 1990, Alan was diagnosed with a recurrence of lymphoma. He had first been diagnosed with non-Hodgkin's lymphoma while in custody in 1986. He had noticed an enlarged lymph node under his arm and had had to fight tooth and nail for a diagnosis and treatment. Up until this point in his incarceration in D.C., his cancer had been in remission for four years. He was supposed to get CAT scans every six months to monitor the remission, but that had not happened. He had been seven months past due for a scan when he felt a mass, this time in his abdomen. He said it was the size of a meatball.

Immediately, the lethal nature of neglect that served as prison health care went into effect. The jail did everything it could to hinder his fight for life. He could not go to the hospital because there was not enough staff. He could not get the right tests because no one could schedule them. He was not allowed to move to a different unit because it was not secure enough, and on and on. There was an air of premeditation in all of it. It took organizing and intervention by those on the outside to get Alan the minimum level of care.

Alan had spent the past two years living in a unit under the hardest and the worst conditions. The men's maximum-security block was in an utter state of turmoil. Every week there were fires, flooding, and the whole tier was maced. He got even less sleep than the rest of us and almost never went outside. The stress, the anger, the constant waiting to go on trial, the uncertainty of whether he would get another forty years added to his sentence, and the denial of parole after he was already eligible all combined into what felt like a fait accompli.

Everyone was sick. Marilyn had been diagnosed with thyroid cancer, Laura was sick with migraines, Linda had developed asthma, and Tim repeatedly had pneumonia. But Alan's cancer was life threatening. We tried to joke—we called it a "war of attrition" and we said we were the "attrited"—but for us, Alan's illness was a deadly serious matter. We asked our lawyers to begin discussions with the prosecution. We wanted Alan sent somewhere else for care and treatment. The medical negotiations began, but the prosecution fought to keep him in the filthy D.C. jail and have him treated at the D.C. General Hospital. We wanted him to go to either Georgetown Hospital or to the Mayo Clinic in Rochester, Minnesota.

The government's appeal of our successful double jeopardy motion was still in court. We thought a decision would be issued at the end of the summer of 1990. Alan was too sick and could not stand trial. The estimate for his return to medical fitness was now nine months away in January 1991. The prosecution's case was weakening if only three women remained in the case without evidence of weapons or explosives.

The statistics were not good. Having cancer or AIDS or any other life-threatening illness in prison creates the greatest fear inside, the fear of dying. For us, it represented "parole by death." At the time, I wrote: "I chronicle Alan's illness to keep a record of the malevolence of the authorities and to remember the repression that has been targeted against him. I chronicle this because the saying that the attacks on one are an attack on all and without unity there can be no victory is a truth we all put into practice and lived through."

The story ran like this:

Finally having been permitted to receive care, Alan was sent to D.C. General for a CAT scan. The oncologist said the results were normal. Alan noticed that the date on the scan was 1988. The doctor retrieved the current scan and noted an abnormal swelling in nodes located near the iliac, deep in the abdomen. The doctor said it was nothing and not to worry. Alan argued for another scan in a month. Eventually, the doctor agreed. Later that night, Alan did a self-exam and located a mass in the area.

In May 1990, Alan was given a biopsy that came back positive for lymphoma. He was told by the security personnel who accompanied him to D.C. General that if he were not a doctor himself he would never have been diagnosed at all. In mid-May, Alan began experimental chemotherapy conducted by Georgetown oncologists at D.C. General Hospital. The government refused to allow him to go to Georgetown.

In June, discussions began with our lawyers and with the government about a possible deal so that we could avoid a trial and get Alan moved. On June 17, Alan was returned to the jail. He had eight days between chemo treatments. He was getting extremely high dosages of an experimental combination of drugs and he was profoundly weakened by it. Chemotherapy destroys white blood cells; consequently, Alan was in constant danger of becoming septic. He was given steroids to ward off septicemia. He was housed on the medical ward of the jail, but there was an active tuberculosis epidemic on the ward and no one took preventive measures. This was not a safe place for him to be.[1]

On June 23, Alan was back in the hospital. He was taken abruptly off steroids by an intern. As a result, he went into adrenal shock. If he had been septic he would have died. After being dosed with steroids and antibiotics, he stabilized. This was the closest to death he had ever been. This is how lymphoma patients die—from the side effects that cause infection that result in death.

On July 26, Alan sent us a letter from the hospital. He knew we had made a deal, in part to ensure his continued medical treatment under better conditions. The deal was that Marilyn, Laura, and Linda would plead guilty to one count of conspiracy and one count of bombing—the bombing of the U.S. Capitol. Tim, Alan, and I were dismissed from the case. The other proviso to this plea was that Alan would go to Rochester to the BOP Medical Center and be treated at the Mayo Clinic.

Alan wanted to come back to the jail to say good-bye; he was expecting to die. We were all in the deepest state of grief when Alan returned to the jail. He looked like he was a hundred years old. He was gray and frail.

We met together in our legal room, where we had been meeting since 1988. We whispered old jokes and told stories, and each one of us also spoke to him by ourselves. I could barely keep from crying. It was nearly impossible to keep it together. Alan and I had been friends for almost twenty years, and we had had an incredible ride in this life, both together and apart. I flashed back to an earlier and easier time in 1977 right after Alan's daughter Sarah was born, when he had been delirious with joy and had played "Isn't She Lovely" by Stevie Wonder. I remembered standing outside his living room, hearing him shout the lyrics over and over. Every one of us had a deep love for him. We wept, but we did not let the guards see our tears. The guards took Alan away from us in handcuffs. Throughout every medical procedure, he (like all high-security prisoners) had been surrounded by automatic weapons and chains. The hospital was locked down, and the medical staffs were terrified by the guns and all the overly dramatic security to create an aura of submission. Very few doctors will stand up to that kind of armed power to assert medical need over security. Having to fight for his own care, to be his own advocate, took additional energy that Alan didn't have to spare and this was part of what made Alan's treatment so difficult and so wearying.

In September, Linda, Laura and Marilyn changed their plea from not guilty to guilty. It was a hard day and we had struggled with the choice for months and months. The three who pleaded guilty felt that they were accepting the government's definitions of their history and actions. It was a compromise with a personal and political cost: automatic sentences of twenty years for Laura, ten for Marilyn, and five for Linda. That made Marilyn's sentence eighty years, Linda's forty-five, and Laura's twenty. It was a sacrifice they made in real terms. Despite the incredible public display against all of us, the prosecution had no evidence of actual participation in any of the acts in the indictment. My friends took the plea so that Alan would not face another trial and would get the medical care that he desperately needed, and so that Tim, Alan, and I would not face possible exposure to more prison time.

Alan was scheduled for an evaluation in October. He was still very ill, but he was alive. When the Resistance Conspiracy case finally came to an end, the future for Alan and for the rest of us held out years of prison, and a return to federal custody.

Once the plea agreement was reached and the legal case ended, it was as though all the energy we had spent in resisting had been utterly wasted. It was like air from a balloon that had escaped and the balloon turned out to be but a plastic shell. It was too soon to try to understand what the last two and a half years had been about, but I was overwhelmed that we had won anything at all. I thought about all the factors that had gone into our struggle over the time we had spent in the D.C. jail. I thought about our commonality with all political prisoners everywhere who fight with every bit of brains, heart, and soul to live under the most difficult and depressing conditions in order to give meaning to their incarcerations, and I thought we lived up to our counterparts. I thought about our friends, our families, and our lawyers (who were also so much more than lawyers), who visited us, fought for us in the world, and brought our cases to the attention of everyone who would listen. I thought about the supporters who built a defense committee and organized to defend and free us, and who helped us carry on. They were extraordinary. I thought about the deepest success of all, which was that after two and a half years, we the "codefendants" were still speaking to one another, and still filled with a commitment to our solidarity. We rose above our history and differences, our conflicting interests and views, and built upon our strengths to fight the government. This could never have happened without our fundamental love for one another.

When we arrived in the D.C. jail, the government's goal was to destroy us through isolation, through exile, life sentences, medical negligence, and horrible physical conditions. In that they failed. We made lifelong friends, life partners in some cases. We also found old friends we had not seen, or thought had forgotten us, and new friends, as well. I met William Wardlaw, "B," an anarchist and peace activist, who along with a friend, refused to stand up for Judge Parker during my court appearance in the Lexington case. They were arrested, beaten up and charged with assault on a federal officer. The case would go on in court for years. Our correspondence turned into a great dialogue and deep friendship. Only much later would I find out that he was scion to one of the wealthiest families of Atlanta, Georgia. I also met Shirley Cloyes, an activist, intellectual, writer, and editor, who visited me at the jail. Shirley was the publisher of Lawrence Hill Books. She had edited and then published Assata Shakur's autobiography. Through that project, she had come to know Mary O'Melveny, who was then working for the law firm that had represented Assata after she was targeted and later apprehended as a leader in the Black Liberation Army. Mary in turn introduced her to me. Both B and Shirley would become great friends of mine and would later be crucial to winning my release. I read more, studied poetry and writing, and wrote more than I had ever written in my life. I fell in and out of love with unattainable women and men who helped keep the heart beating. I lived side by side with women whose entire lives were worse than my time in the D.C. jail. I tried not to weep. If I did, I was afraid I would drown in the waters of my soul.

I felt the suffering and pain around me. At times, it was so bad, I extinguished the difference between my own pain and others. As before, I thought about killing myself as a way of release from the cursed consciousness of suffering when I was beyond the point of caring or compassion. But in reality, suicide was counter to my beliefs. I held on (admittedly at times by a shred) to the notion that people can change, that societies can change, and that my life in prison was not a waste. My understanding of American history—that our history of slavery, stolen land, occupation, and exploitation that had led me to make the choices I had made in my life—was now filtered through the lives of individuals who were no

longer abstractions of systems and causes. Theresa had died, others
with whom I had been living side by side were dying: Celeste, Re-
gina, Frederika, and on and on. Outside, too, people were dying:
Elliot, David, Arawn, and others in the gay liberation movement.
And not only Alan, Marilyn, and Silvia had cancer. My father did,
as well. All that dying and sickness was impossible to rationalize.
The structural violence that resulted in genocidal death in the jail,
or in the black community, or the failures of government to respond
to the AIDS epidemic seemed to me to be part of a war against
the marginalized of America. And as in all wars, the dialogue with
death was a constant. I wrote a poem to reflect my understanding
of this:

We Are Not Well

Our deaths inconsequential
Where one day more is one day less
I have met Death in the cold
of this prison.

Her imprint etched on every wall
in every crevice, in every corner,
screaming with despair.

Wind whips through howling
as if a frozen vapor alone can
hold back her onslaught.

Cold shoots through me
leaving its tracings
where veins should be.
And I

arrogant enough to believe that even death
can be reasoned with
converse.

Her nocturnal visitation
where we debate polarities between
reason and justice
cause and effect
have shown me that
while equal measure of hope and despair can put this
    death march on notice
it is but a temporary holdover.

I have met Death in the cold of this prison.
She arrives in a multitude of forms
In dope
In disease
In desperation
She thrives in a culture where
the dispossessed are disempowered and
disrespect is internalized.

There is no inner peace
between chaos and a hurricane
between racism and genocide.

Ancestral energies explode in minute details
Survival every generation's duty
And while the plagues of modern times
do not obliterate the human spirit
We are not well.

In October 1990, I turned thirty-five. That month, my father's cancer went into remission. I was so relieved. I could not imagine my father sick. He was so vital and filled with a beautiful spirit. My parents had delayed telling me about his cancer, not wanting to worry me, but when they finally did, I was shattered by the idea that he would die and I would be in prison. Alan was evaluated with the conclusion that he needed more chemotherapy and I prepared to leave for federal custody.

At our group's sentencing in November, Marilyn Buck said:

Even in my youthful ignorance and unconsciousness I have always believed in equality. Going out into the world quickly revealed what inequality is and does in a raw and brutal world. It is painful, degrading, demoralizing, and finally enraging to be treated as less than an equal. I know it as a woman and I see it everywhere I look. But inequality can be changed, that I believe and know from history. But if it is not fought for then it certainly will not change. That is why I am here, because I have advocated change for equality, justice, and peace. I stand in the place where thousands of abolitionists, escaped slaves, workers, and political activists have stood for demanding justice, for refusing to either quietly bear the biting lash of domination or to stand by silently as others bear the same lash. I am being sentenced and condemned because I dare to be a white person in a white-dominated country who advocated that black people have the right to determine their national destiny, that Puerto Rico has the right to its independence, that this society must undergo profound changes if it is not to be condemned to the nightmares of worse than we can imagine.

I didn't know exactly when I was being transferred, but the night before I was transferred to Florida's new maximum-security women's prison, I dreamed that I was in a field of wildflowers, as described by the Sufi mystic poet Rumi. This field was quiet and still. The sun was shining, the wind blowing, and I could smell the scent of wildness. It washed over me in waves. I was lying in the field alone. As I closed my eyes, all the terror and horror receded and I started singing. I knew that I did not want to leave the field and I was reluctant to return to wherever that was. I embraced that field. When I woke up, I was calm. Until the security team came all suited up, and I was taken from the jail.

Part Five

Mariana

Chapter 12

Mariana Maximum Security

THE FIRST LEG of the transfer to Florida began with a siren-blaring exit from the District of Columbia. The police and a whole entourage of one van and five cars drove through the back streets until the thruway entrance appeared. Several minutes later, we were entering the state of Virginia.

It was freezing cold in the prison van outside the Alexandria County jail. There were three of us who were all being transferred from the D.C. jail and we had been joined by two other women on the drive south to Florida, to the new maximum-security women's prison at Marianna that lay two hours from Tallahassee. We had been sitting for quite some time and the marshals and local jail officials had been whispering to one another in between steaming breaths while they stood around, waiting. One marshal was cradling his rifle as he paced. Everyone was getting colder and more uptight. The door at the side of the main driveway burst open to reveal two male COs dragging a small woman and shouting at her as they came toward the van. I slid over to the window and peered through the mesh covering to get a better look at the commotion. The woman was wrapped in chains—leg cuffs, handcuffs, belly chains, and black boxes. Even through the mesh I could see that the woman was on some other plane of existence.

They put her in the van next to me. She sat totally immobile, as if in a trance. I spoke to her, but there was not even the flutter of an eyelid in response. Once she must have been delicate and fine boned, but now she was emaciated and her long black hair was dull from lack of care. I thought that she looked Vietnamese. I found out later that she was. I took in her looks and her energy and tried to give off calm and caring vibes. Then I saw her hands. Her wrists were purple and were bulging out around the cuffs, pulsing. Scarred, they looked like she had slashed them over and over. I tried not to blanch, but my breath got ragged. The terrible pain in her was searing me in that cold van. As the van finally began to move, there was a stony silence from all of us in the back. The only sound was the intermittent crackling of the police radio.

Lien (as one of the marshals called her) never uttered a word on the seven-hour drive. When we stopped to use the bathroom— a cumbersome and scene-stopping embarrassment because of our orange jumpsuits, chains, and armed escort—I found myself with another woman, Jackie, who had been in the Virginia jail. She whispered to me not to touch Lien because she had AIDS and was crazy. I whispered back, caught up in some kind of conspiratorial thing, "What did she do?" It did not really matter to me, but I wanted to hear some kind of explanation. "She killed her father, shot him dead through the heart," Jackie said in awe. "Really?" I asked, not whispering anymore. Jackie nodded and stared at me.

The ride to the city jail in Georgia where we stopped for the night was the longest leg of the trip. There was no conversation among us prisoners and the marshals were focused solely on driving us. In the silence, I had a seven-hour meditation on how we had all ended up in the BOP van in shackles, what forces in the universe had propelled us, propelled me, to be sitting next to a Vietnamese woman with AIDS facing the death penalty. I tried everything not to be drawn into Lien's agony. Vietnam, it had all really begun with Vietnam: her path, my path. She and I were the consequences of the illegal, immoral, and genocidal war waged by my government against her people. We were minor characters in an ongoing drama of actions, reactions, and forever-reverberating consequences. I fantasized many scenarios for Lien. She was a boat person, and she had come here to find her father; when she finally met him, he had shunned her and left her to fend for herself in the streets of some U.S. city, where she had become a prostitute to survive and contracted AIDS. I wanted to tell Lien that I had been against the war, that I was an antiwar American who had some understanding of what happened to her country and her people. But as she sat pushed up against me, I saw the vacancy in her eyes and I realized that my thoughts were born of some narcissistic need to feel better, while she was past the point of hearing or caring. My romanticism fueled my imagination as I automatically created my own story about Lien. I really had no idea what the facts were, only jailhouse rumor and what I could see and feel sitting next to her.

When we arrived at the city jail outside of Atlanta, I was put into segregation. By then, my emotions were beyond my control. In response to all the suffering going on around me, I began to cry. I couldn't stop. I didn't think I was crying for myself, but I was. I thought about being both observer and participant, a conscious actor in an ongoing drama, and I rededicated myself to bearing witness, to recording the indignities and the pain so as to remember every detail. Up until that first day of my transfer in late December 1990, there had been moments I had come to call "freeze frames": visual experiences—an image, a scene, a dialogue, an encounter—that took my breath, made my heart pound, or knocked me backward off my feet. These moments shattered the repressive tedium, and they always, at least metaphorically, kicked me in the head. They distilled the surrounding conditions into pure crystals of truth that brought me back to who I was and why I was there. They became reference points through which I could navigate between memory and the present. The journey sitting next to Lien became a profound experience for me. Whether it was because she and I were unable to communicate yet forced to touch, our thighs pressing against each other, or because of my machinations and explanations regarding her circumstances causing me to reflect on the political meaning of my own life, I felt her suffering, and it allowed me to feel my own.

The next day when we left, Lien was not with us. I never saw or heard anything about her again.

We arrived in Marianna, Florida, that day. The trip had been grueling, and as we passed through gate after gate, I got quieter and quieter inside myself. We drove straight to the heart of the complex, a prison within a prison as Lexington had been, only instead of being a basement, the Florida complex was housed in its own building. The sun glinted off the rows and rows of razor wire. As I was pulled out of the back of the van onto the tarmac road, my laceless sneakers sank into the hot asphalt.

The building was big and clean and flat. It had a fake-adobe look, with stones and potted plants at the front entrance. We walked past a row of portraits hanging in the lobby. The one that caught my eye was a grinning President George H.W. Bush. It was the middle of the afternoon, and there was no one around. The building reminded me of Lexington, and in the midst of the terrible heat, a cold chill swept through me. *If Tucson had been the preparation for Lexington and the first physical assault, and Lexington had been systematic psychological torture, and the D.C. jail the most physically arduous and emotionally consuming years of my life—what would Marianna bring?*

As we crossed the lobby and walked through a set of steel doors that popped open, I knew that the well-oiled machinery of the surveillance and security mechanisms were functioning in high gear. There were no people around and no sound, only the whirring of the air-conditioning and the humming of the electronic doors and gates. I was definitely back in the federal system, and it was familiar and worse than I had remembered. At the end of a long hall, a final door opened and I found myself on a tier with locked steel doors. The Beatles song "Back in the USSR" played in my head as I realized I was back in the hole.

I stood in the cell and tried not to drown in the alien, soulless waters of this new place. I was still suffering trauma from the previous six years. For the first time, I wished that I could go to a psychiatric clinic to get help. I wanted to go to a clinic for victims of torture. I wanted to talk to someone about my time in Tucson, Lexington, and in the D.C. jail. I had been so dehumanized and humiliated by the previous years of incarceration that my very being felt frozen. At such a clinic, I would not have to explain all my politics, yet still get help. I had never previously admitted to myself that any torture had occurred, much less that it had left me damaged.

In all the years at the D.C. jail, I had not stopped to deal with the effects of my incarceration, although my friends outside and my friends and codefendants inside had tried to make it clear to me that doing so would not be a sign a weakness or a fall from "revolutionary grace." But I could not admit that I needed to keep the anger going to fuel the action. Anger was a source of energy for me, and I had lots of things to be angry about. I believed that to stop and admit the effects—to acknowledge them even to myself—would open me up to a psychic invasion by the authorities, and I could never let that happen. So by keeping the external conditions primary in my mind, I did not look beneath the surface of my own psyche. I could never get to the internal demons that propelled me. But as I reentered the federal prison system, I had a fleeting sense that a time to look into the caverns of my own mind and heart would come soon.

My cell was bigger than any other cell I had seen. It was clean and new and it had a window I could slide up and down. There were metal bars outside the window, but at least I could regulate the temperature in the cell. *Bang!* I opened the window. *Bang!* I closed it. It made me ecstatic to perform that simple act. I opened and closed the window dozens of times a day.

After the first day and a half had passed, I demanded to know why I was in segregation and asked to make a phone call. I could hear voices in the entrance hallway when the guards electronically popped open the door, but otherwise I was alone. My first encounter was with a man who showed up without notice, looking uncomfortable in a brown seersucker suit. His tie was loose, and there was sweat on his graying temples. He walked in front of the closed steel door and peeped through the glass window.

"Hey, Susan, how ya doing?"

I didn't like him calling me "Susan" at all.

"Why am I in seg?"

"That's what your buddies Silvia and Marilyn want to know. They won't get off my back for a second. It's just through classification. We have to make sure that you won't kill yourself or anybody else." He laughed.

"I need paper, and I want a phone call," I said.

"Don't you worry, we're getting you a typewriter, and I have a bag of things that your buddies sent you." He turned to some camera and yelled, "Open it."

The door to my cell popped open and he handed me a shopping bag. The first things I saw were a pack of Camels and several cans of tuna fish.

Then he stepped back and out and pulled the door shut, as though he couldn't wait to erase the open space between us.

"Hey, who are you? Hey, man, you have a match?" I said quickly before he walked away.

"Mr. Doyle. I'm your counselor. There's some in the bag."

Eventually I learned that Mr. Doyle was a BOP man, a cop who just wanted to complete his time and collect his double retirement check. After serving in the Army, he had become a CO and had risen to the position of counselor. It was not a very high rank within the system; they were administrators, but at the lowest level.

After he left, I sat down on the bunk and inspected the bag. Silvia and Marilyn had done a great job. Besides the cigarettes and tuna, there were oatmeal packets, raisins, an apple, an orange, and a Snickers bar. There were pens and a notepad, stamps and envelopes, soap and shampoo, and two paperback mysteries. They had me outfitted. I hoped that I would be out of segregation before I used it all, but it was a pleasure to know that people were out there and fighting for me to come out of segregation.

I sat down, opened the cigarettes, and found the matches. I was perplexed. I had never been in a segregation situation where a prisoner could have matches or a can of any kind. Matches and metal lids can be used as weapons, although not many shanks (knives) were made from tuna can lids. Their letting me have them meant they did not really think that I was going to hurt anyone and that they were keeping me in the hole just because they could. I decided to use the time to calm down rather than to fight. I opened the window and lit a cigarette. I began my bargaining litany. *If this is the worst, then I can handle it.*

At that moment, a CO electronically opened my door and rolled in a typewriter on a metal stand. Neither one of us said a word. I do not know who was more shocked, him or me.

I began to write. First I wrote by hand and then at the typewriter. I was not ready to begin a new phase of doing time. I was not ready to be back in federal custody, even if the cell was clean and they had just given me a typewriter. The D.C. jail had been chaotic and crazy, but it had teemed with life and spirit. The feds, on the other hand, were about mind control. I reminded myself to flush the ribbon when I was finished typing. That, of course, was false logic, since the authorities could seize what I had written on paper, but I wanted to do everything I could to keep them from learning my thoughts.

I had been thinking about Lien, the Vietnamese woman in the van. I wrote the following prose poem for her and for me:

Prison Transfer with Questions

My generation will remember

in an instant the photo
of over one hundred children piled in a ditch.
Naked and bloody.

A photo of an Asian forest made bare from defoliants,
no leaves, only bodies.
The caption read "Remember the My Lai Massacre."
My generation will remember Lt. Calley and his defense,

"I was carrying out my superiors' order."
Carrying out orders. And it's true. He was.

This same generation never healed from the consequences
of that unjust war. That war of aggression and intervention.
No reparations were paid, no relations restored, no bilateral
discussions held. Once the enemy, always the enemy.
And particularly if the enemy wins.

But monuments went up to pay homage to the dead.
(And even that was way too late.)
Marble to substitute for international law, in place of
     resources and respect.
Apocalyptic movies made at great cost, and great profit,
textbooks written, history reworked to fit the current time.
Who won? Why were we there? What is genocide?
Doesn't Agent Orange grow on trees?

The generals learned. Better than we.

Grenada
Panama
Nicaragua
Iraq

The Vietnamese people are suffering still, as they always will
until someone takes responsibility.
And we suffer, but they suffer more.

And yesterday while in transit in a prison van
In shackles I sat, thinking of wars.

And beside me a woman sat. A woman born ten years after me
   in 1965.
A woman born in Saigon. A Vietnamese woman, a woman once
   beautiful and delicate.
This Vietnamese woman named Lien was a prisoner, too, only for her
the black box to immobilize handcuffed wrists.
Her wrists were slashed and the cuffs made her scars stand out in
   bright purple.
And as I looked at this woman from Vietnam, who was born in
   Saigon but raised on
McDonald's, I knew she was sick, I knew she was dying.

A victim of war.
This Vietnamese woman born in Saigon to an American father who
   left her
While she suffers from AIDS dementia, which caused her to attack a
   white man
And kill him with his own gun.

This once delicate young woman with AIDS, demented, in chains, en
   route to her death, in a prison van, a victim of war.

Which war? I do not know.
Wasn't Lt. Calley only following orders?
And doesn't Agent Orange kill more than trees?

I could only hope that writing would help me again as it had before. It had become my means of survival.

The recreation yard was the size of a small backyard plot, It was a fenced-in inner yard, all concrete and surrounded by buildings.

Even with the bright Florida sun glinting off the razor wire, it was bleak. A basketball hoop had been unceremoniously stuck on the wall; otherwise, it was empty. Walking the perimeter took thirty steps, not enough to work up a sweat.

I was walking in circles, trying to get my blood moving while my brain was buzzing around, when the door from the hole opened. A middle-aged white woman with long, scraggly brown hair stepped through the gate. Wearing an oversize orange jumpsuit, she surveyed her surroundings and then me. I did not miss a step. Feeling worn down, I did not want to talk to her. Since arriving in Florida my own internal surveillance system was in full gear and I had not seen one black prisoner. This woman looked like a Midwestern methedrine addict, old before her time. I was not up for conversation.

She fell right in step with me. "My name is Janet."

I nodded, looking at her out of the corner of my eye. Her pale, parched skin and red-rimmed crystal blue eyes told me she had only recently arrived. From her look I guessed she had been shunted from one jail to another for quite a while.

Oblivious to the aloofness that I was trying to send her way, she asked, "Who are you?"

"Rosenberg," I muttered.

She stopped walking. "I know who you are."

I thought for a second that I would have to fight her. Not being able to tell where she was coming from, I kept walking.

"I'm a political prisoner, too." The emphasis was on the word "too."

"Yeah, what did you do?" I asked, getting more exasperated with each turn in the yard.

"I hate the government," she said.

I kept my pace.

"I bomb abortion clinics," she went on. "Me and my husband, that's what we do. We've bombed nine of them."

I took one full look at her and turned on my heel, walking back to the seg door.

She said, "I saw you in that documentary, *Through the Wire*."

"Then you know to leave me alone." I had no idea what I meant by that; all I knew was that I was seething at her, at the guard for putting us together, and at the whole scene I was now in.

She was still talking as I tried to get back into the building. "I'm in the hole for refusing to work. Our hatred of the federal government gives us common ground."

Common ground? I did not want common ground with her. I did not want my enemies' enemy to become my friend. I did not want to be in this white federal world. I missed my black sisters, my community, and the D.C. life that had become my reality. I missed being the minority in an all-black majority. How could I have common ground with someone I assumed was a white supremacist, but whom I knew bombed women's health clinics? I missed living in a black community because I had spent my whole adult life trying to oppose racism. While I was not black, I had come to believe and feel that black people's culture of response to their history of enslavement was the best of American culture. When I had studied at New York's City College many years earlier, I had majored in American history and written my senior thesis on the role of gospel music in resisting slavery.

Years after that, when I and others in my underground group had gone to public and legal gun shows in the Midwest, we had encountered gun sellers and buyers who were part of the organized white supremacist movement. They had been filled with utter contempt and hatred for black people. I remember one booth in particular that was offering AR-15 assault rifles at a discount with free paper practice targets, and the images were caricatures of black people as monkeys and slaves. The sellers were proud of those targets. I remember wanting to destroy the booth and burn those targets.

I could not have foreseen then that I would be in segregation in a federal prison with someone who seemed to me to fit into the same category as those gun sellers. I could hear the cop's argument: "You people are the same; you both bomb to get what you want." It was a perverse argument that I did not want to hear, let alone have to live with on a daily basis. It would become a litany: "Right wing, left wing, you all are terrorists, our job is just to keep you, and it's all the same to us." Back in my cell, I sat on the bunk and wept. It was Christmas Eve, 1990.

The Marianna High Security Unit for women was the first official maximum-security prison for women in the Bureau of Prisons. It followed in the line of experiments and developments from Alderson, West Virginia, where the first behavior modification programs were conducted in Davis Hall, the segregation unit at Alderson. Numerous political prisoners were incarcerated there from the 1960s until the 1990s: Lolita Lebrón, Assata Shakur, Safiya Bukari, Marilyn Buck, Rita "Bo" Brown, Susan Saxe, and Laura Whitehorn were among those who did hard time there. Then the BOP created the Lexington HSU, which had now morphed into the Marianna maximum-security prison. It was under court supervision conducted by the National Prison Project of the American Civil Liberties Union, a direct result of our litigation against the BOP. It was set up for what the BOP considered the most "hard-core" prisoners.

At Marianna, I found women from my past political life and

from previous prisons, along with others that I knew by reputation. Seeing my friends Silvia Baraldini and Marilyn Buck, both of whom I had had court cases with, gave me such relief and happiness that I would not be alone in doing this new part of my time. Sylvia Brown had been at Lexington with us, and Belinda Carter, who had flown out of a federal prison in California in her lover's commandeered helicopter, were the most well-known escapees. There was Lynette Fromme from the Manson Family and Helen Woodson, a Plowshares activist who had violated parole rules over and over again in her unyielding dedication to ending nuclear weapons proliferation. There were several Colombian drug women who ranged in importance from wives of big cartel leaders to "mules" who had become informants and were being housed at Marianna for witness protection purposes. There were several junkies who had undertaken botched armed robberies to support their drug habits, and there was Conchita and Vieja, heroin dealers from the Mexican mafia who each had a single teardrop tattoo at the corner of her eye denoting gang allegiance. There were women who had run a methedrine lab in Oklahoma, and gang members from the Bloods and Crips. There were a handful of black women with nicknames like Princess, Tender, and Miami. Some of them were former crackheads transferred from general population for "bad" behavior. There were mentally ill women who had nowhere else to go, including women who self-mutilated ("cutters" and "bleeders"), who lived in and out of four-point restraint (meaning shackling at the hand and foot to the metal "bed") in segregation. Finally, there were a few *Marielitas,* Cuban detainees with absolutely no charges, no rights, no outside contacts, and no release dates. They had not been convicted and yet they were for all intents and purposes sentenced indefinitely, for as long as diplomatic dialogue between the United States and the Cuban government failed.

I got out of segregation and stepped into what appeared on the surface to be a clean, brand-new unit. It was in a large building whose central structure was a two-tiered oblong that resembled decks on a boat. Everything was in that oblong, including a small building that housed thirty computers to be used for a data entry factory. Most federal facilities have a contract from another part of the government for prisoner labor. This one was a contract from the U.S. patent office. Prisoners would sit all day five days a week, eight hours a day and input patent numbers. This was for seventeen cents an hour. There was a kitchen, a medical wing, the segregation unit, and an internal fenced-in courtyard slightly bigger than a handball court. The outdoor recreation field, the size of a football field, butted up against the men's prison and their factory.

The Marianna HSU had originally been designed to be a protective-custody unit for men. But because of the Lexington lawsuit, the BOP changed the mission of the Florida unit to accommodate the court, and Marianna became the little sister to the prison for men in Marion. Following the opening of the prison, there were rumors swirling that a new, even more hard-core unit à la the Lexington HSU was being built in Fort Worth, Texas, and that eventually we would all be sent there. As long as Silvia and I were in the unit, the legal threads from the closure of Lexington to the opening and running of Mariana still existed, even if tenuously.

The BOP was establishing more and more twenty-four-hour lockdown units and building multi-million-dollar industrial complexes. These complexes, housing all levels of prisoners, comprised hundreds of acres in isolated areas. The first of them had been built at Florence, Colorado, where the administrative maximum (ADMAX) facility had been built to replace Illinois's Marion prison. No facility just for women existed yet. The Fort Worth, Texas, prison complex already included a hospital, a mental unit, an AIDS ward, a minimum-security prison, and a camp—and soon it would have a lockdown wing for the maximum-security prisoners.

Meanwhile, we at Marianna were stuck in a netherworld of isolation, control, and a barrage of verbal assaults. One day when an officer yelled at some prisoners, "This ain't no cruise ship," someone yelled back, "No, it's a shipwreck!" That notion became a metaphor. We were survivors on a shipwreck, and the question was, would we destroy ourselves in lieu of rescue?

For my first few months at Marianna, the administration spent a lot of time observing Silvia, Marilyn, and me; the United States launched the Gulf War; and the first full-blown AIDS case appeared in the prison and its victim died.

Silvia, Marilyn, and I were confronted with a very difficult set of conditions, in which the appearance of things was more important than anything else. We had "free movement" in the building and we were allowed to possess more things than in any other prison I had been in. We had cable TV, our own clothes, and unlimited access to books that we could "donate" to the unit library. We were allowed to go outside in the recreation yard every day for several hours. At the same time our "freedom" was deceptive. We were under the total control of the prison authorities, we were thousands of miles from anyone we knew, and our isolation was extreme. The administration treated us as a bloc; special lieutenants read our mail, listened to our phone calls, and monitored our visits.

I felt that I was suffocating in Marianna, and not even my past rituals and experiences seemed to help. For the most part, other prisoners were pleased with the "privileges" they received. Many had been snitches and had been sent to Marianna for protection. I felt that the place would erode my soul, and my spirit rebelled. One of the deepest commitments I had made to myself was that I would not allow prison or repression to erode my soul, and I felt that my soul was more deeply threatened now than at any time before. For the first time, I felt that my political will was not enough to give me the daily strength to survive.

There was make-believe work like buffing beige corridors on which no one walked, or working as a "librarian" in a small room where there were almost no books and no one dropped in to read anything. There was only time, and it had slowed down to a snail's pace. The only way to resist time was to use it; otherwise, it would just wear one down like sand on stone. I was beyond exhausted; I was burned out. I was so tired that I couldn't even begin to imagine how to rethink my situation and evaluate my past actions. My sanity still depended on my identity as a political prisoner, but what that meant exactly in this new context was not clear to me. I knew in my heart that my ideology alone would not or could not save me this time.

In early 1991, the United States launched the largest aerial bombardment it had undertaken since the Vietnam War. The U.S. forces dropped more bombs on Iraq than had been dropped in all of World War II. Saddam Hussein called for jihad; Iraq shot missiles at Tel Aviv.

From inside, it seemed that the United States and its allies had finally finished their consolidation into a one-world system, run by only one superpower. With the end of the cold war, there was no opposition to speak of. Cuba, Yemen, and Algeria were the only countries in the world to call the war a U.S. invasion and condemn it. There was some European opposition, but not enough to stop the bombing. Meanwhile, we at Marianna were entombed in the midst of a militant and blind patriotic fervor.

In the federal prison system during a war, the links between the prisons and the Army tighten. It is most clear during war how militarized prison life really is. At BOP factories with U.S. Army contracts, prisoners work twenty-four hours a day to meet the increased demand for everything from parachutes to radio mounts for tanks. Many of the COs are active in the reserve and get called up in wartime. The BOP then deputizes others to act as COs in order to continue staffing the institution, and they lock the prison down for long stretches so that they can run it on a skeleton crew. Lockdown means that everyone is kept in their cells all day. Food is brought around to everyone on carts and handed to each individual through the food slot in the door. Everyone at Marianna knew long before the civilian population did that the U.S. Army had sent troops to Saudi Arabia.

One day, a female CO, a Ms. Wilson, came to say good-bye to her favorite inmates. She was off to Saudi Arabia to staff the military brig. Her unit was one of the last to get called because the Army was just finishing its new detention centers. She laughingly said that she was well equipped for the job after dealing with us tough girls. One woman prisoner, who was always the first to take the guards' side in any altercation between them and us, said after she was gone, "That's a good use of her skills, working in the Army after dealing with us." For fear of getting into a fight with any of the patriotic prisoners, I didn't react, but the political irony of it all—the fact that the patriots themselves were not free—was not lost on me.

Several days into the war, the atmosphere took a more somber turn: one of the COs in Saudi Arabia had been killed. The prison staff had an informal memorial in the men's section in the auditorium. We heard about it from the chaplain, who asked us to pray for the CO's family. Later, a group of COs and lieutenants came to our unit and called an early lockdown, screaming for us to get in our cells. "This is a shakedown," one of them yelled. "If you act like a bunch of sand niggers, then you're ours." One by one they shook down the cells. They walked in and systematically took every piece of property, from toothbrushes to books, and threw them out of the cell into the hall. They cursed at us, pulling us out one by one, forcing us to spread-eagle. They went at it like that until they were exhausted. It appeared that they did not find anything worth taking. When they left the unit, they were empty-handed.

Then one of them got on the PA system and yelled, "Listen up, convicts, we have the constitutional right to take you out to the recreation yard and shoot you all in a time of war. This has been a federal directive since the Civil War, since you will likely aid the enemy to obtain your freedom. We have the president's order to take you out first."

Someone yelled back, "Bullshit!"

Then someone else let loose a blistering scream: "We're not fucking Arabs!"

Finally another voice, filled with tears, was heard: "I was in the Army."

The COs and lieutenants left the unit with us still in lockdown. The war had reached us in maximum security.

The BOP viewed all the political prisoners as the enemy personified. We were enemies of the state. And as abstract a concept as "the state" is to most Americans, upon entering its prisons, its inner sanctums, the concept becomes very concrete. You can lay your hands on it, feel it, touch it, and know that the state exercises its pure and rawest form of power in its prisons. The administration hated all the prisoners almost by definition and even more so those of us whose stance was against the war. They increased the repression against us by enforcing even tighter controls over us and cutting off what little connections we had that penetrated the isolation. Visits were denied with greater frequency and mail was withheld. We chafed against our chains to take an active role in opposing the war.

Given the inflamed passions on both sides during this time, it was strange that the administration gave permission to an African American dance troupe from Florida A&M University (FAMU) to perform at the prison. The approval was granted in response to the federal government's mandate on recognizing Black History Month. It was one of many paradoxes that would take me by surprise. I did not expect the BOP to respect advances in the social structure like the establishment of Black History or Women's History Month.

The dance troupe brought more color and music and energy than all sixty of us at Marianna could muster. They danced to Gershwin, Aretha, Coltrane, and Sweet Honey in the Rock. They brought rhythms from Senegal and Jamaica. The dancers were wearing African textiles, and most of them wore their hair in dreadlocks. Their drums and speed and flowing movements pierced my dead heart. I felt alive. Their free spirits brought liberation and joy. As they were packing up to leave, a woman prisoner approached me and said, "Susan, one of the dancers wants to speak with you."

I turned to see the tallest and oldest woman, who had been the lead dancer in several of the numbers, coming toward me. Her eyes were filled with warmth. "I'm so honored to meet you," she said. "Halfway through one of the dances I saw you sitting right in front of me and realized this was the prison you had been sent to after Lexington." She began crying, and tears fell onto the African National Congress button pinned to her chest. I was stunned by the intensity that she exuded.

I thanked her and told her that her spirit had touched me while she was dancing. She asked if she could give me a hug. As we embraced, she kissed me again and again. She said that seeing the documentary *Through the Wire* and learning about political prisoners in America had inspired her life. I looked around for Marilyn and Silvia, but I could not see them anywhere. She asked if she could write to me. I told her yes. Out of the corner of my eye I saw a lieutenant moving, almost running toward us. I knew that I was about to pay for this encounter with the dancer and was grateful that I had been able to speak to her at all.

The cops pushed the dancer off the floor and up the stairs. I tried to resist, but they dragged me into the medical room and ordered me to submit to a total strip search. After feeling so elated, I was inspired to rebel. I did not want to comply when the lieutenant said, "You knew her, didn't you?"

I laughed at him. "No," I said, "we had only talked." He turned and left, but the two female COs advanced on me. I put my hands up and relented. "I'll do it." I stripped. I had been strip-searched many times and I had always given in to the feeling of humiliation that was a main point of the punishment. This time, however, I did not let it get to me. The exchange that I had had that day with the dancer (whose name I later found out was Olibisi) shook me out of myself and intervened in my psychological downward spiral. Unbeknownst to her, that marvelous woman gave me strength.

Chapter 13

Breaking Rank

EVERYTHING IN PRISON returns you to the moment that you committed your crime and reinforces the incident that landed you there. A "prison jacket" is security identification that determines your resulting placement in either a maximum- or minimum-security facility. It is based on the moment of the crime. Because the crime and its severity are frozen in time, this ensures that the prisoner *is* her crime. Because you cannot undo the events that have occurred, you are reduced to the greatest mistake of your life, or the most extreme behavior of your life. Those who maintain the procedures and processes of prison life do not care whether you are remorseful and recognize that you have made a mistake. People who say that rehabilitation is the purpose of incarceration are either ignorant or lying to themselves. The purpose of prison is to maintain control, not to rehabilitate. The impact of this reality on the prisoner is enormous. When you are seen only as the sum of your worst acts, then the past becomes the totality of the present and the present the half-life of prison. The deadening of the present to serve the past is a bitter reality for all those who endure it.

I knew that I was in a struggle for my own life. I was facing years and years in prison and I felt that I had no purpose while "doing time" at Mariana. I had come from the D.C. jail with the idea of doing some kind of AIDS counseling at Marianna. I had become a peer advocate in D.C. after watching HIV-positive status give way to the opportunistic infections of full-blown AIDS; carrying women from their cells on stretchers to infirmaries knowing they would never return; calling families collect on pay phones, bearing news of illness and death; composing funeral messages and raising money for flowers; writing sentence reduction motions and early release papers only to have them denied; and calling, cajoling, and begging initially unresponsive outside organizations to support us inside.

I had experienced a sense of purpose from organizing against the epidemic when I had been in Washington. I had learned that being an AIDS activist is a way to fight for justice, humanity, and dignity inside the walls. It is a way to organize prisoners and to resist the prison regime. It is one of the only vehicles that we the political people inside can use to work as activists within the prison itself. Fighting for the rights of people with AIDS was a way to challenge the lack of decent health care in the prison system. This lack of care showed everyone how health was secondary to security. The National Commission on AIDS criticized the BOP for its woefully inadequate programming and its medical and social neglect of the HIV-positive men and women in its prisons. Yet prison officials were obligated by law to respond to the AIDS crisis and so they allowed prisoners to work against the epidemic. If the authorities felt threatened by sick prisoners demanding their rights or reacting angrily to inadequate care, they subjected them to "diesel therapy," placing them in transit for months at a time. The result was that you were never anywhere long enough to get medical care or appeal to anyone, including your family, and it was usually fatal.

Constantly being bused from one hole to another hole is physically grueling and mentally draining, even for a healthy person, but it could only accelerate death for someone who was HIV positive.

After prolonged negotiation with the prison administration, I was given permission to start an AIDS awareness group. Once permission was given, Marilyn and Silvia joined me and we conducted an awareness workshop with fifteen women for six weeks. We began by asking the women whether any of them would voluntarily cell with an HIV-positive person. Everyone said no. By the end of the workshop, however, they had changed their minds. We ran workshop after workshop until almost all the women in the unit had participated in at least one. The first time a woman came to me and told me that she was HIV positive, I felt that I had played at least a tiny role in reducing the disease's social stigma, which was a first step in successfully battling the epidemic.

We created a panel for the National AIDS quilt project. We tried to help women who were HIV positive but not yet sick get decent care without exposing them to threats and ostracism. Silvia, Marilyn, and I worked every day against the epidemic. Later Laura Whitehorn arrived at Marianna and added her fantastic organizing skills and her great compassion to our effort. Laura suggested, and all agreed to organize a walkathon to raise money to support a local direct-service AIDS project in Tallahassee. Having something meaningful to work on took us out of our heads and our past, and helped us maintain our humanity—the very thing that maximum security was designed to steal from us. I knew that unless I was actively engaged in the business of living, my past would become all-consuming.

The AIDS advocacy work and opposition to the war in Iraq fueled my ability to resist the mind-deadening conditions and isolation I was facing, but still they were not enough for me. I wanted to write, but I wanted to get past writing in a journal and speak to a wider audience. I decided to enroll in a correspondence program with the Iowa Writers' Workshop and I began to write fiction. I hoped that writing fiction would get me closer to my own truth. As I wrote stories, portraits, and vignettes, I began to question myself, my assumptions, and my ideas. How do you change yourself without losing yourself? How do you question your past actions and still believe in the need for radical change? I asked myself if I had been corrupted by my support of armed struggle to make social change. How would I spend the rest of my life in prison when I no longer believed in many of the specific things that had sent me to prison, including and most importantly our own decision to use violence when we thought it necessary? The path to prison also included another decision that now profoundly disturbed me—the decision to submerge my identity to an organization. On top of that I had come to realize that the left had participated in its own marginalization through infighting and lack of democracy. How would I not become bitter? Ironically, writing fiction enabled me to answer these questions because in fiction I could explore what in my own life seemed impossible to challenge. In fiction I could examine alternative states of consciousness and find meaning in differing points of view.

I had to loosen the mental bonds that I had created for much of my adult life. I had to take apart my own rigid left-wing ideology and hold each piece up to the light for re-examination. I had to rethink my positions about revolution. I had grown up and become an adult who believed in radical political change; I had believed that to change things meant going to the very bottom of the problem and uprooting it. The "it" was the entire socio-economic system in which we lived. I had held to the views I had formed in the late 1960s of the need to change the government. I believed that the American Revolution was an example of a time when over-throwing a tyrannical power was an advance in the course of human history, and that the Declaration of Independence gave the people the right to rebel against an overpowering authority. I had believed that if voting did not work, I had to build illegal alternatives to prepare for the day when enough people recognized the need for change.

That was my past. Now I had to liberate my mind from that past in order to stay alive in the present. The world had not developed as I had thought it would and the idea of radical change, however enticing, seemed almost impossible. To live for the future made no sense to me, but to live in the present with ongoing meaning demanded that I effect change in myself. These intellectual struggles were driving me to the very brink. I could have taken heroin, which was readily available in maximum security. I could have stood on line for psychotropic medication. I could have stayed in my cell and withdrawn from everyone and everything. Instead, I told my political friends both inside the prison and outside that I had to rethink my past views. I did not want to renounce anything or anyone, I said, but I no longer wanted to be actively involved in the political movement. What I meant by this was that I wanted to and needed to psychically disengage from group decision making and from working on different projects together. I didn't want to write papers together or issue statements to the outside world as a group. While at earlier points in my incarceration, most specifically at Lexington, I had argued that as political prisoners we had to demand the right to association and recognition as a means of resistance to the BOP's attempts to divide us. Political prisoners all over the world had fought for this, but now I did not want any association at all. I wanted independence from the collective. I did not want to be held accountable to anyone else's opinions about how to live inside the walls and how to co-exist with other prisoners on a daily basis.

When we had been at Lexington four years earlier, we had had a running debate about how "we" should relate to drug dealers. Could we befriend them? Should we befriend them? Could we associate with them, or would doing so taint us and show the government a weakening of our resolve? Would associating with them imply that we were supporting the drug trade? It seemed to me that more than three-fourths of the prison population had been or was still involved in the drug trade in one way or another and that setting a rule against talking to them was more than absurd. With whom would we talk then? Only ourselves? My fellow political prisoners' view on this subject seemed to me excessively narrow, and I was beginning to believe that it was our narrow mindedness that had contributed to our failure.

To underscore my growing psychological need to separate from the past, I became involved with a woman who could not have been further removed from me politically. She was a "good ol' girl" from West Texas who had been in and out of prison for over a decade. She had a hard core and hard edges and had escaped from more prisons than any other woman in BOP history. Kate Baker was her name, but for some reason she was known as K.C. She had walked past the fence at Alderson, the women's prison in West Virginia, and then at Texas maximum-security prison, and at a Colorado women's prison. She had cut the fence at the Pleasanton, California, federal women's medium-security facility located in the middle of a U.S. Army base, and had been on the run for almost a year when she finally got caught. She had been at Lexington and had struggled against the psychological torture. She was not a part of the lawsuit that we had filed at Lexington because she was not considered a political prisoner, but she had resisted the manipulative divide-and-conquer tactics of the BOP.

She had enormous anger coursing through her and proclaimed herself a sociopath. She did not seem like one to me, though. She had two children she loved with all her heart and they communicated with her and loved her right back. In fact, it was that love that motivated her attempts and that kept bringing her back to prison. The cops went straight to her children and busted her each time she escaped because that is where she physically returned every time she got out. While in Lexington, K.C. turned forty-five, and by the time we were in Marianna she was tired of being locked up. She said that she could escape from the prison, and I believed her.

I respected her toughness and loved her fearless heart, but her temper was extreme and she did little to control it. She was only five foot one but afraid of no one. We had a strange and charged relationship. Some of my comrades were furious at me for getting involved with her. They did not trust her. They thought she had been used by the government when we were at Lexington. They thought she would try to escape again and that we would get blamed for it. Some called her a snitch and said she was just using me to conceal her identity and would break us all apart. Others thought that the relationship was my own private business but that it reflected bad judgment on my part.

I really could not figure out what K.C. might be using me for, and I rejected my friends' opinions. Getting involved with K.C. was, for me, the beginning of an unraveling of the rigid, ultra-sectarian, holier-than-thou kind of arrogance that I had embraced in my youthful attempts to organize for politics and platforms. In the free world, I had been part of a small group that had simply gotten smaller and smaller, by blaming everyone but ourselves for our failures. We were quite capable of repeating that history of blame in prison. I did not want to be a part of that history anymore; the days of toeing a "correct line" were over for me, even though I had been one of the people creating "the line." I was done with that.

I could not see how having a personal relationship with someone outside the group was a betrayal or a violation against anyone. Instead, I saw my relationship with K.C. as a means of keeping my own heart alive and finding some comfort. As it turned out, my relationship with her ended up causing an even greater schism in our group than did my declaration that I would no longer work cooperatively. All of us tried to keep the division hidden from the COs, and I think for the most part succeeded.

While the group of us were having disagreements over how to do time, what things were and were not politically correct, and how to co-exist in the prison, the unit was filling up with greater numbers of women. Marianna housed almost one hundred women by 1992, and increasing numbers of them had been convicted of aggressive and brutal crimes. The prison was a hotbed of hostile and angry young women that the authorities chose to control through regimentation and lockdown.

In every federal prison, it is the unit manager who sets the tone for how life is lived. Our unit manager, a Mr. Deveraux, imprinted the routine with his own brand of psychology. He was an African American from a small city in South Carolina and had begun his law enforcement career by racially integrating the local police force. He brought a small-town mentality with him when he graduated to running protective custody units and special security units at federal corrections facilities. He found being assigned to work with women ludicrous and pathetic and considered us irrelevant to the real work of corrections. He figured that to control us, all he had to do was pit us against one another. He enjoyed playing with us and dehumanizing us with his incessant verbal contempt.

Deveraux had been brought on board, he said, because he was black and a good public relations advantage for the BOP. He told us that he knew how to deal with "bullshit" from the ACLU and the National Prison Project (NPP) lawyers. He hated Adjoa Aiyetoro, the lead attorney for the NPP, with a seething passion. When she came to monitor the unit for her reports to the court, Mr. Deveraux oozed a smarmy glibness that I did not think helped the public relations campaign of the BOP, but did seem to work for the local Florida media. He called his job "babysitting a bunch of bitches," and it seemed that he hated us and blamed us for being responsible for his transfer to unit manager. Everyone knew that he was counting the minutes until he was promoted to associate warden and transferred to another institution.

Mr. Deveraux allowed the unit to be turned into a brothel for his officers, which made it a most difficult place for everyone who wouldn't play along. The sexual undercurrent was omnipresent. We were guarded by male COs and lieutenants, with very few female COs or administrators. There were a few female counselors, teachers, and psychologists, but almost everyone else who dealt with us was male. Officers and prisoners were having consensual sex throughout the unit—in the factory, the kitchen, the segregation unit, broom closets, and laundry rooms—wherever they could steal a few moments of privacy. Prisoners traded sex for everything from perfume, makeup, and drugs to merely a momentary sense of being desired, of something more than being an inmate. I understood the need it fulfilled for the women. The longing to be touched, to feel something, was overwhelming. I also understood that the men did it because they could get away with it, and because of the way in which they viewed us and hated us for transgressing. For those of us who witnessed the sexual dynamics it was painful and upsetting, and unless we constantly looked the other way we were in danger of being hurt, locked up, harassed, or raped into silence or complicity.

Mr. Deveraux allowed the abuse of power to continue unchecked for a year. Then, one day, a lieutenant caught a white CO pants down with a white woman prisoner in the laundry room after the night lockdown. The woman was whisked into segregation and then sent to another prison a thousand miles away. The CO was escorted off the grounds and quietly fired. This, however, was only the first of many such instances; in each case, the white prisoner would get transferred and the white officer would be escorted off the grounds, his job terminated. We joked that it was the only way to get a transfer out of maximum security.

One day, a month later, a clique of five white female prisoners who worked in the data entry factory took their break on the recreation yard. This was a rare occurrence; we knew there were gangs, but they never met openly. It had to be something important for them to be meeting in plain view. The rest of us noticed this get-together immediately. There were no cops in the vicinity and the prisoners were taking their time. When they finished speaking, they casually filed back into the building and returned to work. There was great speculation as to what had happened.

A few days later, a rumor began to circulate that an African American CO named Johnson had raped a prisoner named Deborah. It was an open secret that the two had been having sex, but the relationship had appeared to be consensual. Deborah, a white woman, was in prison for her participation in conspiring to murder her husband. It had been a brutal murder and she had received a thirty-year sentence. She was desperate to get parole, but there was no way anyone in maximum security was getting parole. She wanted a transfer out of maximum security badly enough to do just about anything. Deborah claimed that Johnson had raped her. The six-month investigation that followed produced enough fear and loathing to rival the Salem witch hunts. Led by the U.S. attorney general's office, it began with a grand jury that called in more than ten prisoners and many BOP staff.

I was called to the unit manager's office; the civilian investigators wanted to know what I knew. They said my cell was visually in line with Deborah's and they knew that I knew something. Though I had expected them to call me in, I was angry about it. I told them that I had not cooperated with Justice Department officials in the past and I was not about to start now. I told them that their in-house oversight was never effective and that I did not talk to police; I was not a snitch. They did not try to coerce me because they knew that I would make problems for them if they used this investigation to further harass me or the other political prisoners in the unit. They told other women that new charges against them would be filed if they didn't cooperate, that they would be charged with perjury, and that they would be denied parole and put in administrative detention indefinitely. In the end, they got an indictment against Johnson, who was charged with rape and other crimes. They took him to trial and he was convicted on the basis of inmate testimony and given a twenty-year sentence. Deborah got sent to Danbury Correctional Facility and Johnson went off to spend seventeen and a half years in protective custody in a federal detention facility.

After the trial, I could not help thinking of that meeting on the yard those many months back. My visual memory placed Deborah at the center of it, with the clique from data entry sitting or standing in a semi-circle around her. I kept mulling the scene over and over. I knew that I had done the right thing by not talking, but no one had even mentioned Deborah's possible motive—transfer and eventually parole. Still, I did not really have the facts.

I brought it up with my friend, Sue Gambill, a paralegal and my most frequent visitor. Sue had been visiting all of the political women since the week we had arrived. She was a lifeline for me, working in conjunction with my lawyer, Mary.

Sue—a radical activist, a writer, and a lesbian organizer—helped me stay sane. She had first written to me when I was in the D.C. jail. She had heard about our case and sympathized, although she thoroughly disagreed with our methods. I liked her letters and thought that we had more commonalities than differences. She lived in Tallahassee, about seventy miles from Marianna, and worked as a Legal Aid defense investigator for death row prisoner appeals. She visited monthly, communicated with our friends and families, organized visits, and opened her home to our political support networks. She also helped me write, resist, and change within those hideous walls.

Regarding the rape case, she said, "Write about it, Susan." With those words I began to think through all the implications: I had observed what might have been a legal lynching of a person who was, by definition, my captor—yet I had done nothing. I pondered the never-ending sexual dynamics involving incarcerated white women and African American male guards. I rewrote the events into a short story with a point of view that was not my own. I walked the yard and talked with Laura, one of my oldest and dearest friends. She had missed the events around Johnson, having arrived at Marianna only recently. She had come out of D.C. and organized the first women's support group at the women's general population prison in Lexington, Kentucky, and had been sent here on a disciplinary charge after leading a sit-down strike in response to racism and brutaity against women by male prisoners. I was sorry that she would have to suffer under the conditions that we were living in because I thought they were probably worse than in Lexington, but I was happy for myself that she was coming to Marianna. She descended on the unit in an airlift straight from the hole at Lexington. Soon, she and I had logged hundreds of miles jogging in circles. Laura had me look at the rape case from every point of view imaginable. What if Johnson had in fact raped Deborah? What if he had been white? What if she had been black? What if the other prisoners had told the police the truth? In the back and forth of our dialogue, we gave ourselves permission to step out of our own black-and-white worldview and consider shades of gray. In the end of that process, writing the story was liberating. It freed me from the dogma of thinking things were always all one way or all another. I began to write other stories, too, and the more I played with words—finding exquisite pleasure in creating a character or describing a scene—the further I got from my cell. The further I got from my cell, the more I was able to live in the moment.

With Laura's arrival, the humor and laughter quotient went way up. Being inside with Laura always offered a relief from the repressive, hostile dictates of the police because she made fun of all the petty rules and attacks. We made jokes about the COs' stupidity and we imagined them on the outside. We wrote a prison sitcom that revolved around the security procedures of the administration. The first episode we wrote, "The Shakedown," involved ten grown men running into a woman's small cell, unscrewing the lights, and searching the cell while the prisoner stood outside and let loose a running stream of banter. We came up with titles like "The Wrath of Con" and "Convictions," and most important, we were able to laugh at ourselves. Our laughter was a defense against the terrible conditions of our lives, which we characterized as the "continuing existential devolution."

I was sitting on the bunk bed in my cell one day when the door swung open and a huge, red-haired woman, six feet tall and well over two hundred pounds, walked in. She filled the whole doorway. "I'm the new unit manager, Ms. Nolan," she said. "I'm taking inventory."

I jumped up and stood with my back against the far wall. I had no idea what to expect.

Ms. Nolan went on, "Now, I want you to know, Susan, that I know you all are political prisoners and not terrorists."

I stared at her. I had never heard a BOPer say anything even close to that. My fellow politicos and I were the "terrorist bitches," the "cop killers." To hear the words "political prisoners" from her lips was totally shocking. She went on to give a lengthy speech that appeared to have been prepared. She talked about the 1960s, her teenage years in the early 1970s, and her opposition to the war in Vietnam. She said the difference between her and us was that she had been smarter—she knew that to make change she would have to "bore from within." I snorted at that. She went on to say that by joining the most entrenched of the law enforcement agencies she had more effect than if she had stayed outside the system.

I know I must have looked at her as if she had two heads. I said, "Yeah, so, if you know who we are, then send us to population. You know we don't need to be buried in this hole."

She said, "I wanted to work this unit."

"Good career move," I retorted.

She turned and strode off down the tier to give a version of her rap to the other political prisoners. That first encounter set the tone of our relationship for the next several years.

Ms. Nolan had been born and raised in Texas; she had gone to college in Austin in the 1970s and had studied psychology. She had a failed marriage and a teenage son, drove a Mustang, and always carried a Walther PPK .380. We thought she was a lesbian, but she insisted she was not. Things did change with her in charge, but whether for the better or not was a matter of opinion. She relaxed the internal controls, yet strengthened the isolation by tightly monitoring the communication between us and our supporters. She gave permission for some women to grow a garden that ultimately helped feed the entire unit. She allowed the animal shelter to come in once a month and bring cats and dogs for us to play with. Some of us had not seen an animal in over a decade. She gave us permission to run an AIDS program that brought AIDS service volunteers on the outside into the prison to talk and work with us. But she personally read our mail, stopped our visits, and paid mere lip service to our continual requests for transfer.

Ms. Nolan believed that the way to control us was to rule with a gentle hand. After she read an article about the innovative cosmetics company The Body Shop and its founder, Anita Roddick, she decided that the company should be allowed to sell its products to us at a discount. She understood that for many women in prison, looks and self-esteem were integrally intertwined. She understood that if we had good makeup, we would fight her less about being buried alive thousands of miles from nowhere. So in came the youthful saleswomen from the Tallahassee Body Shop (all of whom had to have special training before meeting us). I have to admit that although I knew full well we were being placated and manipulated with the soft hand of repression rather than the hard end of the whip, having mango body butter and avocado creams were a fine treat. Between The Body Shop and the puppies, it was like being in the Twilight Zone.

Chapter 14

My Father

IN JANUARY 1993, my parents came to visit. They spent a month living in Panama City Beach at an oceanside motel owned by our friends Bob and Arlene. Bob and Arlene had heard about us from Sue Gambill and had become supporters of ours. Everyone who came to visit us at Marianna stayed at their motel. My folks came to see me in Marianna several days a week. These were the most extensive visits we had ever had, and they was marvelous. They took my friends and me away from the visiting room with their tales of the beach and the movies and the lives we were not living. We played cards and Scrabble and ate awful prison visiting room food. (We had gotten the prison administrators to put yogurt and bagels in the visiting room food machines. The bagels were fake, but we ate them until we were silly. It had been years and years since we had seen bagels.) My folks visited all the political prisoners and everyone enjoyed their love and support.

My parents had struggled on from the horrors of Lexington and the near death of Alan Berkman, whom my father absolutely loved, through my father's own prostate cancer to my mother's transformation into a public speaker on U.S. political prisoners. They embodied grace under pressure and were simply and completely amazing. They never lost their cool in front of the cops; they gave respect and demanded it in return. Even the worst of the correctional officers had to speak to them with decency. My parents had come to believe that my friends and I were in fact political prisoners. They thought we were all extremists who had made irrevocable and costly mistakes—we had been "stoopid," as my mother put it. But even when they were angry with us, they believed that we were motivated by deeply held views on justice and racism, and that we wanted a world of equality and peace. One could scoff and say, "Of course they were like that—they are your flesh and blood," but no other Marianna parents were as committed to us as they were. Many of the political people made peace with their parents and brothers and sisters, but my parents were a special gift in my life and in theirs.

Both before and after that month-long visit, I talked to my folks once a week on the phone. For almost all the years up until then, I would call collect and we would talk in what I came to think of as "repression snippets." Every conversation was listened to and recorded. Anything deemed irregular was investigated. In every prison I was in, the COs knew my business from the tapped phones. But in those snippets my parents and I succeeded in conveying our feelings, which strengthened our understanding and thus allowed me to continue to resist.

In none of our visits, phone conversations, or letters did my parents and I ever talk about my getting out. Instead, we talked about everything and everyone else but that. I do not know if my parents thought I would do a life sentence. I think they believed that eventually I would get parole. They rarely revealed the pain they felt about my incarceration, and when they did, it was not with an intention to hurt me. During the first years, they were angry. During our visit at the Manhattan detention center right after my sentencing, my mother had sat furious but stone-faced, refusing to utter a word. She said later that she had been angry at how predictable it all seemed, and that my radicalism had been played out by script, in which she was an unwitting but central actor. But my mother understood that the government would treat me with a massive amount of security overkill, and her anger at that eventually overshadowed her anger at me.

In those Marianna visits we began to sort out the prior years of incarceration. We talked about my parents' experiences of Lexington and D.C. and my own. Three years earlier, when I was in the D.C. jail, my parents and I had finally won the right to a contact visit. My mother had not touched me in almost three years, and all she could do the entire time was grip my knee until it was black and blue. Being able to have physical contact with me distracted her so (all she could think about was how bony my knees were), that she forgot to tell me that my father had cancer. In a Marianna visit, my father told me how he had thrown up after their first visit to Lexington. Yet in telling me all this, my parents were not trying to make me feel bad. As a result of these conversations and in the more relaxed visits during their stay in Florida, I began to gain insight into their suffering and to see the consequences of my choices. They had embraced all of it with dignity, but doing so cost them a high price.

My father recounted some of the experiences that had helped him cope with my imprisonment. He had, for example, gone to Puerto Rico on a speaking tour organized by the Committee to Free the Puerto Rican Prisoners of War; I had been given honorary citizenship from the independence movement and he had accepted it on my behalf. In 1990, my father, who was not a religious man, met Rabbi Marshall Meyer at the B'nai Jeshurun Synagogue on

Manhattan's Upper West Side, two blocks from where my parents had lived for over thirty years. The social action committee of B'nai Jeshurun was showing the documentary film about Lexington, *Through the Wire*, and the rabbi and my father were on the panel.

My father told the rabbi that he had last been in a synagogue to bury his parents, but as a nonbeliever he felt far removed from organized Judaism. He knew from his organizing experience with the Puerto Rican independence movement that having religious community support was crucial to its success, but he said that the organized Jewish community was too self-absorbed and too preoccupied with Israel to support U.S. political radicals who had resorted to illegal and violent means. It was many years in the past from the days of the black and Jewish alliance of the civil rights movement. Yet in Rabbi Meyer my dad found a kindred spirit, a man of prophetic and joyous influence. It struck my father dumb, he told me. He went back to the synagogue, for the small measure of peace it gave his raging soul. He stood at the back of the pews and listened. Friday nights, he would revel in the celebratory practices of Shabbat and, being a man who loved to dance (his friends called him "Gene" for Gene Kelly), he joined in.

Rabbi Meyer had fought for the disappeared of Argentina. He had struggled to secure human rights for Argentineans affected by the junta-led "Dirty War," in which over thirty thousand people were tortured, killed, imprisoned, or exiled during the late 1970s and early 1980s. He understood prisons and he accepted my father's view that his daughter was a political prisoner being repressed by the Reagan and then Bush administrations. At Rabbi Meyer's suggestion, his student and friend Rabbi Rolando Matalon began to work in our defense. Roly, as we came to call him, was himself Argentinean and completely understood the power confronting us.

My parents had been longtime Upper West Side Democrats. They had helped to found the early anti-nuclear organization called SANE and the antiwar organization Peace Now, and they were friends with Democratic Party members. They had supported Congressman Ted Weiss and later Jerrold Nadler. As fate or luck would have it, Nadler was a member of the B'nai Jeshurun congregation. Upper West Side politics and connections were a world away from Marianna, yet there were people there who understood the harsh conditions and treatment, the injustice of disproportionate sentences, and the aftereffects of psychological torture.

In early April 1993, a few months after their long visit with me in Florida, I learned that my seventy-five-year-old father was selling his dental practice and going into a semi-retirement of sorts. This meant that my mom and dad would have more time to spend in their country house on Candlewood Lake in Danbury, Connecticut. On one of my weekly calls to them, I reached them there.

"Mom, how are you? What's happening? How is the country?" I asked.

"Your father is gardening," my mother said, her voice dripping with sarcasm. "He's never gardened in his life. He has raked a lot of leaves and shoveled a lot of snow, but gardened?"

"What is he planting?" I asked.

"Your father saw these crocuses and daffodils, and they need to go in the ground in April, but the ground is still frozen."

We laughed and went on exchanging news. When I hung up, I thought about my father and his complete dedication to life. I thought that he probably decided that because he was semi-retired he should take up new hobbies and that creating beauty was probably one of the better ones he could choose. I imagined he would become a great gardener.

The next time that I called, they were still in Connecticut. My father said, "I hurt my back, but I sure did plant those flowers, in frozen ground and all."

"Ah, but was it worth it?" I kidded him.

"We'll just have to see in July, won't we?"

My mother told me that my dad couldn't be too injured because he was still playing golf. But by the end of April, my dad's back was worse, and although an X-ray showed nothing, the doctors at Danbury Hospital had ordered an MRI. He went for the test at the beginning of May, but he had such a profound attack of claustrophobia that the technicians had to stop. He told me that he felt as if he were being buried alive and he panicked. There were no results from the incomplete test. At the beginning of June, my father was in such severe pain that he and my mom went back to Danbury Hospital. He could barely drive. When the doctors looked at the X-ray, they ordered immediate back surgery. He had a malignant tumor that had snaked up and down the inside of his spine. To get to the spot, they had to remove pieces of his spine and replace them with metal tubing.

A phone conversation with my mother revealed the gravity of his situation. I think I asked what the prognosis was, although it seemed obvious. She said she had no idea. I hung up the phone, went to the law library, and typed a request to visit my father. I photocopied it and put the copies into envelopes to the unit manager, the chaplain, and my lawyer, Mary. I was more than aware of the BOP's policy regarding visits to dying family members, having written countless requests on behalf of others over the years. A prisoner may request a two-hour deathbed visit or (and the "or" is big) attendance at the funeral. A prisoner may not request both. If granted permission for the visit, the prisoner must pay the salary of the accompanying security detail. The payment must be made up front and in cash. In less than one in a thousand cases, the BOP will let a low- or minimum-security prisoner take a death furlough unaccompanied by security.

In the middle of June, I went to Ms. Nolan, the unit manager, and repeated my request in person. Ms. Nolan already knew about it from the transcripts of the taped phone calls. Knowing this made me feel more violated and invaded than surveillance normally made me feel. She opened my "cop-out" in front of me. A cop-out is the first level of request, grievance, or complaint initiated by a prisoner. Once in the Tucson FCI, I had seen a unit manager's office in which every inch of wall space, from the ceiling to the floor, was papered with cop-outs. It was the manager's way of saying "Don't ask me for a thing." For the most part, a cop-out was not worth the paper it was written on. But for the persistent among us, those with a sense of self, filing a cop-out was the way to begin a paper trail.

Ms. Nolan sat behind her desk with a long shatterproof, bulletproof window at her back. She always repeated to anyone who entered that it was "state-of-the-art" glass. The view was a straight look onto Marianna's double electric fences with their multiple rows of razor wire. Off to the side, at a break in the wire, was a low tower next to a gate. In the distance was the officer and visitor parking lot, and past that was arid land as far as the eye could see. Except for the clear sky above all the metal, it was a most depressing vista. Whenever I stood facing Ms. Nolan in that office, I trained my vision to look above the fences to get a clear view of an unfettered sky. I was always longing for a pure horizon.

Standing there that day, I wondered, *Can you like your enemy?* Even though Ms Nolan's purpose was to keep us all tightly locked up, and her training dictated that she rule as if presiding over her own little fiefdom, I could see her humanity. I could see that, for all her power over us, she was big and overgrown and just as insecure as could be. She always wore flowery or patterned dresses that yelled, "See me." Her nickname, in fact, became "Big Dress." Despite being a tough Texas woman, she, too, was out of place in the midst of maximum security. Her marriage had failed, her career was not challenging, and she was trying to raise a son in the middle of the no-man's-land we were all in. She said she was a Southern Democrat, a risky claim given where we were. And for all those reasons, and whatever other inexplicable reasons she had, she saw in all of us something that she could not help but like and respect.

"I want to see my father," I said. "It is very important to me."

"It's okay with me," she replied.

I thought that her response was a trick, that having been informed about the situation she already knew I would never go anywhere. I stood there burning.

"Really, it has my approval," she went on. "But you need to get me a lot of information. I need a certified letter from your father's primary care doctor verifying that he is dying and estimating his life span. I need to talk to another family member assuring me that they will pay for the cost of the security detail, and I need a letter from the hospital stating that he is actually there."

"Okay," I said. "You think it can be approved?"

"*I'll* get it approved."

It was hard to believe her, but I wanted more than anything else to think she was telling the truth, and at least she had not given me an immediate and flat-out no. I knew that she would have to go to the highest echelons of the bureaucracy of the Bureau of Prisons and the Department of Justice, but she said she would try. I left her office thinking it was against the odds, but it was nevertheless possible. I desperately wanted to see my dad.

I was not able to speak to my father for a few weeks. He was always in rehab when I called. I assumed that he was dying and that, without parts of his spine, he would be permanently immobile. But he had announced to my mother and his doctors that he would walk again, and with all his might and will he was working at it.

The next few months felt like one long march. Every day I woke up thinking about my dad and every day I strained harder against my incarceration. The line between my acceptance of my circumstances and anger at those very same circumstances of confinement grew with time. The mental accommodations I had made to accept my circumstances and "do time" as productively as possible were being shattered bit by bit by my father's impending death. I came to understand how precarious those mental acrobatics really were. I was still drawing from a muted well of hostility, and I had to keep myself from jumping Ms. Nolan every time I saw her. She merely kept repeating that things would be fine.

My father left the hospital at the end of July. He needed full-time care, and parts of the house had to be remodeled for him. He was paralyzed from the waist down, but the fact that he could use his upper body at all indicated remarkable physical progress. I could not imagine him unable to stand upright. My father had been a very physical man. He had been an all-around athlete, a golfer, a tennis player, a champion Ping-Pong player, a swimmer, and above all a very good dancer. As a dentist, he had stood on his feet his whole career. Even as my mother relayed his progress, I could hear the anguish in her voice. Neither of us broke down, at least not on the phone.

I called one day and my father answered. I was flooded with such relief that I had to sit down. I got a folding chair from the common area and set it in front of the phone booth.

"Susie, how ya doing?" He was shaky but definitely alert.

"Hey, Dad, thought we'd lost you there," I said with a smile in my voice.

"Not yet, no way. I'll be golfing again."

We chatted for a while, and then my dad became serious.

"Susie, I've been thinking a lot about you and all the others, and I want you to know that the last ten years have been really important to me, too. You know, because of your being in jail, I have met a whole group of people that I would never have met otherwise, people who have shown me that humanity and solidarity and love are the most important qualities. I haven't always agreed with you, and at times I've violently disagreed with you and all your friends, but with all your sacrifices, you all have made me proud to be associated and proud to be your father." He went on, gaining strength with each breath. "Susie, don't take this wrong, because I am deeply upset at the terrible suffering and deprivation, but you all have restored my faith in human beings."

Tears were spilling down my cheeks.

"Barbara, Alan, who had survived his bout with cancer and been released, Mary, and the others who have visited me in the hospital gave me the most love I have ever felt."

I could hear from his manner and the formality that was coating his voice that he had been preparing to tell me this. My father wrote notes to himself whenever he had important things on his mind and in his heart. He had told me that he did this because he would get so emotional that he would forget what he wanted to say, and that writing things down made him clearer.

"Where are you?" I asked, wanting to get a visual picture of him in my mind.

"I'm in the bedroom in the back, your old bedroom."

I told him that what he had just said was very important to me, but that I had already known it from all his actions and all his work. I said that I felt his enormous heart enveloping me all the time. I told him that I was still getting letters from other people behind the walls who he had visited, or sent money to, or had supported by treating their families as a dentist. I told him that I would get out of prison one day, I could not say exactly when, but I would get out.

He said, "I am so happy to hear your voice. I have missed you so."

That was when I started really crying. I had to get off the phone. "Dad, someone wants the phone, I gotta go. I love you. Get better."

"Susie, give my love to all the women."

"Right." I hung up and went to my cell. Wrung out, strung out, and hurting more than I could stand, I threw myself on my bunk and cried and cried and cried.

Laura came looking for me. Laura always helped make things feel lighter—with humor and warmth, she took on and shared my burdens and pain. She did it with everyone she was around. It was as though she was a natural weightlifter for whom no burden was too heavy. Sometimes I thought her heart would burst under all those loads. But it never did. Her magnificent spirit radiated compassion.

In the early 1980s, when we had first gone underground, Laura and I were sharing a safe house when word came that her mother was dying. Our group did not allow any of its members to go home or attend funerals, since important family events offered the FBI some of the best opportunities for catching or tracking fugitives. Laura was not wanted officially by the FBI but she was a member and the rules applied. We were too slow in overturning them. Laura's mother died before she could get there. I had met Laura's mother only twice, but I knew that Laura's humor and wit had come from her. I could see their similarity in their smiles in the one good photo she carried.

As I lay on my bunk ten years later, Laura knew what I felt. "You can't lie there all day," she said.

"Yes I can."

"No you can't. Let's walk."

"No."

"Let's go see what Big Dress has to say about your trip," Laura prodded.

I told her what my father had just said on the phone, and she got all teary herself.

I said, "You're moved, I can see."

"Yes, I am deeply moved," she answered, and that turned into a joke about how a group of people who never went anywhere could be so "moved." And then we did move ourselves to the rec yard to walk in big circles.

I tried to talk with my father again, but every time I called he was sleeping, or indisposed, or doing rehabilitation work. I talked with my mom, Rabbi Matalon, Mary, and Sue Gambill every other day. We were keeping vigil. In the first week of August my father became incontinent and the pain came back in full force. His cancer had returned with a virulence that frightened everyone. He was re-admitted to Danbury Hospital. My mother and Mary called Ms. Nolan to inform her that my father was dying and that I had to come now. Ms. Nolan relayed the message.

Over the next few weeks, an enormous emergency effort was undertaken to make it possible for me to see my father at his deathbed. On August 20, 1993, my father's kidneys failed. In the belief that I would be coming to see him, he asked for a horrifyingly painful, yet life-extending measure that involved inserting a shunt directly into his kidneys. Letters from the hospital, from all the doctors, the oncologist, the surgeon, and his main doctor all concurred that his life was about to end. My mother wired the money to cover the cost of security for my visit, a sum in the thousands. Ms. Nolan kept telling me to hang on, but I grew more and more tense and angry.

On August 23, Mary was informed by the general counsel of the BOP that the warden at Marianna had denied my request because of the length of my sentence and the nature of my conviction. As she relayed the news over the phone, she was in tears and absolutely raging. She told me that she was writing to Kathleen Hawk, the director of the BOP who had replaced Quinlan, to Attorney General Janet Reno, and to everyone else she could think of. She said my mother and Rabbi Roly Matalon were meeting with New York Congressman Jerry Nadler. I hung up the phone and flew across the walkway, down the stairs past the officers' station, across the common area, and into the hallway that led to Ms. Nolan's office.

I walked into the office and stood shaking with anger. "You lied, you lied, all along. You knew this was all an exercise in bullshit."

"Sit down," she roared.

"No. My sentence length has been fifty-eight years for the past nine years. My conviction will be my conviction until I die. It is always the same thing." I wanted to shout obscenities and hit her. I wanted to overturn her desk and destroy her office. But I did not do any of those things.

"Susan, sit down. I just found out, too. Will you sit down, for Christ's sake!" She went on to say that she disagreed with the decision, that she had told the warden this and that it was not over yet. She said there was a "good ol' girls network" and that she was in the process of calling in favors.

"But it's been denied. It is always harder to undo a decision than to get the one you want to begin with—you know that," I said.

"Let me work on this. I told you and your mother and Mary that I am still working on this."

Mary? I thought. *Big Dress is calling my lawyer by her first name?* But I was not placated. As I walked out, all I could think about was what they would tell my father.

They did not tell him anything, however, because no one involved was taking no for an answer. On August 26, Mary wrote the following letter to Janet Reno:

Dear Madam Attorney General:

I know that you are now aware of the tragic circumstances surrounding my client's requested compassionate visit with her dying father. I write hoping that you did not participate in the BOP's decision earlier today to uphold the Warden's denial of the request, and you will permit this visit to take place.

The BOP's action today, according to Mr. Ron Allen in BOP Director Hawk's office, was based upon "the best interests of the BOP." Mr. Allen cited two alleged considerations: Susan's "offense severity," a possessory offense not involving violence, and the "severity of her sentence." According to Mr. Allen these factors present a "risk to the community" if Ms. Rosenberg is allowed to visit her dying father (accompanied by four U.S. marshals), even though her security classification is low security and her conduct excellent by any measure.

This "Catch 22" situation means no sentenced prisoner has any motivation to change because they will always continue to be penalized over and over again for their conduct that led to their incarceration and their sentence used against them at every subsequent point. My client's 1985 sentence of fifty-eight years for a possessory offense was sixteen times longer than the average sentence for such offenses. Had she been sentenced under the new guidelines she could have received months rather than a lifetime.

Unreversed, the BOP's decision sends several messages, all of which seem inconsistent with your stated standards for the administration of justice: First, that blind retribution alone sets the standard of treatment for federal prisoners. Second, that prisoner self-development is of no value. Third, that the BOP's own system of evaluating and classifying prisoners is inaccurate and unreliable, with no meaning. Fourth, that the opinion of BOP professionals who live and work with prisoners cannot be credited.

Finally, and perhaps of most importance here, this decision says that this government is unable to forgive anyone who opposes its policies and that instead targets such individuals forever because of their political positions. Thus, while lip service may be given by government officials to matters such as basic standards of decency, fairness, and human rights, these are illusory matters to be freely ignored and disregarded when it comes to our internal workings of government. We are quick to criticize such action on the part of other nations, but willing to engage in them here nonetheless.

I beseech you to correct this injustice and to do so now before Dr. Rosenberg dies and needless pain and suffering which this situation has caused becomes etched forever in the consciences of his family and the many people who have asked you to exercise compassion and fairness in the face of this tragedy.

On August 27, Ms. Nolan called me to her office. She was joined there by Chaplain Raftry, a Franciscan nun. They both looked at me while Ms. Nolan told me that the visit had been denied and that there was nothing further either of them could do. I could, however, make a phone call to the hospital with the chaplain.

Perhaps the poison in my heart was misplaced, but at that moment I hated them both with every ounce of my being.

I walked out. I wanted to lock down. I wanted to be alone so that no one could look at me with sympathetic eyes, so that no one could invade me with a smart remark. Even in maximum security, there was no privacy until the cell doors were locked. I went to the yard and ran in circles, I sat in the laundry room on the side of the machines, I paced in my cell.

Eventually, I found Laura and we raged together. She wanted to go curse out Ms. Nolan, to scream at her and the nun. Right before lockdown, I was out in the inner courtyard pacing in small circles, going around and around. All of a sudden, something inside me told me to calm down. Listen. And a feeling of repose settled over me. It was magical and total, and I thought, *I will see my father again.* Lynette Fromme (of Manson Family infamy, in federal prison after her purported attempt on President Gerald Ford's life) was also sitting in this little courtyard, watching the sky through the wire netting. She said, "Susan, it is going to be all right." She spoke abruptly, as though she, too, had felt a force of calm, or maybe she had sent me the energy herself. However it happened, my deep agitation was gone.

"Yes, Red," I said, using one of her nicknames. "I think so. Thanks."

They called lockdown. I felt better.

I was awake at the midnight count and slightly asleep at the 2:00 a.m. count. In my semi-conscious state I heard a key in my door and knew it was out of place. I opened my eyes and there was a large, looming shape in the doorway of my cell. I jumped up, understanding it was Ms. Nolan.

"He's dead, right? My father is dead," I said.

"No, Susan, get dressed. You have ten minutes. You're going to see him. Come to my office when you are dressed, and be quiet."

It all happened that fast. *Hang on, Dad, I'm coming,* I thought.

I put on my best clothes and picked up my only jacket. It was a blazer left over from court days. Ms. Nolan began talking as soon as I entered her office. She listed all the people who were going with me: my counselor, the lieutenant who was in charge of special ops, and two COs who were part of the prison SWAT team. They had all volunteered; it was considered hazardous duty. She went on to say that Lieutenant Rocker was the commanding officer and that I had to do exactly what he said.

As if on cue, the lieutenant walked in and said, "We're out of here. You will have two hours with your father and not one minute more. We will be back today."

Ms. Nolan put a paper and a pen in front of me. "Sign it."

I read the paper quickly and smiled quietly. It said that I swore not to escape. (I imagined what Laura's sense of humor would do with this scene.) I signed and stood up. The lieutenant cuffed me, but did not wrap me in chains. I thanked them both as we walked to the front doors of the prison. I was actually leaving, it was really happening. It felt like the federal wall had been shaken and that I was somehow slipping through the crack. It was an exhilarating feeling. They put me in a car and drove me to a small airport, where we boarded an eight-seat Learjet. We flew with the rising sun the whole way up the East Coast. No one spoke the entire trip. It was eerie and strange, but I was so withdrawn that I could not have uttered a word. And they were very serious because they knew the situation that awaited us at the Westchester airport.

We were met by a small army. There were more than fifty agents of every variety and rank: state police, Westchester County police, airport security, Danbury BOP personnel, FBI agents, and U.S. marshals—all of these people assembled merely to drive me to the Danbury Hospital. It was so over the top that all I could do was laugh, despite the awesome firepower at their fingertips. They literally picked me up and put me in a white van with two marshals sitting up front, separated from me by a screen. The one on the passenger side was riding shotgun. He had an M-16 in his lap.

They drove like crazy. The plane left at 4:30 in the morning and landed in New York at 9:15; we arrived at the Danbury Hospital at 9:50. As we were walking to the back entrance, I glimpsed Mary O'Melveny and Susie Waysdorf getting out of their car. I glimpsed them as I was whisked inside. I was escorted up to the eighth floor and was greeted there by more officials. All of us were standing in a darkened hall in front of what I presumed was my father's room. Other than all the security, there was no one else around. A tall, sandy-haired man in a tailored suit stepped forward and identified himself to me as "Justice."

I looked at him and he at me, and then much to my embarrassment my eyes filled with tears. "Thank you, sir," I said.

He mouthed, "You're welcome."

I stuck my arms out indicating the cuffs. Someone said, "Leave them on." "Justice" turned to whoever had said it with a look implying "Are you nuts?" He then nodded directly at Lieutenant Rocker, who unlocked the cuffs. I stepped into the room.

A nurse said, "Thank God. I didn't think you would get here. Your father was very agitated, and I just gave him some morphine."

"Oh no," I said, thinking that he would be too sedated to know I was there.

I took in the scene. My dad lay in the bed with IVs running. He looked like he was asleep. The view from his window was quite startling to me. It was an open New England sky and landscape.

It was like a fairytale picture with houses and a steeple nestled into hills. As I approached the bed, three of the Marianna team came into the room and took up positions around it, with their backs up against the wall. I drew a breath to protest, locked eyes with my counselor, and withdrew. I realized I could fight with them and lose precious time, or I could ignore them.

I went toward my dad and the nurse followed me. She put her hand on my arm. "Let me tell him you are here. We don't want to scare or startle him." She very gently shook him. "Dr. Rosenberg, hello. Doctor, I have a surprise for you, a wonderful surprise. Your daughter is here."

Her gentleness was beautiful. As her words penetrated my father's consciousness he gave a start, tried to get up, and turned his head toward me. He whispered, "I knew you would come."

And I whispered back, "I knew I would see you."

I kissed him, touched him, and massaged his head. I then laid my head on his chest and talked into his ear. I held his arm and his hand and rubbed his shoulder. I felt the bumps on his chest and presumed they were tumors; I could not stop holding his hand tighter and tighter as the seconds ticked on. Knowing it would be the last time I would ever touch him, I decided I would remember how he felt, his arms, his bristly curly hair, his head, and his face. He was mottled with cancer and he looked totally exhausted, but I saw him only as my handsome and terrific father.

The next thing I knew, my mother was standing in the room. Her eyes met mine and we both started crying out of relief, sadness, and happiness. We grabbed each other so tightly that she almost cracked my ribs. I had not realized how strong she was.

My father looked at us and said, "My beautiful, favorite women, Bella and Susan. I love you so." He was drifting in and out of consciousness.

We hugged him as best we could, my mother on one side of the bed and me on the other. My mother mouthed to me across my father, "They weren't going to let me in, but they changed their mind. I saw all those men and thought he had died."

At that point, Dad woke up and said loudly, "I want everyone to know that if you want to carry out my wishes, you all will fight harder to get Susan out of prison." He went on to give a speech about the injustice of my imprisonment.

Finally, Mom said, "Manny, it's us, me and Susie; we agree with you."

"Oh, right," he said, "but I want everyone to know." He was aware of the police in the room.

Then we all held one another. We were crying as Mom said, "We're a trio, we've been a trio a long time, and we are a great trio the three of us, right, Manny?"

Then one of the officers said that we had ten more minutes. Those were the hardest ten minutes of my life. I wanted to break free, I wanted to turn back the time, years back, I wanted to wail and scream. I apologized to my parents for everything I had done and all the suffering that my actions had caused. I promised my father that I would be free, and that I would take care of Mom. There was so much emotion in that room, and so much love, it was overwhelming. I glanced at my counselor and saw tears streaming down her face. And then as quickly as I had come, I was gone.

The Marianna security detail moved me out and cuffed me in the elevator and once again picked me up and carried me to the van. I felt deeply alive and awake, but also in a state of shock. My heart was torn up and my spirit was in rebellion. But by the time that I was sitting on the jet with my forehead glued to the window, saying good-bye forever to my father, I appeared completely calm and still.

We were back in the unit at Marianna before the 4:00 p.m. count. Few of my fellow prisoners—only Laura, K.C., Marilyn, and Silvia—knew that I had been gone. Ms. Nolan had had the unit phones turned off for the day, which caused a minor stir. But that died down when the phones went back on after the count.

At six o'clock Monday morning, August 31, 1993, I felt my father die. I sat up in my bunk unable to breathe and felt that he had been in my cell and was now gone. As soon as the cell door opened, I went to call my mother, who was about to go to the hospital because word had reached her that my father had just died. My old friend and acupuncture partner Jackie Haught had spent the night with him, helping him let go. Jackie was a Buddhist and had become an expert in helping the dying because a lot of her practice was with AIDS patients. Her compassion and humanity had been more than helpful. It had been her gift to my father.

On the morning of my father's death, Rabbi Roly Matalon came to Marianna to visit me. He had arrived late the night before. It was not the first time we had met, but it was a formative visit. His being there that day felt no less miraculous than my visit to Danbury had been. Roly told me about the events that had transpired in the forty-eight hours prior to my visit. There had been an emergency response to the BOP denial by all the people and groups who had supported me over the years. The BOP had received several thousand faxes and phone calls from all over the country. Mary had tirelessly hand-delivered a barrage of letters to all the relevant officials. Congressman Nadler had intervened. He had called Kathleen Hawk, the BOP's director. When she told him that moving me was too dangerous—since people would try to free me and I was a terrorist threat—he had responded that that was a tired line. He then said, "We take over governments in secret, but here you are telling me you can't move one person in secret from

Florida to Connecticut. If you want a human rights nightmare, don't do this. But I suggest that you *do it*!"

The months that followed the death of my father were the most difficult. They were filled with a deep grief, a reckoning with consequences, and a fall into an abyss. I remembered a dream that my father had described to me. He was in the Lexington HSU, both as a visitor and a prisoner. He woke up screaming because of our pain and his inability to stop it. He knew my imprisonment was a direct result of my choices, but on a deeper level he felt that he was a failure for not protecting me against those choices. He was distraught over this, and the longer I was in jail, the more he cried. His sadness at our suffering was apparent. His sadness and compassion were intimately linked. And as I began to realize this, I hated myself for having created the situation.

Perhaps because I was so isolated in maximum security, or perhaps because I was coming up on ten years inside, or perhaps because my father's death made me feel as I had never felt before—whatever the reasons—my extreme grief drove me mad. I could not get away from it. I marked all time by Dad's death. This birthday, that event, each was the first without him. Every time I thought about his being gone, my chest would constrict and I could not breathe. Sometimes I could hear his voice; other times I could not remember exactly what he looked like. I was angry that I didn't know, and had no way of finding out now, his favorite season or his favorite color. I was angry at being gone for ten years and wasting time, as though time were unending, as though we had lifetimes. I realized that our family line would end with me, and that made me the saddest of all. It was hard to grieve in maximum security. I missed my father's fierce love, which had broken through every concrete wall. I thought of his heartfelt politics and his goodness. I wanted to be more like him. I felt that I had to have his goodness in me. It was hard to locate under the conditions I was in. To be good and kind was viewed by the authorities and prisoners as a sign of weakness. But I wanted a fresh start in my own self.

That year, 1993, was a year of grave loss. The inability to take on the normal role of child burying a parent, or beginning to care for the remaining parent is a terrible part of the state's punishment. I don't know whether being aware of such consequences beforehand would have functioned as a deterrent for me. I like to think it would have, and yet in this strange and unpredictable dialectic, the bonds of love and responsibility I felt would not have been as strong without the suffering and the separation I had experienced.

At the same time, my health, and that of my friends, was deteriorating. Medical care at Marianna was nonexistent and we suffered. Marilyn had a bum knee from a poorly healed kneecap and a shortened tendon; Silvia had developed a rare form of uterine cancer and had radiation burns from the treatment she had received in 1991. Laura woke up one day so dizzy she could not walk a straight line. She was diagnosed with shingles, and later Ménière's disease, and her illness lasted for years. For months the authorities' only response was to constantly give her breathalyzer tests because her weaving suggested drunkenness. I began to lose my teeth, one at a time. I had arrived at Marianna with only twelve because of terrible periodontal disease and equally terrible care from the authorities, so that by 1993 I had only six left. We had all endured prison under extremely difficult and terribly stressful conditions for five, seven, nine years, but because we were not dying, no one was sent to the outside hospital.

I was in despair: grieving for my father, for me, and for all of us. When I finally lifted my head up several months later, it appeared that the revolutionary impulse around the world was in decline. Social justice, equality, and peace were no less needed now than they were thirty, twenty, ten years ago. But the vision and means and capabilities had been transformed in the last decade. Activists had been demobilized around the globe. I, too, had been transformed. I had gone from being a passionate militant and a committed revolutionary to being . . . I was not sure what. I wanted to think that Che Guevara's great pronouncement that "revolutionaries above all else are motivated by love" was still true for me. But my own vision now functioned in a much narrower framework. Had I gone from social revolutionary to social worker? No doubt it was all more complex than that, but without a revolutionary movement or theory or radical or socialist camp in the world, I was not sure that one could continue to be a revolutionary. How could I, or anyone for that matter, operate in a complete vacuum? I did not feel that I could separate myself from history.

In 1994, Ms. Nolan made good on her collective promise to us. She succeeded in chipping away at the security wall encasing us and got first Silvia, then Marilyn, and then Laura transferred to general population. Our classification had been reduced and we political prisoners were no longer to be confined in maximum security. I decided to apply to the parole board and test the waters of opinion.

Going up for parole is a wretched process. Laura joked with me that I would need fleece-lined knee pads to survive the parole request. In our brief time together at Metropolitan Correctional Center, in 1985, Irish Republican Army prisoner Joe Doherty had told me that courts in England and Ireland had railings on the dock to prevent prisoners from having permanent knee injuries. Baring one's soul in remorse is hard to do, but when your release depends on it, and yet whatever you say never seems to be either apt or sufficient, it is painful indeed. Ten years inside is a long time, and now I was in the midst of a growing desire and pressure to get out. I had made a promise to my father that, although unrealistic, I wanted to keep.

For years I had put release on the back burner of my mind. A fifty-eight-year sentence felt like a life sentence. But I was eligible to try at ten years, so I decided to file for parole at Marianna.

Going before the parole board would reveal what the government's legal position was; the government had always used the conspiracy charges in the Brink's robbery case to bolster its extreme classification and treatment of me. But because those charges had been dropped, if they used those charges against me now in a parole application, I would have grounds to fight for release. My grounds would be strengthened by the fact that the average sentence for weapons possession was five years in the United States.

I was exhausted by prison. Every bit of it offended my sensibilities. But prison was only one piece of my life. I tried to rekindle an earlier time when my blood had boiled and I had raged against the crimes of the state, when my own savage heart had beat to an oppressive pulse and what had compelled me to act was a vision of social justice and social liberation. As I sat in Marianna, that time seemed so far away that I could barely reclaim it. Life for me at this point was a series of compromises about coexistence with the authorities in the most deadening situation imaginable.

There were varied opinions among us about what our relationship to the parole process should or should not be. "Us" included other political prisoners, the lawyers who had represented us and who continued to defend our rights, our families, and our associates, both past and present. I had come to the conclusion that every individual who had come out of the left in the 1960s and 1970s and was now doing time had a right to develop his or her own position, whether that meant refusing to admit any wrongdoing, refusing to be self-critical, or begging the government for mercy.

Yet I also feared that I was succumbing to self-preservation and by taking part in the parole process I would lose much of my integrity. My friends outside took a more objective view, saying, "Of course, you should apologize to try to get out, what difference does it make?" It made a difference to me.

I vacillated for months as my desire to get out of jail and help my mother grew. For every single choice I had made, I could blame no one but myself.

I decided that I would apologize to the parole board. I would admit my actions were criminal and dangerous. I would agree that having dynamite was an endangerment to innocent people, regardless of intent. I would acknowledge that the terrible antagonism Tim and I had put forth at our trial was my doing, against the advice of our lawyers, and had grown directly out of a refusal to take responsibility for my actions and a lack of remorse. I would further admit that I now believed that violence is wrong and that we were lucky no one was killed. I would say that I would never, ever repeat such actions, nor would I counsel anyone else to use such methods. I would not talk about anyone but myself. I would bend as far as I could without breaking.

In late November 1994, the government canceled my parole hearing because the parole commission wanted the Southern District of New York to explain in writing why they had failed to prosecute me for any involvement in the Brink's conspiracy case. Parole officials wanted to know what the evidence against me was. The U.S. Parole Commission stated that unless the Southern District said that it had dropped the case for lack of evidence, then any evidence it had would be used against me in a "release determination." Since the charges included murder, it would be a "no-release" type of ruling; it would mean a fifteen-year set-off. This meant that I would not be considered for parole until the fifteen years were over.

This was all communicated to me by a blank-faced parole examiner whose desk stood in front of a bare wall. His droning words receded as my thoughts raced around and around until one took hold: a recollection of the men who had rebelled at Attica prison in 1971. I recalled their lack of vindication, although they proved their case over and over again. Forty-three men had died, most of them simply demanding decent and humane treatment. I thought about the state's lack of accountability in that case, and its acts of retribution in so many other cases. Accountability, retribution—did either bring justice? I did not think so.

I thought about the state's ability to remember its enemies and their acts and the long reach of punishment as the droning examiner told me that very probably I would live on until I died in prison. I recalled the statement I had made at my trial in 1984—that the system would not last as long as my sentence. I had been so cavalier about that—yet so off the mark. I thought of one memory ending and another beginning. I thought about the policemen who were killed in the Brink's robbery on October 20, 1981, the shoot-out between Sekou Odinga and Mtyari Sundiata, who had been accused of participation in the robbery and had been hunted by the police and FBI. And how they had been spotted in Queens on October 21st, the next day, and had been in a shootout. Mtyari had been shot to death and after Sekou had been arrested, he was tortured for several days in a Queens police precinct. I thought about the children of all the different people on different ideological sides who had grown up without parents, who were now teenagers and grown-ups themselves. So many lives had been changed forever by that one horrific event in Nyack, New York. It was a terrible thing, and the consequences were unending. *The futility of it, God,* I thought.

Daniel Singer, French writer and intellectual, in writing about the Italian Red Brigades, said that when a self-appointed guerilla group declares itself the leadership of a movement, it actually does harm to the social struggle. By substituting political violence for organizing people where they are, it shortcuts the necessary work of winning peoples' hearts and minds. This description fit us to a tee.

By Christmas, 1994, I had been at Marianna for four years. Silvia was in Danbury, Marilyn and Laura were in Pleasanton, California, and K.C. was in a Colorado state prison serving the end of her sentence. Others at Marianna had come and gone. I was the last one of us still there. The Southern District of New York did not answer the board's request for months, and I withdrew my parole application and applied for transfer instead. However, my application for transfer was denied. Again, the reason given was my sentence length. I was losing ground in every quarter. I was back to where I had started. I had nothing to do but turn to life in the unit.

When Sue Gambill came to visit me after everyone else had gone, she said that not one person had signed the visitors' log from her last visit six weeks earlier. There were no visitors to Marianna. My friends and I were the only people who had ever gotten consistent visits. Every one of the Marianna prisoners was hundreds, if not thousands, of miles from home.

Those of us remaining at Marianna were an odd assortment, considered the worst of the worst, because of our crimes, sentences, levels of organization outside, or behavior. This was a group ripe with the potential for betrayal and vengeance. Every day, our lockdown time increased, and shakedowns were coming fast and furiously. The little garden for food that we had cultivated in the rec yard was suddenly filled in with concrete, and the UNICOR factory that had employed thirty-five women in data entry was closed. The GED classes ended, and the little world that we all existed in was shrinking. As it did, people started fighting. One day a woman took a twenty-pound dumbbell to another woman's skull and blood spattered from one tier to the next. The prison guards locked us down for a week and charged the woman with attempted murder. My anger at everything returned.

And it was just at that point that I was transferred to the brand-new, multi-million-dollar Oklahoma Processing and Detention Center and held incommunicado for three days, only to surface at the Danbury Federal Correctional Institution the following day.

Part Six

Danbury

Chapter 15

Danbury General Population

I ARRIVED IN the early evening. It was late spring and the New England sky was pale, with streaks of blue and white. It was familiar, that light, and I could actually see the horizon. So I did not even care when the cops dumped me into the old and worn room that housed the Danbury prison's receiving and discharge (R&D) area. In fact, the light filled me with an almost uncontainable excitement as I stood waiting to be unchained. I had spent ten and a half years locked inside one space or another: cells, corridors, tiers, "dog runs." Now it was the very first time I would be in general population. I was only seventy miles from New York City and my family and friends. This meant that I would have regular visits. On top of that, the unbelievable irony was that the prison complex extended right to the shore of Candlewood Lake, the same lake on which my parents had owned a house for over twenty years.

Waiting in the R&D area, I let my mind wander. Here in Connecticut, I would no longer have to listen to Christian "rock" radio. Maybe I would even get to hear jazz again—Thelonious Monk and Ella Fitzgerald, Erroll Garner and Billie Holiday. Surely some university station would breach the walls. Yale University was near by, the University of Bridgeport and other schools, as well. Before all the officials came to inspect me, read me my non-rights, and get me prepped for population, I was happy. The Danbury prison would mean less repression, less control. It was an incredible relief.

And then I took in my surroundings. I remembered reading that there had been a fire at Danbury that had killed some prisoners years back. It smelled dank even in May; everything at Danbury appeared old. The stone and brick walls needed paint; the furniture looked like old prison issue. Only the high-tech equipment—the surveillance cameras and the metal detectors—were modern. I remembered reading that Danbury was one of the oldest federal prisons in the country and that it had housed many famous and iniquitous people: the Plowshares movement antiwar activists Philip and Daniel Berrigan; G. Gordon Liddy, the former FBI agent and Watergate burglar; international marijuana dealer-turned-author Richard Stratton; a number of mob members; and various high-profile, white-collar criminals. It had been changed to house women only in the early 1990s.

As one CO unchained me, I could hear the chatter from the others who were lounging around and watching the process. This batch was young except for the gray-bearded man in charge of R&D. He seemed impatient, as if he had dinner waiting at home. He looked as if he were about to tell everyone to "get out" when the steel door separating the room from the inside of the prison was pushed open. The warden walked in, flanked by an entourage of lieutenants. I knew it was the warden instantly because the lounging COs abruptly stood up and looked down at their feet. He stared at me and I stared back, which was easy to do because he was five foot six, my exact height. He reminded me of Quinlan, the former head of the BOP. They both were balding, thin, middle-aged, bland-looking man. They were the kind of men who had other more physically powerful men do their bidding.

"Hey, thanks for taking me into your institution. Don't worry, it will be okay," I said, my voice thick with contempt.

"Wasn't my choice," he said as he eyed me up and down. As suddenly as he had come in, he turned on his heel and strode out.

The COs were all staring at me. One of the lieutenants, an overweight, shaggy guy only a little older than I, ordered everyone out. The COs dispersed quickly, leaving me alone with the hound dog-looking lieutenant. "I'm SIS [Special Investigation Service]," he said.

"I'm scared of you," I retorted snottily. What made me do this, I don't know. My initial excitement about the light and the prospect of relief from repression had given way to anger—at the way I had been transported, being disappeared for three days into the maximum-security holding facility in Oklahoma, where I had been put into a cell on the men's floor, at the chains, at the armed-camp atmosphere, at the animal-in-a-cage atmosphere with all the COs hanging around. It was not the best way to start this new part of my prison life. I could not help it.

I took a closer look at the man in front of me. His name tag said "Frederickson," and I knew, despite his benign appearance, that he was not on my side.

"Yeah," I said. "Poor choice of friends."

He cut to the chase. "You'll never get parole. This little trip here is a temporary stay. You fuck up and you're outta here."

"Tell that to my lawyers," I said.

"You stay away from the other terrorists," he went on. "You don't associate, and you might get room to breathe."

"Lieutenant," I said, "this is old news. My friends and I did

Lexington together, and they tried to drive us crazy there. It didn't work; they couldn't divide us."

His eyes narrowed into little slits and he snorted; he went from looking like a shaggy dog to looking like a pig. "Laugh, but we know you're a cop killer, convicted or not," he added as he walked out.

Despite my sarcasm and contempt, I realized that this man was my enemy and would hurt me at the first chance he got. That, I took very seriously.

All the higher-ups having left, the COs returned and went to work in earnest. I had been "received" before in many other places, but this time there was a new dimension: a psychologist was brought in to interview me. At that point, I could not tell if I would be sent to segregation first or straight into population. It was up to the doctor to make that determination.

Dr. LeBarre strode in. Her appearance shocked me to the very core. She had short, red hair and a tattooed star on her ear, and she wore a hippie-esque outfit of flowing purple linen. In her early thirties, she looked like someone who could have been a progressive from some movement—feminist, gay liberation, whatever. I was reminded once more that I was no longer in the South, where someone like Dr. LeBarre would have been seen as a foreigner.

"Clear out," she ordered. Once again, the COs trooped out, as one of the younger ones rolled her eyes in disgust. The procedure was becoming comic, even to me. As Dr. LeBarre eyed me up and down, she and I began a verbal dance involving ideology, choice, politics—all of those differing strands bound together—that would characterize our interactions for years to come.

"You don't look all that frightening," she said. "I know your friend Silvia, and she doesn't seem all that dangerous, either."

I did not say anything. I just stood still, taking her in.

Then she said, "I'm a cop first—above all else, I am a cop, not a psychologist or doctor. You have to know that."

"I would never assume anything else," I said.

"I mean, if I think you are a threat to yourself or anyone else, or if I think you are planning an escape or any violence, I will lock you up faster than a heartbeat, and it won't be about treatment or therapy or any of that stuff."

My curiosity about this interesting-looking woman turned to revulsion. I loathed her for looking like a "liberated person," or at least for matching my frozen-in-time image of what a liberated person might look like. I thought to myself, *This is what we fought for? Now we have "feminist" police masquerading as "service" professionals.*

She continued. "It's up to me whether you go to segregation or not. What can you tell me? Are you a threat? Do you want to kill yourself? Anyone else?"

I just shook my head no. She had my file open and was filling out a form. I tried to read the open page upside down. All I could make out was the top line of the first typed paragraph, which said: "Escape risk. Inmate is extremely personable. Do not be fooled." I kept my face still, trying to strike a balance between a normal gaze and the convict stare.

Finally I said, "There's no reason not to let me into population. It won't be a problem."

Dr. LeBarre stared at me hard, and then said, "You're going to long-term housing. If you want to talk to me, I am in Three North."

I thought, *What prisoner would ever tell this Ice Woman they wanted to kill themselves?* I couldn't imagine it. *She probably is studying us so she can write a book.*

But she let me go into population. And when they could

procrastinate no more, the COs walked me down the long corridor with windows looking out onto the inner compound of the prison. They unlocked a door, and out I stepped into the general population, into a big, open inner courtyard and the waiting arms of Alejandrina, Silvia—who I hadn't seen since we had been transferred from Lexington—Frin and Phyllis, both of whom had been at Marianna with me, and many others. I was mobbed by scores of women. They had known I was coming to Danbury before I had. That was the way the prison rumor mill worked.

My first twenty-four hours in Danbury immersed me in a kaleidoscope of feelings. I was ecstatic and at the same time despondent because I realized how sick the past years had made me. The first morning, when I entered the dining room with four hundred other women—all yelling, with guards breathing down everyone's neck to "eat fast"—I panicked to the extent that I had to run outside and throw up. This happened repeatedly over many months.

I was sent to live in one of the two long-term units, which housed prisoners with sentences of fifteen or more years. Most of the people who had arrived from Marianna were living in those units. The cells were small, each had a toilet, a sink, and a bunk bed. They had originally been built as one-man cells, in days when "long-term" meant five years. Now each cell housed two women instead of one man, and "long-term" usually meant life sentences.

My first cellmate was a twenty-three-year-old Jamaican woman serving four concurrent life sentences for drug conspiracy and murder. She was beautiful, as in take-your-breath-away beautiful. Looking at her became painful when the reality of her future struck my heart. She had merely been the "girlfriend"; she had used drugs, but she had not pulled any triggers and had not actually stood in the street and sold dope. She had been in the car when the shooting happened and people had died, and then she had refused to testify against anyone. She had no understanding of what was happening to her. She didn't know how to stand up for herself, how to determine what she needed, and had no outside support to help her with money. Unfortunately, I was too self-absorbed and trying to deal with my new circumstances to communicate with her. I was emotionally overwhelmed by her future and my own.

I had come from isolation and found myself in an unknown prison beset by overcrowding, petty degradation, and cruelty. In my first few weeks there, the energy that I had to expend merely to stay alive was exhausting. While living among thousands of women was stimulating, I was suffering from post-traumatic stress syndrome and alternating between depression and hyper-activity.

In spite of my mental state, I talked to everyone. I talked to women who had ten- or fifteen-year sentences, women who were repeat offenders, women who were parole violators, and women I knew from the D.C. jail, all of whom had been doing time for most of their lives in one state institution or another.

Each day, I perceived the administration's utter contempt toward the prisoners more fully than I ever had before. Whereas the terrible conditions at the D.C. jail were like a well-kept family secret as everyone knew about them but just shrugged at them, and the Lexington officials had been concerned with destroying us and our identities, here a pure hatred of women oozed out of every official pore.

During the hottest summer in Connecticut's memory, when it was 105 degrees Fahrenheit for days running, there was no air-conditioning. Women were packed into cells the size of bathtubs, and there was not enough food in the kitchen to meet daily requirements because of the overcrowding.

Slowly, I began to understand the transformation that had taken place within the federal prisons during the ten years that I had been in maximum security. The most obvious difference was the sheer increase in the number of female prisoners. But the other change that stood out was a shift in the racial balance from half white and half black and Latina to a black majority.

In my almost forty years, I had been witness to a great deal of suffering, racial and sexual oppression, degradation, and indecency. Danbury reminded me most of the South Bronx in the 1970s, where I had worked in a devastated urban community in which nothing worked, in which no needs were met, and expectations were so low that only survival at the barest level was considered a victory. To exist with low expectations about the quality and content of life is a terrible thing, and I saw this crushing reality everywhere I looked. It seemed to me that the Bureau of Prisons was succeeding in its attempts at destroying the mass of humanity at Danbury prison.

A few months after I arrived at Danbury, I found out that my friend Donna Nelson—a soul sister of the deepest connection who had saved me again and again in D.C., first by bucking the police lies about us and then by being the first prisoner to smuggle food to me—had died from complications related to AIDS. Five years earlier, she had not even been HIV positive, and now suddenly she was gone. As the weeks went by, I heard about more and more women who had died of AIDS. My codefendants and I could count hundreds of prisoners that we personally knew. All that wasted life energy, all that terrible suffering.

A lovely woman named Pam Cooper who had been in the D.C. jail and then at Lexington, and who had been a great friend of Laura Whitehorn, had at the age of thirty-six received four life sentences despite her unwillingness to pull a trigger. (A conviction of conspiracy murder does not differentiate between the actual shooter and those who participate in any way. All those indicted are considered equally culpable.) I asked Pam, "How do you deal with that? With four life sentences?" She answered, "I don't lay claim to them, I don't claim them."

Her words gave me chills. In truth, Pam would soon die from AIDS, rendering the concept of "life sentence" almost absurd and irrelevant.

The scourge of AIDS was on my mind when I walked into the prison gym one day and saw seven young black women sitting in the bleachers, all of them new arrivals. They approached me and asked me about prison life, about the commissary, the laundry, the rules, and the housing units. I asked if any of them had done "fed time" before. They all shook their heads. "No," they answered. As we talked, I learned that they had sentences ranging from ten years to life. I again thought of my years working in the Bronx, where I first witnessed the impact of racism, prison, and drug addiction.

Danbury, I learned, doubled as an immigration holding prison for the U.S. Immigration and Naturalization Service. On top of the predominance of African Americans within the population, there were dozens of women from the Caribbean and the whole African diaspora, primarily from Jamaica, Haiti, the Dominican Republic, Ghana, Kenya, and Uganda. On any given day, there were women representing more than forty different countries. As I walked around the compound that summer, I could hear an array of languages. Danbury resembled a small city in the developing world, both poor and cosmopolitan at the same time. Laundry was hanging out the windows; women were carrying buckets of water when the water system broke down. Everybody was dressed in ill-fitting brown, green, or khaki-colored clothes.

The extreme heat of the summer gave way to the coldest winter that had hit Connecticut in many years. There was not enough heat in the housing units, even with all the bodies jammed to-gether. The brick, stone, and steel walls allowed the bitter tempera-tures to penetrate. The pipes burst, leaving more than five hundred women in one unit without hot water. For six weeks, they had to walk through the snow in the inner compound to take a shower. The complex looked like a refugee camp. We were all internally displaced people.

The unit managers at Danbury set the tone for the kind of treatment that the staff meted out. In a closed institution, all things related to the outside world pass through a variety of in-dividuals' hands. The mailroom clerks inspect your mail and de-termine whether or not you get the birthday card, which book is approved, and which letters are returned to sender. The counselors decide who is allowed to visit you and who you may telephone. The unit manager, in conjunction with your case manager, decides which job you have and whether or not you can go to school. The unit manager also approves your application for transfer to an in-stitution closer to home, or whether you are moved against your will to a prison farther away. Nothing happens to you without a staff member's direct involvement. You can limit your interactions with the staff, but it is impossible to evade them altogether. They intrude on your reality every day and in every way. As a result, some prisoners decide that it is easier to live in prison with as little contact with the staff as possible. They either withdraw or resist or do time in segregation. Regardless of their decisions, this team of people, "your team" of people, will interact with you at some point. I have heard prisoners after an interaction with their "team" come away sardonically singing, "You can't always get what you want," from the Rolling Stones song, as a means of relief from the disap-pointment of denied requests.

The adage "The less you need, the better off you are" is

especially true in a federal prison. But needing less is useful only if your goal is co-existence with the set of antagonists on the prison staff. It does not get you anywhere if you want to *advocate* for anything or *help* another prisoner with real-life problems. "They," the prison staff, determine how and when you are able to visit your children or parents, what happens when you get scheduled for deportation to a country where you have not lived in years, what happens if you are sick and your security designation prevents you from going to an outside hospital, or what to do when you cannot pay your fine so your paltry wages are garnished and you cannot even buy so much as a bar of soap.

In October 1995, I had been at Danbury for six months and was scrutinizing all the unit managers to see which one seemed the best and the least intrusive, and which one I could get along with and would leave me alone. It was the rainiest night since my arrival when I walked across the compound into the hallway of Unit 9 in my green army jacket, soaked to the skin. I didn't have a hat and my hair was dripping into my collar and down my back. I was waiting to talk to Ms. Sharpe, the unit manager of the east wing. I had heard that she was unpredictable and spontaneous, always blowing from hot to cold. I wanted to live in Unit 9, which had large cells and single bunks. I had never seen the inside of the unit before because prisoners were not allowed to move freely inside of the cellblocks. We were restricted to the unit that we were assigned to live in. Simply standing where I was at that moment was "out of bounds" and potentially punishable as a violation.

I found myself next to another woman in front of Ms. Sharpe's office. I stood silently as one of the unit staff for the east wing, a Mr. Luce, a short, skinny man in his middle thirties, the most distinctive thing about him was that he had a prominent wall eye, came bounding down the stairs. As soon as he saw the other woman and me, he screamed, "Do you live here? Do you live here? You two are out of bounds. I know every inmate who lives here, and you do not. Come with me. You are in trouble."

The other woman and I followed him to the unit next door, and into his office. It annoyed me to no end that male counselors were assigned offices within the living space of so many women; from their posts, they could watch women walking around at all times of the day or night. I could see that Luce was really reveling in it; he had placed his office desk so that he could see directly into the first row of bunk beds.

One of my friends, Maureen, had called Luce "one ugly black shit." His face now was twisted up in anger, and one eye was way off center.

Luce proceeded to scream at the woman next to me, but she did not reply. I did not know her or why she had come to Unit 9. When she did not respond, though, I assumed that she was African, because I knew that an African American would have yelled back. She appeared to be in her late twenties with very curly, short hair and no jewelry. Her clothes, far too large, hung on her body. She started crying. With each hateful word from Luce, she cowered, shrinking into herself.

Luce threatened her for being "out of bounds," but never once asked why she had been standing in the hall. He railed about "the stupid Africans" and how they could not speak English and could not read. "You look like a fucking wet monkey," he yelled. "That's my new name for you, Wet Monkey."

I gasped. He turned to me and told me not to utter a word. By now he had worked himself into a total rage.

The African woman was wailing. Her body was shaking so hard that I thought she would crack. I put my arms around her to get her to stop. She began to stutter, trying to beg Luce not to lock her up. She said she was sorry and that she should have known. "Please, please, sir, oh kind sir, don't put me in the hole."

Luce was loving it, loving her distress so much that his bad eye started twitching and swiveling around in its socket. Then he smiled and said, "You are both stupid bitches."

The other woman started crying all over again and within thirty seconds had completely fallen apart.

Then someone from outside the window, a prisoner who had apparently been watching the whole dreadful scene, blurted out for all of us to hear, "That wall-eyed motherfucker! Look at that shit!"

Luce jumped up and ran out of the office in pursuit of her, but the woman who had vilified him was long gone.

I put my arm around the hysterical woman and whispered to her, "Stop crying, please stop, nothing is going to happen. He can't really hurt you."

He walked back in and said, "I heard that. I *can* hurt you. I can hurt you both."

And then a look of rage passed between Luce and me. I held his gaze, and he looked away first, his eye twitching.

"What's your name?" he barked at me.

I spelled it out for him as slowly as I could.

He said, "Both of you, get out. Next time I will deal with you."

I grabbed the woman and we walked back to the hallway and then outside into the rain. She went to the barrack unit on one side and I returned to my own unit, where, needless to say, I remained for the next several years. The gratuitous pleasure that Luce had taken in witnessing a prisoner's profound agony astonishes me even now.

About three weeks later, I encountered Luce in the mess hall, surrounded by his fellow officers. He said, as sweet as pie, "Ms. Rosenberg, next time you have to be out of bounds, make sure you have permission." I ran into the African woman several times after that. Her name was Mae. She thanked me every time she saw me.

After that incident, I began to think about my friend Donna Nelson, from the D.C. jail. I kept cycling back to when I had been in the D.C. jail. Much of Danbury reminded me of it and it made me think of the many women I had met there, many who were now at Danbury. I recalled how Donna had been my first real friend inside prison; I thought of her big heart. I envisioned her big gap-toothed smile, her constant disrespect for authority, and her fearlessness. I remembered that first orange she had thrown into my cell, which had broken the police rhetoric about us.

I thought that she would escape the plague of AIDS, that somehow she would slide through it, or around it, or miss it altogether. But she was dead at thirty-four. For a long time Donna's spirit was my guide, and even in death she helped me navigate the hateful circumstances that surrounded me and all of us in that prison.

After my arrival at Danbury, I talked incessantly to women whose sentences varied greatly in length. I was obsessed with the lifers, and had been since my first days in prison. I had met a few lifers over the years, and had done time with women who were waiting to go to death row, but I had never lived with so *many* women who had life sentences. I simply could not fathom the idea that all these women would live out their lives in prison and die on a prison ward. I knew that in a certain way I had a life sentence, with a fifty-eight-year sentence and a minimum of twenty years. But it wasn't life. Though it seemed unlikely, I did have an outside chance of parole. I could not allow myself to think that I would die in jail. Dying in jail seemed the hardest thing of all.

The punishment of a life sentence for the many women I had met was disproportionate to their crimes. My experience with drugs had been primarily as a medical problem, in a community where addiction was understood as a disease and people sold drugs to support a habit. But that was old history from the 1970s, and it no longer fit the current conditions. In the 1990s, the war on drugs had become a war on women in the drug trade: the wives and girlfriends of drug dealers, the drug runners—called mules—and drug users. These were the women who were, and still are, doing life at Danbury. For the most part, these lifers are first-time, nonviolent offenders whose convictions are related to drug conspiracies. The unfairness of their sentences is compounded by the fact that, although most drug users in America are male and white, the majority of those who are behind bars for drug-related offenses are black or Latina women.

Though some women in prison are fortunate enough to have family members who remain unscathed by the criminal prosecution—a loved one who can hold some semblance of family life together—many have no one to care for their children. Without family at home, these women lose their children to the state. In a matter of minutes, a woman's life is over and done with. Gone. Only prison time lies ahead, often more time than there are years left to live.

The lengthy sentences and the often great distances that family members or friends must travel to visit prisoners make it nearly impossible for a woman to maintain ties with the outside world. When there is little hope of release, women prisoners quickly lose touch with those that they leave behind. Under the current sentencing laws, if you are thirty-five years old and you get a forty-five-year sentence, you must do at least forty years, which means you can walk out free and clear at age seventy-five. If you have a natural life sentence, you never walk out; you die in the women's prison hospital center at Carswell Air Force Base in Texas.

The severity of punishments in drug-related cases is intended to be coercive. Women targeted by drug agents are pressured into becoming snitches; the agents typically offer sentence reductions in exchange for information. Prisoners who have no information to trade are stuck with lengthy sentences. And those who *do* have vital information, and who cave in to the pressure to implicate others, essentially become government property. They have been bought by the government and can and will be used again and again. It is the government that holds their fate in its hands; it is the government that must be obeyed. Other prisoners are seen as a threat. Thus, building unity among women prisoners becomes close to impossible. The trading of information in prison may not rise to the level of informant trial testimony, where facts have to be verified, but prison informants can and do prevent women prisoners from exercising collective power over the difficult conditions of their lives.

The Bureau of Prisons plays an active role in this coercion. The BOP claims that it is neutral and only carries out the directives of the courts, that it is involved only in custody, not in the terms of punishment. But this is not so. No longer is prison itself sufficient punishment. No longer is the loss of freedom enough. Now the purpose of imprisonment is to ensure total "cooperation," total subservience.

Most people who get arrested do not think that they will ever wind up giving information to the government. But the threats of lengthy sentences begin before an indictment and continue several years after conviction. Before the implementation of mandatory minimum sentences, prisoners had the right to request a sentence reduction: the Rule 35 motion I had brought in Tucson and had failed to get granted. There were various grounds on which one could bring this motion, including family hardship. If a prisoner could demonstrate to a judge that her imprisonment was causing her family undue suffering, the judge could reduce the sentence.

Though not common, sentence reductions under Rule 35 gave prisoners hope, a chance for a break in the unrelenting prison time.

In 1987, many of the sentencing laws were changed and a Rule 35 motion was one of them. Now it can only be brought to a judge by the prosecution. The rule has been transformed into a government tool whereby compliance is the only grounds for sentence reduction. The motion has been reduced to a one-page list of categories with a box for a check mark next to each. Under the first category, "debriefing" (meaning an interview with the FBI giving information about the crime), are four subcategories: debriefing on own role; debriefing on other principals; debriefing on general activities of the conspiracy; debriefing on criminal acts. The sentence reduction depends on how many boxes contain check marks.

In the years during which I was in Marianna, I witnessed the process of breaking women prisoners. The women's unit in which I was housed is unique in the federal prison system as the only super-maximum-security unit for women. Prisoners are sent there directly from sentencing proceedings, not because they are security threats and need more supervision (studies show that very few women require maximum security conditions), but rather to give them a taste of the way the rest of their lives will be lived unless they acquiesce to the government.

I saw women with life sentences, from forty to one hundred years, pass through Shawnee's five electronically controlled doors. As they lay in their cells, the impact of their new lives hit them. They soon called the special agents or prosecutors, or responded when law enforcement officials contacted them. Rule 35 motions were offered, prosecutorial powers were exercised, and the women walked out, transferred to easier prisons with ten, seven, or four years left to go, accompanied by promises of protection and even money.

In Unit 1, where I lived at Danbury, I observed a woman for weeks before the government approached her. Her name was Belle and she was a forty-year-old African American woman with a life sentence for her involvement in a drug conspiracy. She was the mother of several children, teenage and younger. Before her arrest, Belle was the backbone of her family. She is a large, smiling, expansive woman whose eyes crinkle at the corners when she tells a story. The full life she once knew as a mother was gone. Though she tried to stay involved in the lives of her children, her family ties were unraveling with each passing month.

Along with twelve coconspirators, Belle sold about a kilo of cocaine a week. They didn't make millions of dollars; there were no murders or any bribes or threats to public officials (the Colombian cartel, they were not). They were local people involved in a small-time operation that was labeled "big-time" by the U.S. Drug Enforcement Administration. Several of those convicted in the case and sentenced to decades in prison had no knowledge of the overall conspiracy. They were selling cocaine on the side simply to make ends meet.

When the DEA agents arrested Belle, they told her they would put her away forever. They told her that her best friend had already rolled over on her. They said several others were ready to roll, as well. They brought Belle's teenage daughter in and told her that if her mother failed to rat on others, she would be wheeling her mother's body out in a cheap pine box after she died in prison. "Debrief!" the agents screamed at Belle over and over for months. Her options, they explained, were to live her entire life in prison or to cooperate—and the latter would mean at most five years in prison, three years with good conduct.

Belle was the first to admit that selling cocaine was wrong. Like many other mothers who got caught up in the drug trade, Belle told herself she was selling cocaine to give her children a better life. Because of the difficulties she faced in providing for her family, she opted for existence in the underground economy. "It was an easy way out of a bad situation," she said.

It was later that her own addiction took hold. "I know that crack addiction destroys people, and I am glad it's over," she said, not to justify her actions, but to place them in context. Belle is one of the few convicts I have met who would admit to her crime.

However, Belle refused to get past that first check mark on the Rule 35 motion. She felt that since she did the crime, she must take the weight. She refused to implicate anyone other than herself. She was four years into a life sentence when I met her. She did go back to the DEA agents and prosecutors to explain her own role in the conspiracy, but that was not enough for the U.S. attorney to recommend a sentence reduction. Again, they told her, "Give us what we want and you can walk out in eighteen months."

It is difficult to imagine how one might face such a choice: eighteen months versus life in prison. Belle chose not to talk, and she struggled with this decision every day. I saw it in her face when she thought no one was looking. When she went back to be debriefed on her own role, through mirrored glass she saw her children sitting on the other side, unaware of her in the next room. The children had grown beyond recognition. She told me that at that moment her beliefs were more deeply challenged than at any previous point in her life, and she wished that she could die. It is the foulest of bribes—your beliefs or your life—an unconscionable dilemma created by an all-powerful state.

Soon, Belle would no longer be of any use to law enforcement. If she held out and resisted the pressure to become an informant, her options would close. Her punishment, the forfeiture of her freedom for the remainder of her life, so exceeded the crime that it is difficult to comprehend. I could comprehend it only when I considered the government's desire to break the back of the drug trade—but I am angry that it tries to do this by targeting those who are the weakest, those who are the most vulnerable.

Everything that I believed in the 1970s about the influx of drugs into poor black and Latino communities I saw even more clearly and more sharply in prison. The men who run the international drug cartels have the power and money to buy and bargain their way out of prison, often by snitching. When the most callous and cynical manipulations of sentence length are the main device the government employs in its war on drugs, a total corruption of the system prevails. That the government, through its law enforcement agents, can say to a woman, a mother, a person with hopes for a future, "Your life means little to us, and your freedom nothing at all," it is a fundamental betrayal of human rights and one that degrades the life of every individual.

This disregard for the value of life, and particularly nonwhite life, is part of the fabric of American social relations. This was confirmed for me again and again during my time at Danbury. I had to come to grips with it even while it broke my heart. I could not find peace and live with this.

I found that the poem "Four Quartets" by T. S. Eliot helped me to think about the terrible quandary that Belle and others found themselves in:

> *In order to arrive at what you do not know*
> *You must go by a way which is the way of ignorance.*
>
> *In order to possess what you do not possess*
> *You must go by way of dispossession.*

In order to arrive at what you are not
You must go through the way in which you are not.

And what you do not know is the only thing you know
And what you own is what you do not own
And where you are is where you are not.

Chapter 16

AIDS Epidemic

AFTER SEVERAL MONTHS at Danbury, on the eve of my fortieth birthday, two years after the death of my father, eleven years into my incarceration, I fell in love with Frin Mullin, who had over-lapped with me in Marianna for almost three years, but to whom I had barely spoken during that time. Frin, who had not liked me at first, but who was good friends with Silvia Baraldini and had a premonition that we would become lovers but never told me for years and years. Frin, the elusive, beautiful, disdainful "Brit" with all the dry wit, cynicism, and sophistication of the infamous drug dealer to the English counterculture that she had been, who sold drugs to prominent musical celebrities. Frin, who when we were in Marianna had avoided me like the plague until right before my father died, when she decided to tell me her story.

She had been born to an Irish mother and an English father stationed in the colonial service in Uganda, was raised in India, sent to Catholic boarding school in Europe and then to school in London, and at last brought back to India in the late 1960s. Frin was one of the people in the 1960s who had trekked through India and the Himalayas, worshiped the god Shiva, followed the Bodhisattva, and lived on the beach in Goa. In the 1970s, she became a mother and a businesswoman. She did eighteen months in an Indian prison for selling drugs until her sister arrived and bribed the authorities to release her. Although I never was privy to the story of Frin's drug dealings, I learned that she was enterprising and successful, with an exceptionally long run in the business until she got arrested in New York in 1982.

She brokered a deal and got a ten-year sentence, but her young daughter needed her. And so she escaped by walking away from the federal prison camp for women in Alderson, West Virginia, in 1984. She lived on the run in Europe, with her daughter in tow, until someone recognized her and reported her whereabouts to the British government in 1990. Having shamed and angered the U.S. authorities, she was extradited quickly and deposited into maximum security in Marianna. She was moved to Danbury in 1994 and had been there a year before I arrived.

Frin and I danced around our affair for months—yes, no, maybe, should we, could we, what if, what if not, who would be upset, who would not care. Our back and forth was in some ways irrelevant because the sheer energy that consumed us in the discussion was the very beginning of our loving. She finally made it happen, after we consulted the *I Ching* over and over, both of us being long-standing adherents to that ancient text, the Chinese Book of Changes, which melds thousands of years of Chinese philosophy and wisdom. I had first been exposed to the *I Ching* when I was in high school and later again when I was studying traditional Chinese medicine and the application of the five elements and yin and yang to the treatment of illness. Later, in prison, I used the *I Ching* as a form of meditation, as a way of reading text and using the text to bring a new perspective to whatever situation I was confronting. The Book of Changes is one of the world's great books and to me was as important as the Bible, the Torah, and the Koran are to their adherents. It always helped me. So in the matter of loving Frin, when the *I Ching* kept advising yes, in multiple hexagrams with multiple interpretations, I took it seriously.

I was in awe of the way I felt. I had often thought that I would not or could not love again, and so I felt lucky to have another chance. Without passion, it is most difficult to maintain hope and I did not want to become deaf to a joyful noise. The passion I felt for Frin gave me a reason to keep on going and her love gave me power. She gave me power to create in the midst of a destitute reality, power for my own soul, and power to love her back. Even if my joy was tinged with a feeling of guilt—I had made "doing time" a most serious way of living and to fall so completely in love seemed frivolous—but I couldn't help it.

Frin was an artist. She was a photographer, a writer, a chef, a conceptual artist, a woman of taste, and a woman who could fix things with her hands. She could craft and create; she could design and sew and make things grow. She worked in the education department in what we both thought was the funniest position possible: she was in charge of the pre-release program, the set of steps prisoners nearing the end of their sentences must go through so that they are "prepared to re-enter society." Since Frin was a European who knew nothing about American benefits, the health care systems, social services, or employment and educational opportunities, having her in charge of pre-release was like having a blind person lead a mountain climbing expedition. But Danbury was like that, an alternately absurd and deadly place. In order to survive years of it, I had to understand both aspects. I already knew about the deadly part; Frin showed me the lunatic side, and lightened the atmosphere all around her.

We read poetry together and her poetic imagination took us

far and wide. She helped start a program called Poetry for Prison Walls, in which she and others selected several poems a week, graphically laid them out with bars superimposed over the text, printed them on bright-colored paper, and posted them (with approval, of course) all over the compound. Frin's picks tended toward John Dunne, William Shakespeare, Philip Larkin, and Elizabeth Bishop, but she allowed others in the program to incorporate into the mix more contemporary poets, including poets of color. You could be using the toilet in the gym bathroom or walking across the yard and you would run across June Jordan, Maya Angelou, Pablo Neruda, Roque Dalton, Adrienne Rich, and on and on.

One day someone got the idea of putting up Oscar Wilde's "Ballad of Reading Gaol" (his seminal poem about his experience in prison) in the center of the education building bulletin board in large-size type. The head of the education department, Ms. Cotter, could not help but notice it, although she did not read it until it had been up for a week.

> *For oak and elm have pleasant leaves*
> *that in the spring-time shoot:*
> *But grim to see is the gallows-tree,*
> *With its adder-bitten root,*
> *And, green or dry, a man must die*
> *Before it bears its fruit!*

Once she comprehended the text, poetry in the education department, especially the Prison Walls program, was banned. When several education workers went to Ms. Cotter's office to appeal her decision, she screamed at them, calling them elitist and anti-American.

Frin and Silvia brought films to the prison. They convinced

their boss, a teacher/cop known as Mr. Z., to borrow them from the Marist College film library for an adult continuing education class that Frin taught. We saw films by Charlie Chaplin, Luis Buñuel, Akira Kurosawa, François Truffaut, and Orson Welles. We even saw the silent films of Salvador Dalí, which were Frin's favorites. Women who had never seen a foreign film in their life watched them and then discussed them. The imagination unleashed during that year at Danbury was, for me, a leap to a new depth intellectually. Frin, in a most quiet way, was the main architect who transformed the sterility of prison into a splendid little island of stimulating beauty.

While I was falling in love, the HIV epidemic was raging. In our AIDS education classes, our outreach programs, our counseling sessions, and the literature we distributed, I and other peer advocates emphasized that being HIV positive was not a death sentence. The AIDS organizations from the outside that were granted permission to come inside for programs and education emphasized it, too. But we were lying for the purpose of our own success. Before the discovery of anti-retroviral drugs, an HIV infection almost invariably led to death, so much so that the BOP built an AIDS ward for women at the Carswell Medical Center in Texas as a unit in which to die. Even in the rare instances in which compassionate releases were granted, the affected women were almost always too sick to go home, and had to enter nursing homes, shelters, and hospital wards. The vast majority of women with AIDS died behind bars.

As lower-level participation in the drug trade became criminalized in the 1980s and 1990s, more and more drug addicts were locked up. The women's population in the D.C. jail was moved almost en mass to Danbury. This population, 95 percent black, was a mix of the older and younger generations ranging in age from eighteen to sixty. The bulk of the HIV-positive population came from D.C., and I knew many of them.

When Silvia Baraldini arrived at Danbury in 1994, she began an AIDS awareness group and began building an extensive AIDS resource center and library. When I arrived, I helped build the group and teach the classes. Besides Silvia, Frin, and me, the group included Kemba Smith, a twenty-two-year-old African American woman who, under the mandatory minimum sentencing guidlines, was sentenced to twenty-five years for being the girlfriend of a drug dealer. We wrote to members of ACT UP and other anti-AIDS groups, some of whom Silvia and I had known in the political movement from the 1970s and 1980s. We secured donations of videos and organized AIDS educators to come into the prison and lead workshops. We got to the point where we were talking to the medical department about setting up a buddy system for HIV-positive women. We used ACT UP posters with political statements and pictures of condoms, and we quietly distributed information about such things as using bleach to clean needles and lesbian transmission of the virus. Our curriculum covered topics that included exposing the myths of HIV/AIDS, basic prevention education, care of HIV-positive patients, and prisoners' rights in care and treatment.

The prison's psychology department was our sponsor, but we also got support from the education department and the chapel. My prison job was working as a clerk in the chapel. The head chaplain was a Franciscan nun whom I had first met at Marianna. Chaplain Sheridan hired me almost as soon as I was transferred to Danbury to work for her and help her create an inter-denominational library. She knew that I had been a librarian at Marianna. She was sympathetic to the plight of HIV-positive women, and allowed the chapel to be a resource for the AIDS work. We made use of every resource we could to push and organize for AIDS awareness. We all felt, however, that HIV peer advocacy which included helping HIV-positive women analyze their treatment options, going with them to the medical department, helping them if they were sick, teaching prevention and education to challenge the discrimination they faced, helping them file motions for treatment of early release, exceeded the boundaries of what the prison wanted to allow. The officials did not want to talk about or allow us to talk about sex and drugs or how to develop prevention strategies. They would have rather closed their eyes and pretended that it wasn't there. We knew that we were pushing the limits that the administration had set, but we also knew that the epidemic spread through stigma and through fear of the unknown.

We were working hard and everything seemed to be going well until one day in October 1995, when the warden extended his usual five-minute walk around the grounds into the long hallways of the recreational building. The front hall led to the gymnasium on one side and to the chapel on the other. It was the most-traveled hall in the prison. On the wall leading to the gym we had placed a poster that we had decided was rather benign: it depicted a heart pierced by an arrow that pointed to a condom. Underneath the image were the words "Fabulous Sex = Safe Sex." The warden saw the poster, stopped, pulled it off the wall, and marched into the chapel where I worked as a clerk. I was sitting at my desk, organizing the lending library, when the warden and his entourage (wardens never walk alone, just as they never ever eat food prepared by prisoners) stormed in.

One of his nicknames was the "Short Warden," but some of us called him the "Catholic King," for his professed devout beliefs. He was on great terms with my boss, the head chaplain.

"Katherine Ann," the warden bellowed, calling for the head chaplain.

I went into the hallway where he was standing and I said, "Sir, the chaplain is in a meeting."

"You?" He shook the poster in my face.

I tried to calculate how to respond. "That poster was approved," I said.

"Not by me, it wasn't." He crumpled it up and threw it on the floor.

Not very respectful of the chapel, I thought. Then for a moment I forgot who was standing before me, and who I was, and I kept talking. "Warden, this is important information; people need to know this."

"This is disgusting, this promotes filth! No one has sex in my prison." He was turning red. "We have zero tolerance. I know you know what that means," he said, and then stormed off.

The next day the SWAT team descended on the chapel, the education department, and the cell of every member of the AIDS-prevention groups. They tore up literature, pulled tape out of cassettes, and searched through books. They ripped up some Good News Bibles while examining their spines. We watched silently, knowing that the officials were merely trying to intimidate the staff who had supported and approved our work. For us, this kind of tactic was old news, and we knew that eventually we would rebuild. It served us all well never to become attached to anything, and we tried to have multiple copies of materials in multiple locations to increase the chances that at least part of our resources would escape destruction.

At Danbury, the senior staff was easily scared and always embroiled in internal power struggles. It was a corrupt kingdom in which alliances were always shifting and petty contrivances could set off great suffering. I say "kingdom" because the warden *was* king; he had subjects, not prisoners with rights, and he had serfs, not employees, who did the back-breaking work required to make the prison run and turn a profit. He had an army at his disposal to compel his subjects to cooperate, and ultimately he had control over life in the face of death. Most important, he had little accountability: he had enormous latitude in the interpretation of regulations and was subject to scrutiny only from afar. Whatever legal or governmental checks and balances had been set up to ensure the safety and security of all federal institutions had long ago been so disregarded that the federal prisons were as corrupt and mean-spirited as their infamous maximum-security counterparts in the Southern penitentiary state system. The BOP policy of abstinence-only was enforced with a vengeance by the Catholic warden.

While we were trying to survive the many attacks on us by the administration, we decided to create a panel for the national AIDS quilt. We thought making a panel would be the most benign project we could do and would create a break from the administration's growing fear of our work. After all, how could sewing be considered subversive? We first discussed making a panel in the fall of 1995 because we knew that the saying "If you are not infected, you are affected" was particularly true of this prison population. Everyone knew someone who was infected with the HIV virus and if they thought that they did not know anyone, it was because whoever they knew was afraid to tell them. We hoped that making a panel for the Names Project for the quilt would bring HIV out of the shadows. The chaplain contacted the Names Project local Connecticut chapter and they were given permission to bring in several panels of the quilt to show us. We were very excited to have AIDS activists come to Danbury to help us.

The gymnasium filled up with several hundred women. We met with the quilt team in the chapel for a few minutes right before the program began. The chaplain wanted to turn the program into an ecumenical service, but we did not want to do that. The volunteers had never been in a prison and were overwhelmed by the security, the rules, the searches, and the briefing that they had had, even before they could set foot inside the place. They did not care if there was a religious cast to the program or not. They had four panels and a very organized and dramatic way of showing them.

In the end we had a religious service because we had no choice. The choir began the program by singing "Amazing Grace." The choir was an all-black Baptist gospel choir. If the soloist was good and everyone clicked, then they could tear the roof off. But if the soloist was off, then the whole choir could sound terrible. That day, I have to admit, they rocked the gym. The soloist, a high soprano, a young woman named Janelle whose voice was a marvelous mix of clarity and depth, not to mention perfect pitch, led them beautifully. She led them and they followed, singing more sweetly than normal, their demeanor infused with hers.

The quilt group members were all dressed in white and as they unfurled each of the panels and placed them on the floor, they walked around in a circle, holding each end and moving in a very stylized way. As each panel of the quilt touched the ground, one of them read the name stitched on the panel. They did not have to explain anything. There was a hush in the gym after the panels were spread on the floor. We invited everyone to stand up and look at the panels. Everyone ended up forming a large circle and then a larger circle around the first panel. People were staring to see all the individual details. One panel was stitched with glitter glued to colored threads that spelled "Sarah Millner—our beloved sister," and there were different cutouts of felt and cloth illustrating bits and pieces of Sarah's loves and life.

The chaplain gave a brief speech about God's love and then we asked everyone to come up to the microphone and name someone they knew who had died of AIDS. There was total silence until finally Silvia stepped up to the microphone and said, "My friend Aaron, I miss him." Then a woman named Zulma stood up and said "Jimmy Rivera," and then I took the microphone and said, "Donna Nelson and Celestine Washington, and Jon." Then an influential and popular woman who had been incarcerated with many members of her own family got up and walked to the microphone and whispered, "John Henry, my baby brother." I thought that if this woman, whose name was Amma, could help break the silence and come out against HIV, then maybe we had a chance in combating the ignorance and stigma. Within the structure of prison life, prison families are central to how people live, how information is transmitted between the authorities and the prisoners, how privileges are doled out. Informally, Amma was as powerful as any prison official. Her willingness to stand up and acknowledge that HIV had affected her own family would have an enormous impact on our ability to get support from within the prison population.

After this stunning display and the first public breakthrough against discrimination on the compound, we decided to create our own panel. How to design the panel was the next question. We could make only one panel, but we needed to be able to memorialize hundreds of names on it. The core group of women who did AIDS education met with the women who liked to sew. Another group met with the education department to get permission to sew the quilt panel inside the building, and get some help in collecting bits and pieces of felt and threads and materials with which to make it. Finally, it was determined that we would make one panel equivalent in size to four and that the design would replicate the inner compound of the prison with the housing units facing in. Each window of the cell blocks would be an individual panel. Women could make individual eight-by-eleven-inch sections that would then be stitched onto the big panel. Seventy women worked on the quilt for more than seven months. Fifty-five women made small individual panels, and another fifteen met four times a week to create the quilt's overall design and creation.

We started in September 1995 and ended in April 1996. When the quilt was finished, we laid it on the chapel floor and people came to add a name, to write a paragraph about someone they lost, or to simply observe. Hundreds of women filed through. The normally raucous prison chatter was still. I stood in front of the quilt, overwhelmed that we had succeeded in making it. The fifty-five individual panels and the names that were added as the quilt was on public display equaled 195 names, and the number kept growing. The sheer number of the dead was overwhelming. This quilt meant so much to those who made it. For Bea, Jane, Maureen, Jennifer, Frin, and the others, it was the first time that they had publicly claimed their loved ones and shared their losses in a common community.

As we closed up the chapel and put the quilt away, I meditated about many things. My own grief was overwhelming. I personally had known more than twenty people memorialized in the panel. I thought about the political struggle that had taken place in the late 1980s, a struggle I had learned about from people I had known in ACT UP who had rejected the idea of the quilt as being too reformist and not challenging enough to the powers that were responsible for treating and stopping the epidemic. I thought that in the context of prison, the quilt was an effective symbol of protest.

I thought about the class and racial divisions that are so great that they prevent those who should be natural allies from unifying. I thought about those who need so much more than quilts. As we locked up the chapel, my last thought was the need to figure out how we could force the government to acknowledge and respond to the suffering of all these women.

The next day was the final day for public viewing. The following week, the Connecticut chapter of the Names Project would collect the quilt for transfer to the "big quilt," where it would be stitched on. As I and others from the committee were getting the space ready for more women to come to the program, the head of the special security team from the captain's office accompanied by his entourage strode into the chapel. They had a video and thirty-five-milimeter camera with them. They demanded that we leave the room and that the chaplain come to speak with them. The whole team spent more than an hour with the chaplain behind closed doors. When they finally opened the doors and walked out, no one was smiling. When the chaplain closed the front door and spoke with us, her Irish brogue got a bit thicker. "Well, girls," she said, "it seems that the warden and the captain have a problem with our quilt. They object to the tombstone on the corner, with the quote 'Mourn the dead, but fight like hell for the living,' and most strenuously, they object to the purple helicopter flying over the fence, pulling the banner. They are convinced that embedded in the design is a message about how to escape." After she spoke, she burst out laughing. We were talking about a three-inch piece of felt cut into the shape of a toylike helicopter. At that moment, I liked her better than I ever had. She was my boss and we had had several bad and challenging exchanges over how she implemented her chaplaincy and my view of the repressive role that religion played. But in this instance, I knew that she had persuaded them that it was a benign expression and so the quilt would not be seized as contraband.

Prison contained so many layers of loss. Frin and I had a joke, really a refrain, for when something truly terrible or wonderful would happen. We would ask, "How do I love thee?" This would begin a litany of descriptions for either love or horror and dismay. How did I find relief from the suffering all around me and then from my own past?

If you seek redemption, then you will have a hard time finding it. Redemption comes when you are not thinking about it at all. A woman prisoner that I knew from the compound—a poet who had shown me her work, who had discussed writing, and had read with me—was struggling with her incarceration and trying to make sense out of a senseless set of circumstances. She was a thoughtful young woman who strained at her imprisonment. Pamela Howard was twenty-four years old and had a ten-year prison sentence for selling cocaine to an undercover agent.

I knew her from her poetry and her quiet and thoughtful manner and in how she conducted herself in public, but I did not know the facts or the details of her life. We were not close like that. But one day I was outside the education building and I heard this unearthly howl coming from the short-term living unit. I saw several women run toward the sound. A few minutes later, I saw a group of women surrounding Pamela and walking with her toward the medical building. I did not move to see or find out what was happening. I thought that her friends had it covered, whatever the problem was, and that I would no doubt find out about it later in the day. Bad news travels faster than the speed of light at Danbury. A few hours later, I was at my job in the chapel when the chaplain came into the library where I was working. She asked me to accompany her to the medical building. "Why?" I asked her. This was highly unusual and I became fearful that they were going to tell me some terrible news. But as I sorted out my own responses, I realized that if something was wrong with my mother, the chaplain would have told me right then and there.

"There's a woman in one of the holding cells who wants to talk with you and I approved the request," Chaplain Sheridan said. She was the senior chaplain and she definitely had the authority to do that.

"Who is it?" I asked. But by then I remembered watching Pamela being escorted into the medical building. The chaplain did not answer.

We walked together across the compound, up the stairs, and into the building. I was taken into the area where there were several holding cells. To call this a hospital was a total misnomer. It was one floor in an old building that housed a few medical staff, a few examination rooms, a locked pharmacy, and then several steel doors that led to what in other circumstances would be called strip cells. Typically, people are placed in these cells when they are on suicide watch, or waiting to be transferred to disciplinary proceedings, or when the authorities want them kept very isolated but not in the general segregation area of the prison. That section is called the special housing unit or, in prison language, "the hole." The hole always connotes either punishment or protective custody. I knew that whatever had happened to Pamela was not the result of an infraction, but of bad news, either about her family or her case.

As we walked through the holding cells, I looked through the windows of each one and they were empty. The sole piece of furniture in each room was a small bolted metal bunk with a plain mattress resting on top. When we got to the cell that Pam was in, I looked through the window and saw that she had her clothes on, but that they had taken her shoes and her earrings. She was lying on top of the bunk, eyes closed, very still. She was so quiet that I thought that she must be sedated. I bent down to the food slot, which was open, and looked in. The chaplain bent down, as well. They were not going to open the door and let us in; we could only talk through the slot. "Ms. Howard, this is Chaplain Sheridan. I am so sorry about your daughter. As soon as I can get someone to accompany you, the officers will let you make a phone call. I have Susan here." No movement, not even a flutter.

"Hello, Pamela. They won't let me in. I'm sorry about that," I said. "I'll just sit here for a while until they take you to the phone and if you want to talk I'm here."

The chaplain nodded at me and then keyed the door and walked away.

"Pamela, what happened? I don't know why you're here," I said in a much lower voice.

She lifted her head up and looked at me through the slot. Then she sat up, swinging her long legs over the side of the bunk. She did not get up, but kept looking at me through the slot. She looked pretty bad. Her face was streaked, and her normally neat braids were all twisted up.

"Tynesha died this morning."

"Oh no. Oh God, I'm sorry. Did you talk to your family?" I asked.

"I talked to my mother, who told me, and then I lost it and they brought me up here."

"What happened?" I asked.

"I don't really know, my mom was crying so hard that I am not really sure."

Tynesha was Pamela's five-year-old daughter who had been living with her mother.

"She was jumping up and down on her bed; it was the top of a double bunk bed, and Ma was always fussing with her to stop. She got her robe caught on the hook, fell, and got hung. Mom came in and found her hung up and not breathing. The ambulance came and they couldn't revive her." She started sobbing.

All I wanted to do was sit next to her and hold her. I knew that asking permission to do this would be pointless. I just watched her through the slot and kept repeating how sorry I was. Then I asked her if there was anything I could do, like call anyone, or talk to someone in the prison, or write a request to attend the funeral. That idea affected her.

"You think I could go?"

"I don't know, where does your mom live? And what's your classification?" I asked her.

"D.C., we live in D.C. I am a low security, I have no other record."

"I don't know, but maybe. It's worth asking." I wanted to do something useful and something specific, I did not want to stay much longer staring and communicating through a slot. "Try and get out of here; this isn't right," I said. "Did you say you were going to kill yourself?"

"No, I just couldn't stop crying. I think it freaked everyone out," Pam said.

I stood up trying to take the cramps out of my knees from squatting.

"Susan."

"Yes, Pamela," I answered.

"You know I'm HIV positive."

I got so quiet and even sadder as soon as the words were out of her mouth. I had not known it. "No, I did not know that." I stopped myself from saying anything else.

"Tynesha was negative. I was so happy that she was HIV negative. I was so happy that she would have a whole life." I felt so terribly inadequate and everything that came into my head to say just didn't seem right. So I did not say anything. I just looked at her and tears came out of my eyes. I felt that I could not stand it. I do not know why, but there seems to be a much higher percentage of women in prison who have lost their children, either through violence and then death or through the foster care or child welfare system. So I was familiar with the kind of grief that mothers exhibit when something happens to their children. One of my best friends inside had lost her son and her broken heart never healed. I felt that awful sinking feeling for Pamela.

I sat down on the floor cross-legged and said, looking at her through the slot, "Pamela, come here please." She got up and came to the slot and squatted. I put my hand through the slot and she gave me hers. I pulled her hand through the opening and kissed her hand.

"Anything I can do, just ask," I said. I stood up and banged on the dividing door between the medical department and where we were. A CO came and keyed the door and let me out.

Several days later, I was in the visiting room waiting for a visit when a family of about fifteen people was let in and all of them quietly took seats in one corner of the room. It was an unusually large party, one not generally allowed in the prison. When Pamela came out of the strip room and into the visiting room, the way she immediately eyed her mother from the far end of the room was as if an invisible cord was connecting them. Her mother stood up instantly and they walked toward each other and fused together as they wrapped their arms around each other. Their embrace and the feelings that I felt watching them left me breathless. There was so much pain and grief and empathy and love exchanged between mother and daughter that it was staggering. The energy vibrated around them and throughout the room. *Her mother looks only ten years older than me*, I thought. Her hair was in beautiful braids down her back and her darkly colored skin was very clear of blemishes and signs of age. Cowrie shells were carefully woven inside her braids. She was wearing a purple knit pullover sweater and blue jeans. Holding her daughter with such intimacy, without a shred of privacy, seemed most generous, and if she was filled with guilt I could not see it. Watching the scene, I had never seen such compassion exchanged between two people. There appeared to be no anger or blame emanating from Pam. Maybe that would come later, but her eyes were clear. Their arms encircled each other as they stood, whole bodies touching for a minute and then another and then another.

The rest of the family was silent and stood in a circle around the two women. And then they separated. The mother whispered something to her daughter and the daughter nodded. Then the daughter turned and faintly smiled to the others. They each in turn hugged her and quietly sat down. It was one of the loveliest and ritualistic of exchanges of human emotion and particularly of grief I have ever seen. I thought, *How marvelous to be able to grasp the reality that life is temporary and that things happen without reason and we can either be destroyed by misfortune or come to understand that it is all part of the picture.* I felt honored that we had exchanged enough about poetry and prison life that Pam introduced me to her mother and that I could convey to this beautiful woman how terribly sorry I was for her suffering and her loss. I was happy to share, if only for a moment, in their community. How strange to have felt strengthened from that loss and not devastated. As my visitor arrived and the spell of Pam's family and their emotional journey was broken, I knew that I had just learned something very important about the lifelong relationship we have with suffering and grief and the ways to respond to it, move with it, be changed by it, and not be destroyed by it.

The HIV/AIDS epidemic forced me to live actively in the present. Becoming an HIV peer advocate pushed me beyond the limits I had established of my willingness to serve. Working against the HIV epidemic allowed me to find my own reservoir of compassion, a place that was free of all ideologies and structures. As a result, fighting the epidemic touched the deepest emotions in me. I found that touching emotion was a way to keep my heart from dying (even though people were dying all around) in an otherwise overwhelmingly sterile place.

Chapter 17

Parole

WHILE I WAS dealing with HIV and life in general population and reconnecting with old friends and making new ones, my codefendant, Timothy Blunk, had been at Lewisburg Penitentiary for three years. He was applying for parole after previously having served time at the federal penitentiaries in Marion, Illinois, and Leavenworth, Kansas. At Lewisburg, he was closer to his roots in Pennsylvania, as I was at Danbury, Connecticut. This made doing time for Tim a little easier. He was with other political prisoners at Lewisburg, and they had a small community around which visitors and prisoners alike revolved. There was Alberto Rodriguez, one of the Puerto Rican political prisoners, and Larry Giddings, an anarchist prisoner who had come out of a radical prisoners' support organization in the early 1970s. Larry and Alberto had been doing time for nineteen and thirteen years respectively.

Tim had built a network of support on the outside, and he did creative and social work as a painter, a musician, and a teacher's aide. He was planning on getting married to a woman named Mary who had become his greatest advocate and defender. He applied for parole in February 1996, after eleven and a half years in prison. At the end of his parole hearing, he was given a tentative release date of November 1996, twelve years to the month from the time of our arrest.

All of Tim's friends or associates were astonished that he was given a release date. Although he surely deserved it, given the disproportionate length of his sentence, his demonstration of remorse, and his clear conduct record, it was amazing that he was given a date because of his ill treatment during the past decade. Those of us who were classified as political prisoners had developed an entrenched view that none of us would ever get out of prison. It was not something we could talk about, but we all felt it in our own ways.

I never allowed myself to think, *When I get out of prison* . . . I did not live for the fantasy; instead, I spent enormous amounts of energy dealing with the present and creating life in the present. But upon hearing that Tim had gotten a date for release, I took a flight of fantasy for him, for me, and for all the people I knew and loved inside. My flight was a freedom ride. It would hit me in the dining room; it would attack me while in a particularly rotten moment at work; it made me shake with hope that I would get out and see my mother alive; and it fueled my heart when I looked at Frin and thought I might see her again after she got out of prison. It felt like a threatening indulgence to the very secure mental structures that I had put in place to survive. These lines of demarcation functioned to limit my emotions of joy and agony, happiness and sadness.

The idea of Tim getting out rocked my ossified world. I was thrilled for him and then for me because his release would have direct implications and help create grounds on which to argue for my release. The government had always viewed us differently because of the more extensive political history I had and the dismissed indictment from the Southern District of New York that had sent me underground in the first place. But, fundamentally, Tim and I had been convicted and sentenced for exactly the same thing.

Tim's date was ten months away. There was nothing to do but wait and see what happened. I did not want to go to the parole board until Tim was released. I did not want to upset any process that was in motion in relation to his parole process.

I became a woman in waiting. I was waiting for enormous life changes, none of which I had any direct control over. I was waiting for Tim and his release and I was waiting for Frin to finish her sentence and be extradited to England. Their impending freedom now served to reinforce my incarceration. Waiting for their transitions weighed on me relentlessly. I tried to practice how I thought I would feel when Frin left. I would pretend when we went our separate ways during the course of a day that this separation was final. Then when she would saunter back into the unit or cell, I would be so relieved to see her that I would start crying. She would look at me and say, "You've been practicing again," and shake her head and then take me in her arms if we were in our cell or just look at me if we were in public. "You silly girl," she would say. But then she would give me a stricken look and we would both know that we could not predict the half of it.

We had a lot of fun in those last months. We wrote a screenplay together called "More Than Suspect." It was taken from a short story that I had written several years earlier called "Lee's Time." It was based on events that took place in Marianna prison where an African American male guard was falsely accused of raping a white female prisoner and the subsequent investigation and trial that took place. Neither of us had ever written a screenplay before, but we read lots of them, along with several how-to books, like Syd Field's best-selling guide. We stole index cards from the education department and sat on our cell floor, writing and talking and arguing and writing some more. When we finished, we dreamed of getting the story produced so that it would help to free me, even though it had nothing to do with me or my real-life story. It became part of the mythology that we created to sustain us.

Then, in early September, Frin's extradition came through. The day it happened, she was at work in the education department and I was at work in the chapel. A friend of ours named Paula, who worked as the orderly in the captain's office, came into the chapel and told me, "They are taking Frin to New York this afternoon." My heart closed up as I overzealously thanked her for giving me the heads-up. I asked one of the other clerks to cover for me and returned to our cell.

Frin was standing in the middle of the cell doing nothing, just staring out the window. For the first time since I had known her, there were no quick quips coming out of her mouth and no smile on her face at all. "This is it," I said stupidly, over and over. "This is it."

Frin had a long, narrow cotton scarf in multiple shades of purple wrapped around her neck. She took it off and gave it to me. She then rummaged through her locker and pulled out our copy of the *I Ching*. She had embroidered a cover for it. I knew that she had been working on it, but did not know that she had finished it. Now she handed it to me. It had all our symbols on it—her Native American symbol, a brown bear, and mine, a raven. We had helped the Native American community at Danbury build a sweat lodge and as thanks, one of the religious leaders of the community had told us how to find our totem animals, the symbols that fed our spirits. Frin had also embroidered the beautiful old oak tree from the recreation yard. That tree was our best place, a place where we had sought and found refuge. On the side of the book were the trigrams that made up the hexagrams that had defined our use of the text. It was quite a beautiful work of art. I started crying, making gasping sounds.

"See the red string?" Frin asked.

I nodded. It was in the center of the book and served as a book marker.

"That's from the Dalai Lama. That's what I have been wearing around my neck. Now I give it to you."

This was very hard. We had talked so much about her leaving and my staying, how we would stay in communication, continue to collaborate on another screenplay, how it was not the end, and on and on. But somehow it felt like the end, as if we had deceived ourselves into thinking that the rest of my sentence would magically disappear, or that the prohibition against ex-felons re-entering the United States would not really be applied to Frin, or that being on different continents would not have an effect on our relationship. And yet, here at this moment, as she was about to walk out of the cell and through a series of successive doors and never come back, it felt as if we were dying.

I quickly gave her one of my favorite earrings, which I had been able to smuggle from one prison to the next for over a decade. It was a tiny ruby embedded in a gold leaf. Then we traded watches and she gave me her earring. We said that we would trade them back one day. And then she walked out. I sat in the cell frozen, unable to move, think, react, or comprehend. I wanted to follow her, but we were extremely private in our relationship and never made any kind of public scenes. We never had and we wouldn't now. Most people in the prison did not know that we were lovers and I did not want to be subjected to staff harassment or ridicule. So I simply sat for a long time in what had been *our* cell, where we had lived *our* lives. I heard the lunch bell ring, but I did not get up. Then Frin suddenly appeared.

"Your transfer was canceled!" I stood up expectantly.

"No, they told me to get lunch in the dining hall. They did not have any food back there, and the marshals aren't coming until later this afternoon."

We looked at each other and started laughing.

"That was only fifteen minutes. I don't think I can live through the rest of my life."

We hugged and kissed each other for the next hour, and it was that reprieve, that totally random extra hour, during which I located a small place within me to always keep for Frin, a place that I have to this day. Then the guard came for her and she was really gone.

I got an excuse from the chaplain to leave work and I sat in our cell for a day, smelling her, dreaming about her, and examining all of her little knickknacks and her prison junk that she had left me. That moment turned into weeks and then unrelentingly painful months. I could not figure out how to live without her. I did the minimum at work and fortunately, I was not reassigned a cellmate for a few months. What I had known in part while we were together, I realized in full after Frin was gone. I had never been so happy loving someone. And the incongruity of this happening under the worst of circumstances had only intensified my joy all the more. I became despondent. I carried my sadness indelibly, and the only thing that I actively wanted to do was sit under the oak tree.

Frin was held in detention in England for only a short while. Afterward, she moved to Dublin to live with her sister and help take care of her aging father. She began corresponding with me and we began to write our second screenplay. Frin went to the Dublin School of Film, where she worked on our script, "Sanctuary." The script was about the faith-based social movement in the U.S. that helped undocumented Central American refugees who were fleeing political persecution from right-wing dictatorships and civil wars. Our contact was the critical thing that kept me going. She urged me to go to school, write, keep living, and working to get out. I could not see any end in sight. There was no word about Tim. His November release date came and went, and I was sitting in legal limbo. Eventually, I began thinking about going to graduate school.

I enrolled in a long-distance learning program. The only graduate school I could find that would waive the residency requirement was Antioch University in Yellow Springs, Ohio. I was accepted into Antioch's McGregor Graduate School with the goal of completing a master's degree in writing. I first had to research the requirements of such a degree at various top U.S. schools, and then I had to find two professors in my field who would become associated with Antioch for the duration of my program. I was also assigned an adviser from Antioch and I had to coordinate the communication between this adviser and the professors. Then I had to create courses or find professors who were willing to let me take their class via correspondence, or a combination of writing, visiting, and phone exchanges. After I completed the course work, I would write a thesis. If Antioch and my academic committee approved the thesis, then I would be awarded a master's.

The prison's education department was as unhelpful and skeptical as they could possibly have been. To do anything related to working with a nonprison program I needed permission, and getting permission was difficult. Using the phone in the education building, using the library, asking the librarian for help and using inter-library loan, bringing volunteer professors into the visiting room, all of that the prison was reluctant to approve. The biggest hurdle was getting a typewriter I could use whenever I needed. There was a computer lab that taught short-termers word processing and finally the head of that program helped me work there part-time so that I could use the equipment for my courses. Since the Pell Grants that gave scholarships to prisoners had ended in 1994, no one had completed a college degree, let alone a graduate program.

Despite the repeated studies showing a lowering of recidivism with increased educational levels, higher education was considered a luxury and not a priority. The prison considered college courses elitist and since they were out of the ordinary, conducting them was considered a bad security risk. In prison, anything that is not part of the routine is deemed a threat to security, and security always comes first.

The only mandatory educational programs at Danbury were general equivalency diploma (GED) classes and English as a Second Language (ESL) classes for non-English speakers. Like the prison psychologist Dr. LeBarre, the prison teachers were first and foremost cops. The aides under them used their curricula and taught all their classes. Because the teacher/officers had many hundreds of people assigned to each of their specific sections, the prisoner aides were in effect the primary teachers. To be an aide, a prisoner had to have completed high school. There were several women who had been educated in other countries. They were allowed to teach women from their own countries or in their native language until the first Anti-Terrorism Act was signed into law in 1997. (One of the provisions of the new law was that all Immigration Naturalization Service detainees, whether they were newly in custody or had lived in the prison for years, were labeled high security risks and placed in "lockdown" until they had their deportation hearings.)

Finally, there was an adult continuing education program that was not for academic credit and taught solely by prisoners at night and on the weekends. Attendance was voluntary and the program was the most popular activity in the prison outside of church.

Six to eight courses were running at any given time and they included African American history, film studies, Spanish, AIDS education and prevention, and Latin American literature in Spanish and English. The women who developed and taught these courses were a diverse group. Their convictions ranged from drugs to spying, from fraud to bank robbery. Yet in the back room into which they were all crowded, they were united in their mission to keep developing their own minds and to share their knowledge with others. If they had not carved out that space and pushed the limits imposed by the prison authorities, I would not have been able to enroll in that experimental degree program at Antioch.

Professor F. Horwitz signed on as the Ph.D. head of my whole program. He had been a professor of English literature for thirty years and was recently retired and writing a book about Henry James. He was a generous, kind, and very sardonic man. Many years earlier, when he had lived in Kansas, he had done work in support of several activists from the Black Panther Party who had been attacked by the FBI Counter Intelligence Program (COINTELPRO) aimed at destroying the black freedom movement. Without his support, encouragement, challenges, and monthly trips to the prison visiting room, my graduate program would not have happened. Professor Horwitz had a wry sense of humor and always understood that unless one laughed at the total absurdity of arbitrary power, it was impossible to survive and create real work.

I began the program in January 1997. I read Homer, Euripides, Ovid, Cervantes, Dante, Shakespeare, Henry Miller, Virginia Woolf, Carl Jung, Sigmund Freud, Faulkner, and Ernest Hemingway. The reading was challenging, and my complacency about my own knowledge was shaken. I realized that for all of my intellectual arrogance, I knew very little. I adopted Alejandrina's saying, "I only know what I don't know." The reading did something else: it took me back again to my own life and history, forcing me to re-examine my own responsibilities in the political world that I had belonged to and to its methods.

In April, Tim was finally released on parole. I knew that he must have been ecstatic and amazed. I imagined myself at the gates of Lewisburg at his release and I played the scene over and over in my head. One moment I was inside watching, the next I was outside waiting, and then I was accompanying him as he went through those interminable bureaucratic procedures to gain his freedom. I imagined the administrators giving him the suit of clothes that had been left for him and a cashier's check for forty dollars, which he would repeatedly refuse to accept until, as their last act, they ordered him to put it in his pocket. I imagined that he had his prison ID card in his pocket and that they told him that it would help him get other IDs, as if he would be fool enough to show it at the Department of Motor Vehicles.

Tim was forty years old and beginning life anew. He had significant amounts of emotional baggage, more to negotiate than most forty-year-olds, but he was not without love and resources. I wondered, as I sat in Danbury, if he thought of his life as a waste and how he assessed the past. We had lost our youth, and in some ways had lived our lives through our friends on the outside acting as intermediaries. We had been punished and changed by that punishment. I hoped that he had been changed for the better. I hoped that I had, too.

So Tim was free. Alan Berkman was free, and Laura Whitehorn was expected to get out of the prison in Pleasanton soon. I felt that I had to fight to follow them. My spirit rose in reaction to Tim's release. The relentless grinding down by repression, routine, contempt, and neglect at Danbury got harder to take as the idea of freedom took up more and more mental energy. But when I thought about my friends' release, I could get past myself and my jealousies and desires. Even if only briefly, I could revel in their liberation and at times wake up and hear that particular timbre that flowed from the unique voice of Dr. Martin Luther King Jr. as he cried out, "Because I have been to the mountaintop . . . Free at last, free at last, thank God Almighty, we are free at last."

After thirteen years inside, I had to confront the process of fighting for release. I had done this self-examination before, but I had to reflect on my past this time by taking responsibility for it. Even before that, I had to convince myself that I was worthy of getting parole, that in fact I deserved parole. I would never again be involved with a small group and engage in violent action to fight policies of the government. But my analysis of the ills of society that had defined me were reinforced in prison on a minute-by-minute basis.

Tim's release should have set a precedent for me because he was my codefendant, had been convicted of the exact same charges, and had been given the same sentence. But I assumed that the parole board would deal with me differently as a Brink's defendant. (Even though the charges had been dropped, they were still mentioned in my prison records.) At least that seemed the most likely scenario. Whether the parole board would hold me accountable for charges that had been dropped eleven years earlier (whether or not this was legal under the administrative law governing them) or if they would simply consider my standing conviction of weapons possession could only be determined by appearing before the board.

Dennis Curtis, a Yale Law School professor and national expert on sentencing, parole, and prisoners' rights, and Mary O'Melveny prepared me for the hearing. We met repeatedly from July until the hearing in November 1997. I liked Dennis. He was a hand-some Irish American with a wrestler's build and a gentle smile. His easy and calm manner, his quiet assurance was always a pleasure to see in the visiting room. Dennis had done more legal work to help prisoners retain their rights and regain their dignity over the preceding twenty-five years than almost anyone else in America. I had wanted him to help me with my parole case from the first time I had heard about him. But when I had first wanted to talk with Dennis in the 1990s, he was living in Los Angeles and I was in prison in Florida. He could not make that trip. Then he moved to New Haven to teach at Yale, and I was in Danbury, less than an hour's drive away. Dennis knew how the parole system worked and Mary knew everything about my case and so together they navigated through the proceedings. I felt a gathering of forces in my defense, or rather, a defense of my life and my right to create a new life. It became my greatest hope and my greatest fear. The fact that my mother was also rallying around the idea of winning parole compelled me more.

The summer after Silvia's parole denial was filled with my own preparations, teaching grammar and English, writing, developing my graduate school program, and my rising hopes. So I was sur-prised when Silvia suggested that she and I jointly teach an adult education course about the Jewish Holocaust. The idea behind teaching this subject to a predominately African American group was that it might help black women develop a broader framework for looking at the world and their own history. I did not expect anyone in the course to know much about World War II and the Nazi concentration camps. Silvia and I decided that we would not get into the argument about which genocide was greater, the Atlan-tic slave trade or the Holocaust.

I realized as I read one book after another that the ancient Jews rejected the notion of the state in their religion and their life. Their rejection of this in part led to their outcast status. They were not a nation. They were a people who consciously identified with their religion over and above governments and states. They did not assimilate into other societies because of their religion. Consequently, despite their nonviolent stance, they were always the outsider, the stranger, the outcast, and subject to anti-Semitism. The whole process of how anti-Semitism took root and then evolved with the ideas of conversion, expulsion, and finally extermination all began to make more sense as the various countries in which Jews resided saw them as a threat to their state. I finally understood the true meaning of the ghetto. How basic this was, and yet until this reading I had not grasped it fully.

Silvia and I taught the class for eight weeks to twenty women. We accepted women only with a high school degree because the class required a lot of reading. We watched *Night and Fog*, a silent film about the concentration camps. No one in the class had ever watched a silent film. We got permission to show the film *Schindler's List* and that was an important addition to our curriculum. Later, the film was put on an official BOP list of banned films (supposedly because of the violence). We talked about the tenets of Judaism and the history of anti-Semitism.

Up until that class, I had taught only AIDS education and literacy. I had never written an academic curriculum or thought about teaching as a means of community building. The very provocativeness of the subject and the development of a dialogue between Silvia and me and our students was a lot of fun. We heard all the usual anti-Semitic stereotypes, as well as common criticisms of "Jewish landlords" and yet, eventually the women in the class were changed by their exposure to the facts and understanding of the history. I, too, was changed: I came to understand my dual identity as both "the other" and as a more privileged American Jew who identified with all "the others." More important, I realized that teaching was the way to give back, to be fully present in the world, and to communicate ideas in order to make change.

In November 1997, I appeared before the parole board. I had been in prison thirteen years and I had waited three years past my ten-year eligibility before applying for parole. My family, friends, lawyers, and I were trying with great effort to contain our hopes. Mary had been my lawyer and friend every step of the way for twelve years. Whenever I had won in fighting the courts and the BOP, Mary had been directly involved. Each time my case took a new and more daunting turn, she had said, "I am a civil litigator, a labor lawyer, not a criminal defense attorney or an expert on parole." But when I needed a criminal defense attorney in Washington, D.C., ten years earlier, Mary had become one. In fact, she had become the head of the entire legal defense team for six of us in the Resistance Conspiracy case. When I had needed a prisoners' rights lawyer to fight the hideous conditions at the High Security Unit in Lexington, Kentucky, Mary had become a prisoners' rights advocate and ended up—along with others from the National Prison Project of the ACLU, the People's Law Office in Chicago, and Elizabeth Fink in New York City—winning one of the more difficult prisoners' rights cases in U.S. history at the district court level.

However, when Mary firmly told me that she was not an expert on parole, I knew she meant it, and so I was glad when Dennis Curtis joined the defense team to guide the parole process. We all felt that having an expert might somehow miraculously transform the conditions around my situation and produce a positive result.

Mary did not want to bear the brunt of my disappointment or blame at the continuing defeats that we had experienced. I believed that she did not want her heart broken again by another legal set-back in my struggle for freedom.

I was at work in the chapel the day before my scheduled appearance. It was to be held in the building that housed the warden's office. I was nervous. My biggest concern was whether the administrators would ask me to implicate other people as a condition for my own parole.

Sitting at my desk lost in thought, I didn't hear the lieutenant come in.

"Rosenberg," he hemmed.

I jerked up and just stared at him.

"You should call your lawyer."

I didn't ask why or which one. "Okay, thanks," I answered.

I went to Chaplain Sheridan and got permission to go back to my unit to make a call. I shut the phone room door and called Dennis at his office at Yale. There was no answer, just a machine. I called his home number. After the operator went through the routine of saying, "This is a collect call from a federal prison and you do not have to accept the charges," I heard a croaking sound say, "I'll accept the call." I knew immediately that Dennis was sick.

"I'll be there," he said, coughing.

"I can go alone," I said.

"No, you shouldn't go alone, not this time," he whispered. "I'm staying home today to get better."

"Okay," I said. We hung up. I went back to work to wait out the day.

I awoke to a cold fall day. I put on my prison-issue army jacket. It seemed unfair to me that the one time I needed to wear my own clothes I could not. Not that I had many of my own clothes left, but even a jacket would have been better than the prison garb. I spent a long time straightening out my shirt and pants and combing my hair, and so I missed breakfast altogether. Before I could get to the phone to call Dennis, I was sent to the visiting room. I was patted and stripped and searched, my legal folder rifled through, and then I was escorted into the visiting room. It, too, was chilly. I scanned the place and it was empty except for the CO at the front desk where people were let in. Then I walked toward the legal visiting rooms.

The only person there was Mary, sitting in the corner where she always sat during our visits. She was dressed up in a beautiful suit of fall colors. With her briefcase and bag she looked courtroom ready, as I wished I did. We hugged each other under the watchful camera's eye. She smiled an ironic smile. "Dennis is too sick to be here today." Despite all protestations to the contrary, I was glad. I had wanted Mary to be there. Mary always "had my back," so to speak.

Mary had to walk inside the prison. I wanted to give her a tour, and show her my cell, but of course that was not allowed. I left her and went back to the strip search room, where I was again stripped and searched and then allowed back into the inner compound. I met Mary in the waiting room on the ground floor of the building. There were no other prisoners milling about because this whole building was off limits. While it was still within the double-tiered, chain-link, barbed-wire fence, most of the building was set off and faced the staff parking lot. And most it faced outward and not inward.

We climbed the stairs to the second floor, where a conference room doubled as a parole hearing room. It felt exotic and strange to be sitting with Mary in an open room with no police anywhere in sight. We were almost touching and that seemed odd, as well. Our prior meetings had been spent sitting face-to-face with a table between us. As we sat side by side, I could feel her nervous energy. We waited very quietly for an official to come talk to us. After what seemed like a very long time, the door opened and a tall, African American man gestured us in. He was Mr. Bell, one of the traveling parole examiners and the same one who had interviewed Silvia.

Mr. Bell sat down and ruffled through some papers and then reached across the desk between us to turn on a small tape recorder. He asked me for my statement. I had a prepared one that I half read and half said. I outlined my criminal acts and what I felt about them then and now. I talked about the political ethos of the 1960s and how it had led me and my associates into thinking our activities were acceptable. I detailed how sorry I felt now, how I accepted responsibility for my past actions, and how I would never commit any crimes again. I tried to put my life within the context of the historical period when many Americans thought they could change the world and end war and racism and poverty. I tried to distinguish between my core values and my embrace of the use of political violence. I stated that I now rejected the use of violence. I meant all that I said.

The examiner then asked me whether I was responsible for several deaths that had occurred during the Brink's robbery in 1981. I told him no. He asked whether I knew where Joanne Chesimard was, and if I could tell him how she had escaped from her New Jersey prison. Again, I told him no. He also asked me if I knew Dr. Mutulu Shakur. "Yes," I said. Mary answered him and said that there was no preponderance of evidence to suggest my actual involvement in the specific crimes that he was talking about. She pointed out that the government had dismissed the Brink's conspiracy charges against me eleven years earlier. With each passing second the feelings of fear, anger, and sorrow all rose inside me until I felt like I would burst out of my skin. Then Mr. Bell abruptly ended the hearing by telling us to step outside.

A CO ushered us into a small office nearby and told us to sit down. I stared out the window at the leaves hanging in front of the window. Mary was staring, too. We were silent as we replayed in our minds the entire hearing. After ten minutes and then twenty and then thirty, we began to pace the room and Mary began to get angry. She stepped out of the room to see what was happening. The door to the hearing room was ajar and Mary was surprised to see the examiner engrossed in conversation on the phone.

Forty-five minutes later, we were ushered back into the hearing room. I did not want to live through the next few moments; I wanted to have an out-of-body experience. Mary and I repeated the same ritual as we had earlier. We sat, Bell sat, and then he reached to turn on the tape recorder.

He began by telling me that he was going to have to hold me accountable for the three deaths in the Brink's robbery and murder case. He said he didn't doubt that I was a very different person now, but he reiterated that he was going to *have* to hold me accountable for the three deaths.

Mary turned absolutely white and I heard the air go out of her lungs. I heard the rustling of her clothes and I felt her gathering her energy to rebut. I knew I was not supposed to speak, although I wanted to start screaming at him.

Mary asked what was the evidence to show this. Bell responded that there was enough evidence from the Southern District to indict me and that all the federal parole commission needed to deny parole was an indictment. He pointed out that they have broad latitude in determining no release on parole. Mary shot back that there wasn't enough evidence for a trial and that the charges had been dismissed. She asked how could they hold someone without trial. Her voice was steely and she was annunciating into the tape recorder.

Bell replied that all they needed to determine was whether there was a preponderance of evidence and since there was an indictment, he said there was more than a preponderance of evidence. He went on to say that the Brink's robbery was an attack on the community and if they released me on parole, it would reduce the seriousness of the crime, and they could not do that.

Mary interrupted him and pointed out that Tim Blunk, my codefendant, was out on parole and that he had the exact same conviction. Bell replied that Tim wasn't indicted in the Southern District. He obviously knew all the details of my case. He acknowledged that this wasn't right or fair and he advised us to appeal this decision. He finished by looking directly at me for the first time since this interchange had started. He told me he was sorry but he was recommending a fifteen-year set-off point. Then he ended the hearing, stood up and turned off the tape recorder.

We moved into the hall and just stood there. Mary was furious and anguished at the same time. Even though we both had expected this outcome, it was another thing to actually experience it. I thought, *That man just took fifteen years of my life using less energy than it took to break a pencil.* I felt as if I had just been thrown against a brick wall and every bone was shattered.

Mary said, "We'll appeal; he said it wasn't fair. He was on the phone for a long time. We'll appeal." Mary went home and I had to return to my unit and my job and my prison life. I had to act as though another fifteen years was water off my back. I could not crumple under the weight of another fifteen years, but I was devastated.

I was an old hand at maintaining my composure and not

showing anything to the corrections officers who surrounded me. The sadistic ones took glee in the setbacks that many of us faced. I was always saddened by the gratuitous mental brutality that guards unleashed at us. They knew the outcome of the hearing before I had said good-bye to Mary. But I was determined to remain calm and cool regardless of what I felt inside. I also believed that it was important to be strong for the people on the outside. I didn't want them to be devastated. My greatest fear was that my mother would die before I got out of prison. Now that I had gotten the worst decision that I possibly could have gotten, I was in a struggle with myself not to become immobilized by fear.

I knew that I would have to do two totally opposite things at the same time in order to live: I would have to detach from my fears and desires and many of my own human needs. At the same time, I would have to keep struggling to be free. I would have to come to terms with the fact that no matter how sorry I was about past events it would never matter to the parole board. It was not about remorse. Telling the commission that I knew that I had been wrong would have no impact whatsoever. The option of saying that I had lost my mind for a decade between the ages of nineteen and twenty-nine was not something I believed, and it would not have made any difference if I did.

I knew I had to find a way to persevere. The only good I could find in my recent parole denial was that preparing to go before the board had forced me to journey inward to my core as a human being more deeply than I ever had before. I had found my core self, I had looked at it and held it up to the light in a most serious way. While my soul was tarnished and frayed, I felt it to be essentially good. I had been tested. My principles had not cracked. To this extent, I felt liberated, which given everything that had happened was totally unexpected.

I went back to work. One day several weeks later it was late morning, hot for the season, and the nine o'clock work break was over. The last stragglers were stamping out their cigarettes and returning to their jobs. Lieutenants were all milling about in front of their stations, sporadically yelling at people to clear the compound. Classes had started again and I was working in the adult education program one day a week. All the prisoners who worked there were sitting at their workstations killing time until classes began later in the day. I was reading a magazine when the whistle blew. We all looked at one another.

The whistle meant lockdown, no movement, repeated counts, and a host of other possibilities. A whistle could mean an escape, a shakedown, or a national emergency. I always hoped when the whistle blew that it was an escape. We all rushed to the windows to look out on the compound. We saw several women running to get back inside and out of the open. Once they disappeared, the whole compound was empty and strangely quiet. Out of nowhere, we heard boots slapping on concrete. A team of about fifteen men came out of the control gate at the front entrance of the prison, marching and chanting in step. In helmets and black jumpsuits, carrying plastic shields and clubs, they broke rank and swarmed toward one of the long-term housing units. This was no usual shakedown where a small number of officers would go room to room. This was a bust of some kind because of the sheer number and power that was displayed. As the officers entered the building, the captain, the warden, the two associate wardens, and a slew of other officials converged at the front of the unit. All the women who were in the unit were brought out one by one. I hoped that they all had permission to be there. They were in varying states of undress. They had been sleeping, or taking a shower, or watching TV, or working. They were in their bathrobes or pajamas or sweatsuits.

Each woman was put up against the wall, spread-eagled, and pat-searched. We could see all the interchanges between the cops and the women. Standing in her nightgown and curlers, Phyllis didn't want to be searched by a man and refused to spread. As my friend Lisa and I watched a lieutenant push Phyllis against the wall, Lisa said, "That bastard! You know Phyllis is telling him, 'I could be your mama. Would you do this to her?'" He was rougher than he needed to be. Phyllis was fifty-eight years old and had severe lung problems. As the other women were searched, she was led off to the side of the building to stand at attention.

I asked Lisa, "What is this? Why the SWAT team? You live in that unit—what's going on?"

She looked at me with a raised eyebrow as though to say, "You can't be that stupid." But she did not answer me.

Our boss, Mr. K., one of the few educational officers who had a sense of humor, came into the room and yelled, "Get away from the window, and move to the hall—we're having a count!"

Everybody started in all at once: "What is this shit?" "Why is the warden there?" "We just had a shakedown." And on and on and on.

By the time the education crew was counted and we were allowed back into our area, all the women in the besieged unit had been put up against the wall. The SWAT team was running in and out of the building. I kept trying to find someone who could tell me what they were searching for. Was it drugs, knives, perfume, food? Finally, Lisa turned to me and said, "Susan, you are so out of it." Then one of the lieutenants strutted out of the building and whispered to all "the suits" who were standing around. The warden shook her head, clearly angry, as were several other staff members. Then another lieutenant emerged from the building gingerly holding a large plastic bag with his fingertips. Everyone in our room moaned. I could not see what was in the bag. The officer walked right over to the warden, opened the bag, and with his plastic-gloved hand took out a cylindrical object and started waving it around.

Lisa started laughing and finally blurted out, "They got it. It's the dildo factory. They busted it."

"The dildo factory?" I couldn't believe it. "They brought in the SWAT team for that?"

"Hey, I didn't know they were selling them," someone else said. "If I had, I'd have bought one."

Then several other helmeted COs came out all holding plastic bags. The women at the side of the building were all laughing. Everyone fell out, except the warden. They shook down that unit from one end to the other. We were all locked down for four hours while they did it. Nobody worked, nobody moved. Even the kitchen ceased to function. We knew that we would be punished for this.

"What are they made of?" Elsa asked.

"Plastic," someone answered. "Wow, check it out, they're different colors."

"What were they going for?"

"Thirty bucks a piece."

It seemed that almost everyone knew something about this business. I dragged Lisa off to a corner of the room. "Okay, tell me," I said, laughing.

"It was a UNICOR thing, a sophisticated operation to be sure," she said with a grin, referring to the federal government work program in which many Danbury inmates were employed. "Between the plastic cables for the wire mounts—you know, the ones the Army contracts—and the molding shop, someone collected all the scrap plastic, snuck it out of that shop, and got it into the molding shop, where it was poured into those cylinders. Then they moved it to the paint shop, where someone else painted it according to the order. I can only assume they got them out of the factory and through the security points one at a time, presumably hidden inside someone."

It turned out that a prisoner in the gym had been caught with one of the dildos while showing it to another prisoner in the bathroom. Both prisoners had been taken immediately to segregation, where one of the SIS lieutenants had threatened them with a new charge of stealing government property. One of the women cried, "It isn't mine! I just borrowed it." The other whispered, "It's from the factory." These two women were left in the hole while a full-scale investigation began. The work supervisors at UNICOR were taken to task for a failure to police the prisoners and threatened with "days on the street" disciplinary charges. This meant days without pay and a warning, where three warnings resulted in termination of employment. Allowing the smuggling of plastic out of the prison factory was a serious charge, especially plastic that belonged to the program manufacturing U.S. Army radio mounts and air force cables. One factory supervisor turned in a list of prison workers he assumed to be "butches" with a use for dildos. They investigated anyone who had received over thirty dollars on their books from an outside source—the form of payment for services or goods inside.

And so a virulent and vicious round of attacks against lesbians began. In the end, the charges included possessing contraband, stealing government property, lying to an officer, possessing government property, and of course engaging in sexual misconduct. Despite the fact that no one was ever caught making the dildos or using them, thousands of hours of staff time were expended on the incident, hundreds of files created, and numerous women placed in segregation. The internal name of the security investigation was BTB—some said it stood for "bust the bitches" and others said it meant "bust the butches." Like the original incident, it was so emblematic of the institutional cruelty and contempt that the BOP has for women. This campaign was ugly and went on for months and months. It made doing time even harder.

Chapter 18

Political Prisoners

THE YEAR HAD been filled with so many profound emotions, problems, and changes. I had carried my shattered heart with me every day, and at times it made the pain of living beyond relief. I had allowed my broken heart to define my consciousness, reducing myself to only wounding sadness. I had been unable or unwilling to give up my grief. It had become my protection from my loneliness. But because I had had a relationship in which I had loved and been loved, I now had the courage to examine my past. As long as I did not bring bitterness or blame into this process, then it would be strengthening. Loving Frin had helped me find the humor and the light in myself, and that humor replaced the old ground that was crumbling and giving way to a new ground to stand on.

Yet my desires had overwhelmed me, and that fed my obsession with grief. The two poles of my life I defined as "self" and "service to others" had swung too far toward the self. I resolved to balance the two poles, to make amends not only in the abstract, but also in the present.

I decided that I would write poetry and that I would serve people. I would engage in the business of living in the prison community. But first, I would write poetry. The first poem that I labored over and finally liked was this one:

Distant Milford saw breathless New England fall
A valley green turned to a dazzling array of variation.
Red leaf, gold, orange, and maroon
became a yellow wood.
Whipped by winds made deathly stark.
It was only the natural order of things.

Then winter arrived expectant with dread; lightning did not strike
*   the tree.*
The ancient oak, upper branches bent by time, lost nothing of its
*   grandeur.*

Surely the season would stand still, and dew turned to crystalline
*   droplets*
crunched under thick-soled boots. But the earth failed to shatter;
*   everything kept on,*
nothing dramatic from one day to the next.

The only thing cleaved was my soul.
This altered state has clothed me with
your absence.
My best, most intimate friend through which
I see the seasons.

Your absence is my coat of leaves that I dream of
falling into and dying while wrapped in,

surrounded by your scent, your laughter, your very self.
A natural progression of the natural order.

I began to observe things again. If I was going to fully live in the prison community and live successfully, then I needed to be a participant again. What I saw was an ever-worsening set of conditions. Prison life was becoming terribly bleak, with more and more regulations, an increased institutionalization of control, and less and less solidarity. The idea of solidarity among the prisoners seemed almost nonexistent. There were moments and smatterings of hope and resistance—for example, the constant pat-searching by male guards had been temporarily halted because a number of women had filed grievances against the administration—but overall, life was a repetitive round of work, control, television, people wasting time by screwing around, and then finally "scamming." Unfortunately, people reverted to behavior that they knew from the street because there were no programs—no schools, no sports, no interventions to provide alternatives. There was only punishment for infractions.

It was difficult to figure out how to respond to this. I accelerated my AIDS work. I continued working in the chapel, and I talked with as many women as I could, but internally I retreated to my private studies. I began to read mythology. The "myth of the fallen woman" was an idea that gave me a new view of my surroundings. According to this myth, the source of all human misery lay in the missteps of women who then enticed men to transgress—Eve and Pandora are two well-known examples. I wondered if their stories were behind the prison system's effort to pathologize women who rebelled.

I also traced the history of the witch hunt as a means to conceptualize the life I was living. In fact, during this time, the BOP came out with a new policy that amounted to a witch hunt against lesbians. We woke up one day to find the hunt had begun without warning. Anyone suspected of being in a lesbian relationship with another prisoner was sent to segregation and placed under investigation for thirty days. If you were accused, it was not your "right" to know why you were under investigation or who had made the accusation. No physical contact had to be witnessed—the accusation alone was enough to trigger an immediate lockup. The consequences were real. An investigation of thirty days usually meant losing your job, your phone privileges, and any private property you had. It even could mean a parole denial.

The BOP administration actually held meetings and informed us that lesbianism would no longer be tolerated. They had a list of names and would "vigorously pursue" the matter to the end. Scores of women were put in the hole. Others were called in for interrogation. The administration subjected everyone who was known to have ever loved a woman or who had created a prison family. The little shreds of hope that we had found in reaching out to one another were under attack. The entire institution was filled with paranoia and fear.

I could only assume that behind this witch hunt was the real issue of sexual abuse on the part of prison guards. Pat-searching and voyeurism (manifested in constant intrusions into our lives) were two of the symptoms of systemic abuse of power. More telling was that over the past two years, more than twenty-five male officers had been removed from Danbury for having sex with women prisoners. Hunting for sex between women was a way of deflecting the misogyny of the system.

One hot night while I was walking around the prison compound, I saw four young white women, all of them with varying shades of blond hair. They looked to be about eighteen years old and stood out prominently in the larger sea of black and Latina women. They seemed nervous, again in marked contrast to the women around them, who were eating, listening and jamming to their Walkmans, or just mingling in the oppressive summer night. After that night, I noticed a few other newcomers. As I scanned all the new faces, I saw that there were equal numbers of black and Latina women, all twenty or under. It was just insane—these young women doing hard time in federal prison instead of going to school, working, and having a good time.

Each of the young white women had a hefty sentence. None was getting out with less than a twenty-six-month stay. They had all been minor characters in a plot to rob a bank devised and carried out by two young men. It was a bungled and stupid attempt, and potentially dangerous, but it resulted in no injuries. The young men had been caught and in exchange for six-month sentences, they identified the girls. The girls, who had no one to turn in, got the maximum allowable sentences; one of them had been sentenced to six years. The women in this case fell hard.

I began to think about what I could do to help these women. How could I share my experience with them? Teaching "Prison 101" became my mission. I developed the following speech: "Don't trust just anyone. Don't show your papers to anyone who promises to help you. Don't get caught up in the bullshit. Don't get caught up in slave labor 'working for the man.' Don't get cut by another prisoner. Don't cut yourself. Don't get sick. Don't under any circumstances snitch. When asked a question, only answer it; don't volunteer information. Don't stereotype. Don't join a gang." I followed the don'ts with some do's: "Fight your sentence. Use the time: sleep, exercise, read, think, write, create, get fit, go to school. Keep connected with the outside, Keep your head down, but keep your heart open. But, above all, fight your sentence."

I thought about these girls' youth. How do you keep perspective if you haven't had a broader framework than prison life to draw from? Unfortunately, my Prison 101 speech was merely a finger in the dike, and I watched these young women lapse into patterns of juvenile behavior again and again. As people settle into the role of prisoner, many go crazy, either loudly or quietly. They take heavy psychiatric medication. Others sleep around constantly, diving into an ever-changing stream of sexual partners.

I became friends with one of these young women, Courtney, who was twenty when she came to Danbury. One day, after we had spent some time talking, I was in the visiting room when Courtney's mother and grandmother arrived. All three were frightened at the unknowns and cowed by the security. I sat next to them and talked with them as best as I could, given that it was against the rules to "cross-visit." I told them not to worry, that Courtney would be okay, and that she would not fall victim to violence. I promised I would watch out for her. Her mother started to cry while thanking me. It embarrassed me to no end, but I kept my promise. Courtney was my first "prison kid."

The first time I walked into Dr. Gibson's office, he was playing a Joan Baez tape. I was dumbstruck, as I had been when I first encountered Dr. LeBarre on my first day at Danbury; "Joan Baez fan" was not a label that I would have pasted onto a prison psychologist. Dr. Gibson was the AIDS awareness group's staff sponsor, and he needed to approve everything we did.

He was my age, maybe a bit younger. He was over six feet two and a bit on the heavy side, not fat but beefy. Blond and clean shaven, he wore wire-rimmed spectacles that were small and round. Sometimes I thought he looked like a grown-up Dennis the Menace, cowlick and all; other times he was extremely serious and kind.

He was a devout Mormon and not afraid of ideas, and he had a wife and three children. Somehow, being the chief psychologist in the federal prison system did not seem to mesh with the rest of his life.

I do not know why, but Dr. Gibson never believed the lies about me that the administration had spread. Perhaps because he had been a prison psychologist for over ten years before meeting me, he had learned that even if the criminal justice personnel had written conclusions in stone, it was still better to make your own assessment. Maybe he realized that the information in a prisoner's "jacket" reflected the most extreme and difficult moment in his or her life and was not the best grounds on which to make a summary judgment. Or maybe he was just jaded. He had been the resident psychologist when G. Gordon Liddy had been at Danbury, and he had seen many other high-profile male prisoners. In any case, it was unique in my prison experience not to be pre-judged.

Over four years, Dr. Gibson and I came as close as a prisoner and a prison psychologist can to being friends. He never once asked me about anyone or any situation on the inside, and I never compromised him by asking him for anything he did not think was right, meaning things that would threaten his position. We did talk about how screwed up the prison system was and how he could not do his job anymore (at least as he perceived it) as the emphasis on work and punishment took hold over the more benign form of control known as rehabilitation. Dr. Gibson had worked with a lot of Vietnam veterans at Danbury in the early 1990s when it had been a men's institution, and he had written about the relationship between post-traumatic stress disorder and incarceration rates.

Dr. Gibson and I talked about the course of the AIDS epidemic both inside and outside, and about BOP policy with regard to the disease. We also talked about folk music and even about politics and religion. I once said to him that it was impossible to get psychological help in a coercive institutional environment because the role of the institution was solely to maintain social control. This was our central argument, the one that we always came back to. I discussed with him the French philosopher Michel Foucault's ideas about prisons and hospitals, and he read Foucault's *Discipline and Punish* at my urging. Essentially, Foucault argues that disciplinary punishment gives "professionals" (wardens, psychologists, program facilitators, parole officers, etc.) power over the prisoner, because the prisoner's sentence length and release on parole depends on the professionals' opinions. Foucault further suggests that a "carceral continuum" runs through modern society, from the maximum-security prison, through secure accommodation, probation, social workers, police, and teachers, to our everyday working and domestic lives. All are connected by the (witting or unwitting) supervision (surveillance, application of norms of acceptable behavior) of some humans by others. Our conversations were probably more important to me than to him, but they did affect him, as well. As the head of his department he was always subject to the overriding concerns of security, but he did support programs that were beneficial to women. He agreed that it was wrong for male COs to pat-search female prisoners and he said so openly.

With each administration, the psychological services got buffeted about, depending on the warden's view of psychology. Like Ms. Nolan from the Marianna High Security Unit, a tiny minority of people in the prison system had gone into it thinking that they could make a difference or seeing it as a form of service. They all said, "If we weren't here, life would be worse." It was undoubtedly true, but I always felt that no matter how nice or kind they were, they were still part of a process that trafficked in human freedom and that would eventually destroy their decency and humanity.

Although befriending Dr. Gibson taught me how to work within that horrific system and to push the boundaries of what was allowed by the administration, the power dynamics that existed between the administration and me made me a prisoner first and foremost. I never believed in the system or thought that it could be changed for the good. I was never a prison reformer, although I fought constantly to extend medical, educational, and legal rights to prisoners. I didn't have an ideology that surrounded the service I did. I just wanted to alleviate people's suffering, to empower people to think critically, and to help other prisoners understand the system they were living in and use whatever options were available to them.

In 1998, the parole commission granted me a reconsideration hearing. I had three options in how to approach the hearing: I could bring a lawyer, go alone, or ask a staff person to be my representative. I asked Dr. Gibson to go with me, and he said he would. In fact, he held a meeting with Chaplain Sheridan and others in the education department to discuss how they could support my parole application. I brought letters from BOP staff, as well as from the outside. I also brought letters from the various teachers who were working with me through the Antioch program and other longtime supporters. In the end, the original decision was upheld. I felt I was back at square one. I was being held in prison, whereas Tim, my codefendant, was out on parole. I was still being held because of the Brink's case, which I was never arrested or brought to trial for. Whenever people heard me voice that idea, they were shocked. To hold someone indefinitely without trial was a downright un-American thing to do, wasn't it?

My friends Rabbi Matalon, William Wardlaw, Barbara Zeller, and Shirley Cloyes worked along with my family and my lawyer, Mary, to begin to create conditions and develop resources to build broader support for my release.

An advisory board was organized whose purpose was to build a high-profile group with strong professional and cultural credentials, including people with academic, legal, and artistic backgrounds, who could be called upon if and when there was a need to organize publicly as the "Campaign to Release Susan Rosenberg." Shirley's idea behind this was to develop a public relations and congressional campaign for a parole appeal, or if that failed, then whatever legal remedies there might be.

On a deeper level, I was relieved about the development of this strategy because over the past decade I had witnessed the work that the progressive and radical left movements had done in support of political prisoners. I had felt that while the work was motivated out of the best solidarity and concern, its effectiveness varied greatly. I had come to believe that some of the same reasons that we had landed in jail—principally, our marginalization from American society and our misreading of people's consciousness with regard to opposition to U.S. policies—were reflected and repeated in the work in support of political prisoners. This was further complicated by the different types of political prisoners coming from different movements and holding different strategies and positions. I felt that there was a real failure to communicate between those of us on the left and the rest of the society. I felt that developing strategies to win by finding nonpublicly negotiated methods was at times in direct conflict with the need to use us as public representatives of social movements.

There were several hundred political prisoners still inside U.S. prisons—people who had been involved in various political movements in the 1960s, '70s, and '80s, ranging from protesters of the Vietnam War to the U.S. occupation of Vieques, Puerto Rico, to advocates for civil rights and black nationalism. The list included Leonard Peltier, a member of the American Indian Movement

(AIM); Mumia Abu-Jamal, a former Black Panther Party activist and journalist now on death row; Geronimo Pratt, a former leader of the Black Panther Party (BPP); the Puerto Rican Prisoners of War and Political Prisoners; the MOVE Nine prisoners; black religious and environmentalist organizers; Dr. Mutulu Shakur, a member of the Republic of New Afrika and the Black Panthers; Sekou Odinga, member of the Revolutionary Action Movement (RAM) and member of the Black Liberation Army (BLA); Tom Manning, a leading member of the United Freedom Front (UFF); Bill Dunne, an anti-imperialist; David Gilbert, a member of Students for a Democratic Society (SDS) and then of the Weather Underground (WUO); and Marilyn Buck, who was a leader of the anti-imperialist revolutionary movement. Every single one of them had been subject to the FBI's Counter Intelligence Program (COINTELPRO) during their time in the movement and through the course of their trials and imprisonment.

Over the years, there had been unitary efforts to raise the consciousness of the general public regarding the reality of political prisoners in the United States. The Puerto Rican movement had repeatedly tried to publicize the existence of their prisoners in every avenue they could, including in the Decolonization Committee of the United Nations. Remaining revolutionary groups—from the black independence movement, the American Indian Movement, the Puerto Rican independence movement, the new left and the women's and lesbian movements—had held public forums. There were defense committees or loose structures around all of us with varying degrees of organization and capabilities. Different lawyers, law collectives, and law practices were dedicated to keeping alive the fight to free political activists from U.S. prisons.

Still, the existence of U.S. political prisoners seemed to be a well-kept secret. While there were discussions in the rest of the world about the release of political prisoners, recognition of real civil and political conflict that caused casualties, and the need for reconciliation on all sides, there was absolutely none of that in the United States. After the Second World War and the start of the cold war, there arose an organized and concerted effort by the people of the colonized world to end their colonial exploitation. Out of that impulse had come the political struggles for national liberation and independence in Africa, Asia, and Latin America. Throughout the 1950s, '60s, and early '70s, independence movements had raged all over the world. In South Africa, the anti-apartheid movement was organizing. All over Southeast Asia there were national struggles for self-determination. There were revolutionary movements in every country in Latin America that challenged the role of U.S. profit making and dominance, as well as advocated for the poorest of the poor. A worldwide radical movement spurred equivalent developments in the United States and throughout Europe. The war in Vietnam, the role of racism, the lack of economic equality, and the role of women, all confronted people here in the U.S. Out of this came revolutionaries who took up alternative means to challenge power relations. In Italy, Ireland, Germany, Spain and France, groups of people fought their governments for social change and many of those participants went to prison. Ten, fifteen, and twenty years later, European societies decided to engage in public discussions about what the past had meant, why civil conflict had occurred, who the victims of it were, and whether these conflicts could ultimately be resolved. Over time, this national dialogue led to the call for amnesty for people who had been incarcerated during that period, and if not outright amnesty, then at least recognition that they had been punished enough, and should be released. Mass releases of political prisoners in Spain, in Ireland, in Italy, and in many countries in the developing world occurred. No equivalent dialogue or amnesty took place in the United States.

Even Amnesty International, the world's oldest and most respected human rights organization, was unwilling to recognize U.S. prisoners as political unless they were deemed prisoners of conscience, people imprisoned for expressing their political or religious beliefs in a peaceful manner, or were wrongly convicted, or were on death row. Amnesty *did* recognize Leonard Peltier, Mumia Abu-Jamal, and Geronimo Pratt as prisoners of conscience, and they were willing to examine the horrendous conditions inside maximum-security prisons in the United States. But other prisoners and institutions fell outside of their boundaries. Amnesty placed the majority of political prisoners into the category of "politically motivated/criminally convicted," which was designated for those who had been involved in armed struggle or illegal activities. This included Nelson Mandela and Oliver Tambo, the most famous South African prisoners from the African National Congress, and Joe Doherty and Bobby Sands from the Irish Republican Army.

By the end of the 1990s, there was no unified movement that could articulate one strategy to get people out of prison to win a mass clemency or to figure out a way to move prisoners from the margins of the political landscape and into some vibrant organization working for social change. Without such a movement, it was up to individuals to win parole, serve their sentences, or apply for clemency entirely on their own.

The idea of parole—the idea that if you do enough time and you have good behavior and you are remorseful, you will be released—is a lie. It is an absolute lie. For some reason, there is a set of myths that begins on the macro level with what a great democracy we have, and works its way down to the micro level with our belief in individual rehabilitation. The macro myth and the micro myth are so ingrained that even when one knows—and I know it like I know the blood coursing through my veins—that once you are caught in the criminal justice system you are frozen in your worst, most extreme, bizarre, or out of luck moment, you believe that when you go up for parole some rational and just set of eyes will look at how you are now and set you free. But rehabilitation is a myth that allows fine, upstanding citizens to think that people are put in prison only for their own good. But that justification is merely a mental safety valve to justify the continuing brutalization and destruction of the most marginalized populations in our country.

And so it went. I was furious at being dragged through what essentially turned out to be an exercise in the U.S. Parole Commission's abuse of power. I wasn't broken; I was just angry.

In 1999, Henry Bean, my thesis adviser, friend, and a prominent screenwriter, introduced me to Howard Gutman. Howard was a friend of Henry's brother and a lawyer in the firm Williams and Connelly, the biggest and most prominent law firm in Washington, D.C., which had every possible political connection. One of the senior partners was President Bill Clinton's lawyer. I was skeptical about tapping into this kind of network, but so many different people had told me that "this is how it's done" that I embarked on a brief attempt to use these channels.

When Howard first came to Danbury, I knew from the moment I saw him that he had never been in a prison visiting room and had never met anyone like me before. Howard was rail thin and his nervous energy flitted around him like a moth at a light. He had the strangest watch I had ever seen; inlaid into its thin gold face was a gold paper clip. I spent the first visit with Howard groping to understand what it might symbolize.

Howard wanted to meet with the U.S. District Court of the Southern District of New York and convince them to drop their opposition to my release on parole. Mary Jo White, the chief U.S. attorney for the Southern District of New York, had been the one to voice the opposition. Howard argued that if the Southern District withdrew its vociferous objection, then my status in the eyes of the U.S. Parole Commission would shift to the position that they had taken with my codefendant Tim, and they would release me.

But what did that mean? What would talking to the Southern District of New York entail? I had nothing to say to them that was different from the public record, nothing new to add. Howard argued that just the act of talking to the Southern District judges was a way to demonstrate greater remorse, to show that I understood how the game was played. It would show that I was willing to cooperate with the system. He was convinced that this would help me in the future with the parole board. Mary was opposed to the whole process. She had spent the last fifteen years representing me essentially pro bono, and given her job as a representative for workers in labor law, she was not a fan of the old boys' network. In fact, she had specifically opted out of practicing or working in that kind of environment. I know that it offended Mary, but I felt that my options were narrowing and I wanted to explore this new avenue.

Howard and Mary Jo White danced back and forth for months, but in the end the "negotiations" were a complete flop. I do not know if Howard would agree with this assessment, but the U.S. attorneys working for the Southern District of New York refused to change their position and refused to withdraw their opposition to my parole.

My reaction to yet another denial was multifaceted. I could not really deal with thinking about serving out my remaining time. I certainly could not project what the future held, and so I threw myself into my writing and graduate school. I processed my life through writing about it. I grappled in writing with the consequences of my life choices by creating a set of fictional characters. I wrote one screenplay, scores of short stories, and half a novel. The energy I put into writing preserved my mental well-being and consequently saved my very life. In fiction, I could confront and dissect motivations, morals, and choices. I created some characters that were the antithesis of me and my friends, while others were thinly disguised carbon copies. I loved all those made-up people, even the despicable ones. I felt, as my dear friend and novelist Doris Schwerin said, that I was mining for gold, and that while most writing turned up as fool's gold, the real nuggets in between were worth all the work.

The year 1999 was filled with tremendous highs and excruciating lows. One morning I woke up thinking passionately about Frin with lush impressions and intensities—of feelings, colors, tastes, and pains. I woke up remembering the feeling of diving into the cold ocean waves and the incredible, tingling shock to the system, the feeling of wetness as the head submerges and the taste of the first lick of the tongue as it darts out to touch the salty water, but not to let too much in. I recalled the spray right before the impact of the dive and the feeling of being carried away without fear and anxiety. The Atlantic Ocean was friendly and willing to let me ride its wave and take pleasure from it. To imagine the horizon where the sky and ocean meet blue on blue and to reflect on all the people who had stood for years at the same vista, that same point fixed but not fixed, mutable but not mutable. Impermanence and sameness: the eternal paradox. I thought of the Atlantic as my ocean, because it is where I grew up and its familiarity is deep and profound for me.

I was seeking intensity, from my dreams, from my surroundings, from any tactile and sensual stimuli I could find, because the same place, the same day in and day out, the grinding routine and never-ending days, the violence, the falseness, the artificiality of it all was making me forget the ocean. How could I be descriptive and tactile and remember the feelings in order to translate them into words? I lived by the maxim, "Write what you know." Prison was what I had known for fifteen years, but I refused to let it be my horizon. I felt that my memory, the details of my past, had to be stirred up and then stored up; otherwise, I would have no vocabulary or language. So I forced myself to remember. I lived in a box where freedom was a memory. And then there was the word. I tried to keep writing and to study and finish my coursework from Antioch.

I had been working for four years in the chapel at Danbury and had watched religion become more and more a mechanism for codifying the prison's rules. A system used to serve as a means of meeting prisoners' spiritual needs and of offering them recreation and enjoyment had turned into its opposite. The chapel library, which a small group of us had built almost from scratch with the chaplain's budget, contained more than six hundred books, two hundred and fifty videos, and two hundred audiotapes. The books, in seven languages, contained information about all the major religions and raised questions that readers could think about and learn from. The collection included books about Buddhism, Shamanism, Catholic liberation theology, anti-racism, women's role in religion, the Holocaust, and Rumi's poetry. Yet very few women read or used any of this material.

The Reverend T. D. Jakes's books, tapes, and videos had swept the population. He promised salvation and redemption. Coupled with that was the ever more popular study of Orthodox Islam and Judaism. Testimonials and devotionals had become the sole order of the day, and as prisoners with longer and longer sentences were entering at younger and younger ages, with less and less education and inner experiential knowledge, easy access to an all-forgiving God was the quickest solace. It seemed to give people some modicum of peace. But even Chaplain Sheridan called God a replacement drug, taken from Leo Booth's book *When God Becomes a Drug.*

The visiting Muslim Sunni imam had been replaced by someone stricter, and now members of Danbury's Islamic community were wearing chadors and retreating more and more into themselves. The warm, sympathetic Reform rabbi who had been on part-time contract for several years was underbid for the position by a Chabad rabbi and now the only organized Jewish religious practice was an Orthodox Lubavitcher. Perhaps even more telling was the fact that the most progressive event that the chaplaincy organized was a Catholic mass given by Bishop Edward Egan from Bridgeport, Connecticut. Then, one day, we came back from work and found red crosses painted on the doors of cells in which either Jews or Muslims lived. My door had been painted. Later we found out that the culprits were several newly born-again Christian fundamentalists who were part of the Bible study group led by the inmate choir coordinator.

As a secular Jew, and having been witness to how religious practice was manipulated for the purpose of control within the Bureau of Prisons, I could no longer stand the dogma taking hold in the chapel and its environs. Genuine education was losing ground to a rigid, oppressive, and reactionary set of conditions. Multicultural acceptance and interfaith unity had severely declined since I first started working in the library.

From working in the chapel, I had learned tolerance for belief systems different from my own and I had come to understand why so many people felt it was so important to have faith. But I could not help feeling that the way religion was now being practiced was merely a salve for the gaping wounds that existed among the prison population. I could not see how born-again Christianity could be either a tool for empowerment or the advancement of social skills. I decided that I had to leave the chapel job or I would wither. My best alternative was to go to work in the education department as a continuing education instructor.

I did not know then that all the things that I had taken as immutable conditions for life and living at Danbury were about to come to an end. How do you say good-bye to someone you have been soldiering with for years and years? The person is not your leader and not your follower. She is not your lover, not a parent, not your best friend, but she is more than your road dog, more than your running buddy, more than the person who rides second with you. You've seen the beauty of her soul and felt terror for her as though it was your own when her weaknesses were exposed. You've benefited from her solidarity and suffered the brunt of her individualism and anger. And because of time, place, and conditions, she has seen it all in reverse with you. The time when you witnessed someone who was having a heart attack, and the time you were once brutally attacked, this person helped you. And day in and day out, she gave you a smile that helped you get up and do another day. So how do you say good-bye to a person who has become a part of you as no one else ever again can be?

That was Alejandrina. Doing time with her was one of the greatest gifts I'd known in prison. We were not always friends. We disagreed on things as much as we agreed, and there were times when I could not fathom her actions. But from the moment I met her in Tucson, Arizona, in 1985, until the day she walked out of Danbury in August 1999, in my eyes, she was always a beautiful human being. Alex embodied the revolutionary passion and sacrifice of Puerto Rican nationalism and the movement for independence. I know that her imprisonment hurt every day in a million ways, but Alex bore it with grace. Alex was a true heroine.

When Alex told me on August 11, 1999, that President Clinton had made a conditional offer of clemency for the Puerto Rican political prisoners and signed a sentence commutation, I knew that eventually she and others would negotiate it and get out. The demand from the independence movement had always been unconditional release for all the Puerto Rican prisoners, so this offer was not a total victory, but it was still a tremendous success. It was a profound concession from the head of the most powerful empire on the planet. I knew it was a victory before they walked out the door because the Bureau of Prisons allowed them (all fourteen of them) several lengthy joint phone calls from all the different prisons they were in, from California to Connecticut, from Leavenworth, Kansas, to Lewisburg, Pennsylvania. The authorities had been directed by President Clinton to decriminalize them. By that, I mean that even though the Puerto Rican prisoners had been tried in different cases and had different convictions from different times, they were comrades who needed to talk with one another and determine a joint response. This was totally unheard of within the BOP.

Other prisoners were completely shocked that on the day the clemency was offered Alex did not just sign and walk out the door into the waiting arms of her husband and children. The offer was conditional; it did not include Carlos Alberto Torres or Marie Haydée Beltrán Torres, and there were special conditions for Oscar Lopez and Juan Segarra Palmer. Thus, the other prisoners had to determine what they would accept. As the days of negotiation continued, the tension grew and grew. After a week, not one of the prisoners granted clemency had signed—no one had rushed to get out the door. Having spent ten or sixteen or nineteen years in prison fighting for Puerto Rican independence, not one of them was going to "capitulate." And while the overwhelming response from the Puerto Rican people was jubilation, there was also anger. The commutation carried with it onerous conditions that included the denial of free speech and the right to associate. During the weeks that followed, over 100,000 people in Puerto Rico demonstrated in their defense and demanded no imposition of restrictions on their release.

Having been in support of the Puerto Rican independence movement, and having lived side by side with Alejandrina for more than a decade, I felt that the clemency the Puerto Rican prisoners were receiving was a victory for me, too. The most beautiful aspect of my extraordinary experience with the Puerto Rican liberation movement was witnessing the fruits of their labor to see themselves vindicated. For so many years, I had felt that my political movement was vanquished, even though I had felt that it was right to continue resisting attempts by the state to break my spirit and my heart. But there were not many external incidents that gave fuel to that desire. Rare material acts of social change were the most profound fuel to make my heart beat a little faster and to remember that there are ways to achieve justice. The Movimiento de Liberación Nacional, the Committee to free the Puerto Rican POWs, the Rafael Cancel Miranda High School, the Pro-Libertad committee, Dr. Luis Nieves Falcon—all of the organizations and individuals, despite their differences and struggles, were all victors in this extraordinary event. They had succeeded in uniting the existence of the prisoners and their freedom with the movement against colonialism, which included opposition to the U.S. naval occupation in Vieques and the referendums about the island's political status. As Jan Sussler, the attorney who represented the

Puerto Rican prisoners and helped to win their release, said, "This is a historic moment. The President of the United States recognized that men and women who have dedicated their lives to the freedom of their country deserve to be free, to participate in the political, legal process to shape the future of their country."

Alex was released, and then later that year, after ten years of legal battles and struggles, Silvia was transferred back to Italy. I was now without my political companions while I was facing at least fifteen more years behind bars. The common wisdom in prison was that every seven years was a whole turn in time—you either made it past that point or went crazy. I had made it through two seven-year stints.

Besides my friends and family, I was helped by my cellmate of two years. Jane later told me that when she saw me entering the prison for the first time she knew we would be friends because we both had a kind of "wild hippie look." She was right about that. Jane had become a great friend. In addition to engaging me in intense exchanges about books and politics and prison life, she helped me with my graduate work. We sat in our cell and discussed Walter Benjamin, Theodor Adorno, Hegel, and the other thinkers that I was studying in literary theory. We made the agreement that I had made with other friends in the past, that we would only talk about prison life and prison officials ten percent of the time. We knew that otherwise we would become consumed by hating them, and would have wasted too much time. Our greatest pleasure was playing racquetball, both against each other and as a team. We were among the oldest players in the place, but we could still kick up sufficient dust and beat those young kids.

Jane was smart and, despite what seemed to be an ephemeral quality, she had lots of life skills that always impressed me. She had read widely and had a huge frame of reference from which to draw.

Her numerous siblings (she was the oldest of twelve children) kept in contact with her, as did her lovely daughter. Jane had been a member of the counterculture of the late 1960s and early 1970s. As a single mother, she had gone back to school and become a pharmacist to support the two loves of her life—her daughter and son. Her son was a young man who was just beginning to come into his own identity when he was killed in a car accident. From what she said, he had a beautiful soul. His death sent Jane into a downward spiral that ended with drug addiction and a seventeen-year prison sentence. Jane had a beautiful soul and despite her own grief, a great capacity for empathy that enabled her to respond to other people's suffering. She received an excessive sentence for her sale of drugs to support a habit. We spent many hours discussing what the world would look like if drug use were decriminalized. While I was working and psychically drifting, Jane stayed the course in our joint cell life.

Friends outside stepped up their work on my behalf. Old friends that I had not seen since I was imprisoned reappeared in my life. Some corresponded, and others came to visit. My high school friend, from Walden School, Jon Preiskel, who had also been a radical activist and done extensive solidarity work with different African liberation movements in the 1970s and later had become a lawyer, walked into the visiting room one day. I hadn't seen him in well over a decade. He was with another friend from high school, Tony, also a defense lawyer and activist, and they both apologized for being out of my life for so long. Seeing Jon was a great, familiar relief. He embraced my views and understood my life choices and at the same time he was deeply connected with how I had grown up. His friendship helped me directly challenge the feelings of estrangement from my life before prison. Judith Mirkinson, who had been one of my closest friends for twenty-five years through all of my political sojourns, who didn't let a month go by without sending a book or a letter, visited more frequently because her daughters were now in college on the East Coast. Paulette D'Auteuil, a long-time radical activist and old friend, would drive up from New York with my mother, and the three of us would sit and laugh and listen to Paulette's intricate and interesting tales from her life in the Native American solidarity movement.

Shirley Cloyes visited as frequently as her schedule allowed. Shirley was the person who had always had a plan; she led the formation of the committee that had been organized to defend me at my parole hearing. Shirley was deeply committed to social justice and to a radical transformation of the prison system. She had not been in the same part of the left as I had, but she was politically progressive and understood why I had made the choices I had made. We became friends through the prison walls. Over the years she left publishing and became a human rights activist, a writer, and a highly skilled congressional lobbyist who had built strong ties to people with political power on both sides of the aisle.

Shirley strongly believed in working behind the scenes. She did not confuse publicity with actual organizing or strategy. I loved her visits, because the scope of our conversations always took me out of the prison, and I felt that her political connections, immediacy, and willpower would energize everyone else's efforts to obtain my release. She had this amazing high-speed energy that she slung over me like a blanket in the visiting room. I trusted her.

Howard Gutman wanted to go to court in the Southern District in front of Judge Haight, the original judge, in whose court the Brink's conspiracy charges were assigned, and ask him to rule that the Southern District of New York could not instruct the U.S. Parole Commission to use the Brink's case against me in obtaining parole.

This unique strategy was a long shot because it meant that we were asking a judge to step beyond his normal procedural boundary and curtail the prosecution's power. More than anything else, I thought that it was a way to build support for me and to expose the fact that the Parole Commission had used its discretionary power based on prosecutorial positions, not on the specifics of my case and my conduct. After a case has gone on for years and years, it is difficult to sustain activity around it. Languishing either in court or in prison is in effect a delay of justice, and there is great truth to Dr. Martin Luther King's statement that "justice delayed is justice denied." The prosecution has the power and the resources of the state behind it and can almost always outlast and outspend the individual. Even people who love you and support you cannot sustain their support through years of defeat or inactivity. And so both the people who had been on my side from the beginning and those who were new brought light and movement right through the prison walls. It helped me to sustain my resistance.

Howard filed a motion, got oral arguments scheduled on the motion, and then went to court to argue it. I only heard about it afterward. My mother and people who were working in my defense went to court to support the effort. Howard's strategy was to push the sitting judge, Judge Haight, by using the original judge, Judge Lacey's decision to drop the case against me as a way to limit and put a check on the power of the prosecution in the parole process. It was an attempt to push the very boundaries of jurisdiction and it was a strategy that recognized that the court of public opinion was an important place to court favor in order to one day be in a position to win. This was because even if the court didn't have jurisdiction over the implementation of the decision to have a federal judge on record saying that the BOP was wrong to use charges that had been dropped as the reason for denial of parole, it would be a part of the record on my side. The prosecution took it for granted that they would win this new motion and therefore did not really address the merits of our argument. No one knew how long it would take for Judge Haight to write a decision.

When he did rule several weeks later, it was a mixed decision, a common result within the legal system. Judge Haight agreed that it was unfair for the prosecution to direct the parole board to use the same case against me in which he himself had declared *nolle prosequi* (meaning he would not pursue it further) fifteen years earlier. He said it was not "decent," but he also said that it was beyond his jurisdiction and he could not legally order the Southern District of New York not to actively oppose me and instruct the Parole Commission to use the Brink's case against me. Even so, because the language in the decision was a strong rebuke against the government's abuse of its power resulting in my continued incarceration, my side was able to use the decision on my behalf. It was the first crack in the government's use of the Brink's case against me.

But I had run out of legal options. Howard wanted to appeal the ruling, but to whom could we appeal? I felt we had reached the bottom of the legal process.

Chapter 19

Cancer

SPRING CAME EARLY in March of 2000. Sitting outside the housing unit before the bustle of women left for work and feeling the warmth of the first rays of spring was one of those fleeting pleasures that made me happy to still be alive. The work bell would ring and then hundreds of women would stream out of their units, all moving in the same direction toward the back of the main buildings leading to a gate that opened into the factory. The only way you could get out of work was to be placed on the "callout," a list that detailed where everyone was supposed to be while not at work. Medical callouts, educational callouts, and recreational or legal callouts were the only things that could get you out of work. That day I was on the medical callout list.

Once a month, a mammogram technician would come to the prison to see as many women as she could fit into a day interrupted by meals, counts, and other routine disruptions of orderly institutional life. With a population of more than seventeen hundred women, whose median age was thirty-seven, the callout list for mammography was never ending. The room that held the mammography machine doubled as the visiting eye doctor's exam room. Occasionally, there would be a scheduling mistake and both the mammogram technician and the eye doctor would arrive on the same day.

That morning I was getting a mammogram. There were five of us waiting for the technician and ten waiting for the eye doctor. The technician and the doctor were taking turns seeing patients. There were empty rooms nearby and I kept wondering why they just didn't move the eye doctor into one of them.

Whenever I was having a medical test or exam, I tried to put the practitioner at ease. I went out of my way to be friendly and compliant. I kept in mind that the practitioner was in an unfamiliar environment, and I preferred to make it easy for him or her to do the job well. The mammography technician was a woman I had seen before. She was from the Danbury Hospital's radiology department and she always wore a flowered smock and pink cancer-awareness ribbons from head to toe. She took the pictures, stored them, and carried them back to the hospital, where a radiologist read them. She knew that our care was substandard, telling me that the mammography machine was outdated and that it was terrible how "we girls" were treated.

A week later I was standing in the yard, about to walk to work, when a female officer named Ms. Karel, from the security detail, walked up to me and said, "Rosenberg, come with me."

"Why?" I asked, not wanting to go anywhere with her.

She moved to take my arm and I stepped back.

"Where?" I asked.

She nodded toward the building that housed receiving and discharge (R&D) and said in a lowered voice, "Don't give me a hard time. I told them you would come with me."

I turned to a fellow prisoner and said, "Tell Jane that I am being taken to R and D."

I followed Ms. Karel through the labyrinth of normally out-of-bounds doors into the empty dressing room. No one was there except us. She threw me a jumpsuit and then a pair of laceless blue canvas boat shoes and said, "Strip."

"Can we move to the back, away from the front door?" I didn't want to be naked if someone else came into the room.

Ms. Karel nodded affirmatively and we went into the back area, where a curtain divided the space. She had me strip completely, bend over, and then squat and cough. She inspected my ears, nose, and throat. I put on the jumpsuit. "Where are we going?" I asked again.

"The hospital."

"Oh no. Why are we going there?"

"Don't have any idea," she said.

I thought that she was lying and just refusing to tell me. "I want to see a lieutenant," I said.

She laughed and said I would see one shortly. She told me we were going to "cuff up" and wanted to know if I would comply. I stretched out my clasped hands in answer. She cuffed me, chained my legs, and ran a chain around my waist and between my legs and hands. I was trussed. As we stepped outside the front door and into the parking lot, I surveyed the scene awaiting me. There were six cars, a van, a row of shotguns, and all of it was for me. I looked at them and thought, *When will this end?* They pushed me into the van and off it roared. As we drove down the hill to Route 37, I looked out the window and saw a helicopter above us. I was livid. It seemed that moving me was just an excuse for them to practice their high-tech security routine and show all their guns. I was tired of having my very being used as a justification for repression. We drove the brief distance between the prison and the hospital, the same hospital where my father had died seven years ago.

We drove into the delivery area at the back entrance. The COs picked me up and sat me in a waiting wheelchair, covered me up to my neck with a blanket, and wheeled me into the hospital. Two of them, brandishing rifles, led the two pushing me, who in turn were followed by more rifle-toting officers. The whole route along which I was taken to the eighth-floor radiology department was locked down. Patients and staff had been told to remain behind closed doors until the coast was clear.

It was only in radiology that I learned the reason for this hospital visit. My mammogram was suspicious, and a technician was going to take more pictures. As Ms. Karel uncuffed me, the technician shook from anxiety. She told the lieutenant to keep the guns out of the room. As soon as the film was out of the machine, I was cuffed again. An hour later a doctor came in carrying a clipboard. He didn't look happy. He introduced himself and without further ado said, "We want to do a biopsy on your right breast." He pulled out an X-ray and showed me the area that he wanted to probe.

"Now? You want to do a biopsy today?" I said.

"Well, no, but since you are here . . ."

I don't know why I complied. Maybe it was because I had been so accommodating already, or because I was scared or just exhausted. With my wrists still cuffed, I signed the permission forms.

Everything else happened in rapid-fire fashion. The radiology technician took measurements and inserted a needle, and then the COs wheeled me into a surgical room. They administered twilight anesthesia, and I vaguely remember the surgeon having a loud exchange with the lieutenant in charge, demanding that he uncuff my right hand, which had been cuffed to the side of the bed. I also remember that there was some kind of altercation about the rifles in the operating room. I woke up and asked when they would start, and they told me they were almost finished. I lay on a gurney for an hour, and by four o'clock that afternoon I was back in my prison cell.

I had been an HIV/AIDS advocate for years, and so I knew the procedures and schedules that the medical system followed in patient treatment and denial of treatment. I knew the medical staff at Danbury, from the administrator in charge of medical services to the head doctor to the rotating physicians' assistants. After my biopsy, no one from the medical department called me in for five days nor did my name appear on the medical callout list. I finally went to the medical department and walked into the director's office. The director was on the phone, but when he saw me he whispered into the receiver, "I'll call you back." I could see over his shoulders, past his big desk and through the window, a sharp image of hundreds of uniformed women standing around waiting for work call. It was a familiar image, but I had never seen it from a second story. I thought, *Remember this, remember this view because it looks like every prison work camp all over the world in the twentieth century.*

I looked back at the director, and his eyes were like little black holes that ended in a pinprick. He was sweating and his thinning hair was plastered across the dome of his forehead. I stood there. "Yes, ah, well, ah, yes, Susan, yes, you well, you have breast cancer, and it's lobular, and we are sending you to the Carswell Federal Medical Center in Fort Worth, Texas, for a double mastectomy."

He didn't say "Sit down," or "I am sorry to tell you this," or "Can I get you some water?" or "Do you want to make a phone call?" No, his pronouncement was the sum total of his words to me. Did I expect kindness or sympathy? No, not really. I had seen him display just such a cavalier attitude before with other prisoners. But, nevertheless, his complete lack of compassion jolted me.

"Admirable bedside manner, Doc," I retorted. My heart was

pounding, but I kept my composure. "I want to see the pathology report, and I want a second opinion," I managed to demand.

"Yes, by all means, we will get you the path report," the director said.

"I want to see it now, and I want a copy to show my lawyer. I am sure I have a right to see it."

But I didn't see it that day, or the next, or the next. I kept going back to the director's office, and he kept lying to me. I knew that the administration was simply planning to ship me to Texas, where I would never be able to call anyone, and that I would not get back to Danbury for months and months, if ever. I told the director that if they sent me to Texas, I would refuse medical treatment and so it would be a waste of money. He said the matter was out of his hands.

On the fourth day, by which time I was running ragged, the director was not in his office; a visiting doctor was there instead. I very calmly told this doctor that I was supposed to pick up my pathology report and asked her to look for my file. She said of course, found my file on the pile, photocopied the report, and handed it to me. I went to the pay phone in my unit and called my friend Barbara Zeller, a doctor. I read her the report. It was a single piece of paper that said I had "lobular carcinoma in situ" and that the recommended treatment was mastectomy. And that was it.

Barbara said that she would investigate this and call Mary, Shirley, and my mother. When I called the next day, Barbara said, "Susan, what the director told you is not reflected in this pathology report. If the path report is right, you don't have breast cancer at all."

I was thrilled, yet also stunned. "What do I have?"

"It's a genetic marker that indicates a higher risk or maybe a predisposition, but it certainly isn't cancer." I could hear the relief in Barbara's voice.

"So why are they saying I need a mastectomy?"

Barbara didn't know.

I didn't know what the whole process—from the unannounced biopsy to the director's delays—was about. But I knew that Mary and Shirley would try to prevent my transfer to Texas. They got New York Congressman Jerrold Nadler to write to the prison officials, asking them to halt the transfer and allow a second opinion. Several days later, I was called to the medical department, where a surgeon from the Yale School of Medicine was sitting and reading my file. He confirmed what Barbara had said on the phone. He said that he would recommend "watchful waiting" as the least-invasive treatment, but that there was a drug, tamoxifen, that had proved useful as a preventive. Only in extreme circumstances would a double or single mastectomy be called for. I thanked him, said that I would choose waiting as my treatment option, and danced out of the office.

No one in the Bureau of Prisons or the medical department ever explained the misdiagnosis and miscommunication, nor did the director apologize. I knew that if it hadn't been for those on the outside who loved and cared for me—and whom I had come to think of as my "citizens' committee"—I would have been immersed in "diesel therapy," the BOP's favorite form of neglect. And my body might have been butchered.

I went back to teaching to regain my equilibrium. Having left the chapel, I had taken over Silvia Baraldini's job in the education department after she was transferred to Italy. I was now teaching African American history and HIV/AIDS prevention as my prison job. It was difficult and challenging, but I was having more fun teaching than I'd had in a long time. Also, I had finished the graduate program at Antioch and gotten my master's degree and was now writing stories and revising a screenplay.

I had not wanted to teach African American history because I felt that as a white person it was an overstepping of my role, even if I was a committed anti-racist. I had grown up in a time when black people fought to teach and take control of the interpretation of their own history. But after much back and forth, I was convinced that it was more important to share what knowledge I could than to let the course die. My solution to my conflict over my role was to build a small group of coteachers who could then make the course theirs. I worked with Kemba and Jackie to build upon Silvia's curriculum and update it.

There were twenty-eight women in the class ranging from twenty to sixty years old, eighteen of them from the southeastern section of Washington, D.C. The others were from Ghana, Jamaica, Puerto Rico, and New York. The educational level spanned from seventh grade to college. The experiential divide—my whiteness, their blackness, my age, their youth—was enormous. The hardest thing of all was to get everyone to think beneath the surface, to move beyond the obvious. What my students did not know astounded me and what they did know seemed to me a terrible reduction of history. They didn't not know about Marcus Garvey. Garvey was a national hero from Jamaica who lived from 1887 to 1940 and was a black nationalist, journalist, and organizer who founded the Universal Negro Improvememt Association and African Communities League (UNIA-ACL). He was an important proponent of the back-to-Africa movement, which encouraged those of African descent to return to their ancestral homeland. This movement would eventually inspire other movements and become the largest mass movement of African Americans in American history. At its peak, the UNIA had more than four million members.

My students did not know Robert Williams, the author of the book *Negroes with Guns*. Robert Williams organized African

American armed self-defense in the South. President of the NAACP in Monroe, North Carolina, he led the black community in preventing Klan attacks and opposing the racism of governmental agencies. He was falsely accused of kidnapping charges by the FBI and was forced into exile. Williams lived in Cuba and China from 1961 to '69. From Cuba, he broadcast Radio Free Dixie, which aired the message of black liberation to the Southern U.S. He built strong relationships with world leaders like Fidel Castro, Che Guevara, and Mao Tse-tung and he organized international support for the human rights struggles of African Americans. The women in the class were shocked to find out that there were people who had preceded the Panthers' stance of the right to self-defense, about which they were aware only in the vaguest of terms. They had not heard of Bobby Seale, a founder of the Black Panther Party and a codefendant in the Chicago 8 trial. They had not read Eldridge Cleaver's book *Soul on Ice.* We read Malcolm X's crucial text *On Afro-American History* as a way to analyze the impact of not knowing one's own history. Working with all these black women, and seeing how little they had been exposed to black struggle, was Malcolm X's very point about how much easier it is to enslave a people when they are cut off from their history.

The historical figures they knew something about were Harriet Tubman, Dr. Marin Luther King Jr., and Rosa Parks. When we finally got to the mid-1960s, it was difficult to deal with the topics about power and freedom in the environment that we were in. We read Stokely Carmichael's article "Power and Racism: What We Want," which was the first written statement coming out of the Student Nonviolent Coordinating Committee (SNCC) about Black Power after the march to Jackson, Mississippi. It was after this march that SNCC argued that white people's main responsibility was to fight racism among whites. It was 1966, and it was part of the black movement's transformative process of becoming a revolutionary movement, like many of its counterparts around the world, particularly in Africa and Latin America.

I had previously underestimated the moral component of the early civil rights movement and its importance in forcing the condition of black people onto the world stage.

Teaching the African American history class to the Danbury prison community brought into sharp relief the fact that the United States has always been in the business of human bondage, first through slavery and now through the criminal justice system. This had not changed. The people I was living with had been robbed of the intellectual tools they were entitled to as human beings and the students ate up the knowledge that we offered in that class. They made the intellectual link between the plantation and penitentiary for themselves; we did not have to lecture about it. That it was impossible to close the gap between the parallel lines along which black people and white people had developed was a truth I could see around me every day.

When Howard Gutman had said that he wanted to appeal Judge Haight's decision to deny me parole, I said no. I had had enough of stirring an empty pot. I was in my cell writing Howard a letter when I thought about Bill Clinton. I recalled that, while watching his inaugural in 1993, I had thought that he might be a president who could understand my motivations and consider clemency. During his two terms he had freed the Puerto Rican prisoners, he had sent Silvia home, and he had apologized for slavery. Figuring that I had nothing to lose, I wrote to Howard that I wanted to apply for a presidential pardon, or a clemency, or a sentence commutation. I also mentioned this letter to Mary, Shirley, Rabbi Matalon, and my old friend Jane Aiken, who was now the head of the prisoners' rights teaching clinic at Washington State University Law School, in St. Louis, Missouri.

It seemed like such a long shot, and I was skeptical that it would work, especially because putting in an application to the Office of the Pardon Attorney was usually done years in advance. It was late—Clinton was leaving office in less than a year—and it would be a risky proposition for him to grant such a pardon. But, from my vantage point, looking at another fourteen years, all I could think was, *Why not give it a try?* I realized that it would be an enormous amount of work, and I felt bad asking people to again work on my behalf. But the people around me all recognized that if there was a president who might possibly grant such a request, it was Bill Clinton.

My friends, lawyers, and supporters rose to the occasion and mounted a strategy to apply for clemency. There were differences of opinion about whom to work with, how to work with them, and how to keep the request under the public radar screen yet build support at the same time. My feeling about other campaigns that had been carried out by the left in defense of political prisoners was that they were narrow and sectarian, and that as a movement we had not learned how to appeal to the broadest segments of society. But despite my feelings and opinions about this, I did not feel that I could arbitrate the differences that emerged within the groups of people supporting me. Ultimately, it was agreed to be as quiet as possible about the application. Shirley argued and Mary agreed that conducting a public campaign would draw the ire of the opposition and make it more difficult for President Clinton to go against the tide.

My main role was to write a letter explaining why I was requesting presidential intervention and what I thought of my actions then and now. I worked on this letter for months, writing draft after draft until we reached the filing deadline set by the Department of Justice.

Shirley began to quietly lobby all her congressional contacts. She made the case for my release in writing and made phone call after phone call to convince both Democrats and Republicans to support my release. She strategized about who on the White House staff might take my request directly to the president. The argument ran that I was being denied parole on the basis of dropped charges and that it was a violation of my right to due process that those charges were being used to deny me release. Shirley pointed out that my codefendant was out on parole after having been convicted of the exact same charges as I was. She also mentioned the disproportionate sentencing in our case, highlighted my changed views on violence, and detailed my years and years of good work while in prison.

Mary was in frequent contact with former officials from the administration. Jane Aiken had written the clemency petition and then re-worked it with Mary and others in order to file it on time. Barbara was coordinating the administrative work and providing indispensable practical and emotional support to me and my mother. Other friends who knew politicians or policymakers were trying to contact them. William Wardlaw was helping to fund it all, and my mother was holding the fort. It was altogether a Herculean effort.

One day, I got a letter from the short-story instructor at my Antioch program. I had learned a lot from her and had liked her. She had come to visit me at the prison several times during the course, and I appreciated her effort. The letter said that her husband, John Marks, had followed my case for a long time, and that he had written a novel about left-wing radicals in Germany around the time the Berlin Wall had fallen. Coincidentally, I had read this novel several years earlier and had liked it. He was now a producer for CBS's *60 Minutes* and was interested in doing a piece about me and my case. I later found out that he had gotten the press kit about my case and first spoken to Shirley and then met with Shirley and Mary in Washington, D.C., to determine if I would do an interview or not.

I reeled as I read the letter. My first thought was, *No! The media is not my friend.* While the film *Through the Wire* had done an enormous amount to help me and the others at Lexington, and had brought the issue of political prisoners to an international community, it had also been a personal nightmare. I hadn't wanted to be center stage, ever, and couldn't see how being on television could help me now. Then I got another letter from the senior producer of the team, Steve Reiner. Both Steve and John visited me, and Steve told me that he had been a member of Students for a Democratic Society, the most prominent student anti-war organization of the 1960s and '70s. He said that he had been on a similar page with me back then, and was now sympathetic. He assured me over and over that he would do an honest piece and put out my side of the story. It seemed risky, given that there were so many factors beyond my control, maybe even beyond Steve's control. It was also obvious that if the timing of the piece itself was not good, it could undermine my clemency application. Others argued that, conversely, it could support my release.

In the end, I agreed to be interviewed for the program. I spent four hours with Morley Safer, who asked me every question under the sun about my crimes, my charges, my role, my beliefs then and now, prison life, and on and on. It was one of the most intense and pressured exchanges I had ever had with anyone, let alone a television reporter. I could not imagine how the broadcast would do anything but hurt my chances.

Six weeks later, the episode of *60 Minutes* aired with my brief segment on it. I watched it in the communal TV room along with everyone else in my living unit. I remember thinking that Mary looked terrific on TV and was totally clear in her discussion. The segment was sympathetic toward me; the Parole Commission person seemed rather oafish, and no one from the court of the Southern District had deigned to appear. Despite my incredible anxiety, the piece did no harm. But whether it would help me get out was still an open question.

On December 19, 2000, the Clinton administration released its list of the first round of pardons. The list contained more than seventy names, including that of my dear friend Kemba Smith. I had expected her to get clemency because of the merits of her case and the skillful way in which her supporters, including the NAACP Legal Defense Fund, had been able to organize. They had framed Kemba's case as an example of the terribly unjust federal drug sentencing laws that had been enacted as part of mandatory minimum sentencing.

Kemba, a girlfriend who had answered the door at her boyfriend's apartment and let in a man who purchased several grams of cocaine, had been handed a twenty-seven-year sentence. Her beautiful parents had never given up on her for one second and galvanized parts of the black community to make her case a cause célèbre. Before Christmas, she walked out of the prison and into the waiting arms of her son and her parents.

I was not on the list, but I expected another list to be released before the end of President Clinton's term. Though my friends were counseling caution, I for some totally inexplicable reason was convinced of it. I had been sending some of my books and papers home. As the days went by and the end of the Clinton administration got closer and closer, every action I heard about or piece of news that I received became laden with greater meaning and I got more and more nervous. When I heard that an important congressman had seen President Clinton at a dinner and had handed him a letter from Rabbi Matalon that contained another letter from Elie Wiesel asking to grant me a pardon, I thought I might really get out. Yet I swung wildly from one extreme to the other.

I felt my paranoia level rising. I was talking on the phone more than I had ever done and I was increasingly feeling that my phone conversations were being monitored. The sound booth monitor was a woman officer with several years of seniority who worked for the Special Investigative Service. Whenever I saw her on the compound, she stared hard at me. I tried not to talk about the request for clemency on the phone or mention the president's name, because I believed that whenever I did a red light went off somewhere, a buzzer sounded, and someone was put on alert.

One day I was standing outside the education building, just watching the compound and smoking a cigarette. Without thinking about it, I suppose I was listing to one side. The sound booth monitoring officer was standing in front of the lieutenant's office, also smoking and staring at the compound. She turned and said, "Are you all right?"

I realized that I was leaning and said with a laugh, "It's the weight of incarceration."

She walked toward me and said, "Can I tell you something?"

I nodded.

She said, "Don't take this wrong, but I have always wanted to congratulate you on your master's degree."

I stared at her, taken aback, and then said, "Thanks."

"I know about it because I heard you talk about it on the phone."

I did not reply; I simply stared back at her and I could see that she was getting uncomfortable.

"How is your pardon going?" she asked.

"It's a long shot, but so far so good," I answered, thinking that this woman must have been listening to my every word. I was feeling more than violated by this exchange, but she was oblivious to my emotions.

"I hope you get it."

I turned and looked directly into her eyes and asked, "Why?"

"I read your file. I usually don't read anyone's file, but I wanted to see yours because the staff talks about you and I wanted to see for myself."

"I'm sure reading my file doesn't create a lot of sympathy for me."

She said, "I think the Southern District is wrong, and it blew me away that your codefendant is out on parole."

In the end she said, "Staff is running four to one in your favor. You know that, right?"

I told her that I had to go teach my class and went back upstairs. After years of constant vigilance under surveillance in order not to reveal anything of myself to the authorities, I was shocked that someone could have gotten into my business like that.

Chapter 20

The Hill

I WAS COUNTING the days. I was barely living through them. Every night after dinner I would go to the weight room and lift the heaviest weight I could find. Then I would go play Scrabble with my coworker Mary in the game room, return to my cell to talk to Jane, and then exit for a cigarette in the smoke room, trying not to fall apart in front of anyone else. President Clinton was leaving office on the morning of January 20, 2001. The 17th came and went, and the 18th came and went.

On the morning of the 19th, I woke up and tried not to think or feel anything. I refused to succumb to the utter panic that was a scratch away. I went to work at the early morning work call. I did not want to sit by myself. My coworkers were agitated and wound up but trying to contain themselves. A few hours into our shift, our boss, Mr. K., yelled from his office to ours, "Rosenberg, in here."

Not one of the five of us in the room moved or said a word for several seconds. I got up, shaking inside, as if going to my execution. There was a big glass window between Mr. K.'s office and ours, and so everyone could always see what happened on either side. I left the door open so that everyone could hear, as well.

"You have to go to R&D now." Still no sounds from the other room.

I kept my cool. "Why? Did I make the list?"

"You have to go and pack out," he said.

"Am I being released?" I said, raising my voice.

"I don't know about that. Just get out of here and go," he insisted, trying to be stern.

I had the oddest response. "No way, unless I know I am leaving. I am not going to go pack out in front of the whole prison unless I am not coming back."

Exasperated, Mr. K. looked at me as if I had lost my mind. "Rosenberg, get out of my office and go to R&D."

I walked out of the office back into our area. No one said anything for about thirty seconds. At last, Mary said, "Susan, you are acting a bit irrationally. Go to R&D and find out what is happening."

I wanted to tell her to stop being a shrink (she had been a psychiatrist in her preprison life), but then four SWAT officers walked in. "Come on, right now!" one of them demanded.

I stood up and went with them across the compound. As we walked from one end of the inner prison complex to the other, prisoners came out of their units or stopped picking up cigarette butts or clipping bushes to watch me walk across the yard.

At R&D, the SWAT group deposited me in the main room. Mr. Shelton, the CO in charge of R&D, smiled at me with what I took as a genuine smile.

"Am I on the list?" The question had become my litany.

Mr. Shelton eyed me again and said, "I am giving you two duffle bags and boxes. Go fill them up and bring them back here. We want you packed."

I didn't move.

Then he said, "We don't have a list. But we want you packed since tomorrow is Saturday and no one will be here. In case you make it, we don't want any R&D staff to have to do overtime."

I just looked at him. Now I wanted to punch those upturned lips. "No overtime," I said incredulously. "That's unbelievable."

He handed me two duffle bags. I walked to my unit with them. My fellow inmates were all over me. I kept shrugging and explaining that I wasn't on the list, but that they were packing me out in case, and I thought how humiliating it would be to have to unpack. It was now three o'clock and the work shift from the factory was returning to the housing units. Jane helped me carry the bag and boxes to R&D. Then we went to the education building and she helped me pack up some papers and books. We carried some of them to our cell and left the rest in the office. Then we locked down for the four o'clock count.

At 4:50 p.m., when the count had been unofficially cleared and the kitchen workers were massing at the door to be escorted to work for the dinner shift, my case manager, Ms. Shaloub, who had an office at the front of our block, walked down the hall to my cell. She stood outside and said, "My office. Now."

The whole floor lit up with chatter. Jane walked with me to the office. I went in and Ms. Shaloub closed the door. I said nothing. She said, "Call your lawyer. Call Mary." She pushed the phone across the desk toward me.

I was struck by how familiar people become in times of extremity, as though we were all in this together. I guess it was human nature. I dialed Mary's office number while staring at Ms. Shaloub, trying to read something from her demeanor. Mary picked up. "Mary, hi, what's up? They had me pack out and the whole place is crazy."

"Susan, there is no official list yet, but someone in New York called me and said that on the five o'clock news on Channel 9, you and Mark Rich and several others were mentioned as getting clemency. Then a reporter from another station called me to ask if it was true."

"Really?" It felt like my rib cage was going to crack. "Wow," I whispered into the phone.

"There is no official list," she repeated. I looked at my watch.

"Mary, if I get out tomorrow, I think you should be here to pick me up."

"The last shuttle to New York is eight o'clock. I'll be on it with Susie, and we'll be there in the morning."

"Thank you, thank you, and thank you. Either way, thank you," I said.

"If I hear anything else before we leave, I'll call Ms. Shaloub back. She says she'll be there until seven forty-five."

"Okay, great." I hung up. My case manager and I looked at each other across the desk.

"I hope you get it," she said. "You know I am getting my master's at John Jay College of Criminal Justice, and so I don't intend to stay here, either," she continued.

I hadn't known that. I thought back to when she had first started at Danbury. I remembered that she had been mean and was overly meticulous and thorough. I realized that she had moved up the ranks quickly in less than five years.

"Can I just sit here for a minute?" I asked. I didn't want to go back into the unit and I certainly didn't want to go to the dining room. I sat there about a half an hour and thanked her. Mary didn't call back.

Just before Ms. Shaloub went home, she called me back into her office and said that there was still no word. She wished me good luck. I saw that my very thick BOP file, my "prison jacket," was sitting on her desk.

That night, Jane and I talked for hours. We had shared a cell together for over three years and had gone through bouts of closeness and times when we just struggled to co-exist in our tiny cell. We had lived on the second floor in the last cell on the line with a double ceiling and a tall window that looked out onto the sky and no fences, and then we had lived in a cell on the first floor that had no distinguishing features other than the energy and beauty we brought to it.

I went to breakfast alone as soon as the door was unlocked. It was Saturday, January 20, and there was no real breakfast, just cereal, donuts, and coffee in advance of the Saturday brunch. Saturday visiting hours were 8:30 a.m. to 3:15 p.m., but because of the 10:00 a.m. count, new visitors were not admitted between 9:15 and 11:00. I was hoping that Mary and Susie would be there in that first forty-five minutes.

I also knew that the Bush inauguration would begin at noon. I had only four hours left. At 8:30 on the nose, I was called to the visiting room over the prison-wide PA system. I was ready. I hugged Jane and said, "See you later." I stood outside the locked door waiting for the CO to open it so that I could enter the strip room and be let into the visiting room. It had snowed that week and it was very cold. Despite the weather, I lit a cigarette while I was waiting. The smoke and my icy breath commingled and I blew it out in a straight and powerful stream. *I have to quit,* I thought to myself, *but not today.* I did not have gloves, so I alternated between stuffing one fist and then the other into each pocket as I switched the cigarette from hand to hand. I smoked the whole thing and was about to light another when the door popped open.

The strip room was very cold and I tried to get through the whole embarrassing process as quickly as possible. I had it down to a science, and for once the CO was rolling along as fast as I was. She was cold, too. I walked out into the visiting room and immediately saw Mary and Susie sitting in the larger legal room. They were worried and tired, but still looked wonderful to me. We all hugged as though it was the last time. No word, that was clear, and it was 9:00 a.m. Susie had made an unofficial agreement with the COs at the main entrance and then at the desk in the visiting room that she would be able to go out to the parking lot to use her cell phone and then come back in. It was a violation of their procedure, but this once they had acquiesced. We sat there just kind of looking at one another. At 9:30, Susie went out to call someone. She was back in twenty minutes, but with no answer.

The rest of the visiting room was filling up with families. Every one of the prisoners knew what we were waiting for. It was hard to talk. At 10:30, Susie went back out to call. Mary and I held hands. A little before 11:00 a.m., Susie wasn't back and Mary started to cry. I said, "Don't cry yet. It's not over." But as 11:00 came and went, I kept thinking of George W. Bush putting his hand on the Bible that Chief Justice William Rehnquist would be holding. From where we were sitting, we couldn't see through the window into the parking lot. We couldn't see Susie. By then, the 10:00 a.m. count had cleared and a few other prisoners were greeting their families.

At 11:25, Susie came back in. I couldn't tell anything from how she was moving toward us. She saw us looking at her—in fact, everyone was looking at her—and she was about twenty feet away from the door to the clear glass wall and entrance between us. She paused, looked at us, raised her arm above her waist, and gave us a thumbs-up. The entire room burst into a yelling roar of tears and screaming. People were jumping up and down. Mary and I burst into a hug and tears that took us to the center of the earth. I felt a rushing in my head. I was free.

Susie came into our little room and we hugged and hugged and jumped up and down and laughed and yelled and couldn't stop until a CO from the front came and told us to be still, we were disrupting the visiting room. A woman sitting with her family told the CO, "Leave them alone. They are happy, and we are all happy." But the exchange brought us back to where we were.

Susie said, "You are on the official list released from the White House. I talked to Alan and he saw the list online."

I looked at my watch; it was 11:45. They had waited till the last possible moment. Susie was doing the negotiating with the police and she was calm, collected, and systematic. But I could see the joy around her eyes. All the different prison visiting rooms of the last sixteen years passed through my head. I had seen Mary in all of them, Susie in most.

Susie went to the desk. "My client has received presidential clemency, and we would like to leave. Her mother is waiting for her."

"We have nothing official on that," the CO said.

We sat for an hour. Finally, Mary got mad and went to the desk. "I would like to see the captain or the warden. I would like to speak to someone in charge about what this delay is about."

The officer nodded. A few minutes later, the side entrance opened and in strode the two associate wardens and a slew of lieutenants. They walked up to the doorway and the tall, thin associate warden in charge of operations said to me, "Ms. Rosenberg, you have received a presidential pardon and you will be leaving with your lawyers." He stuck his hand out to shake mine.

I thought of all the encounters he and I had had over medical treatment and living conditions. I stood up and shook his hand. "When?"

The other associate warden, a blond woman who was formerly an education supervisor, said, "We are waiting for a fax, and then we can get the paperwork moving."

I disliked her even more than the other one because she had oversight in education and had happily cut all the programs.

Mary said, "I have a bag with clothes for Susan to put on."

"Give them to the officer at the entrance and he will see that she gets them," the blonde replied. "Susan has to go through R&D."

I was still standing up, looking, at all of them. "I need to go back inside to get the last of my things together," I said.

"Oh no, that's impossible," said the blond associate warden.

"I really have to. I have papers and things I need."

"We can't let you go back there. It wouldn't be safe."

That made me so angry I forgot that I wasn't quite free yet. "That is such a crock. I've lived in your prisons for over sixteen years and I have never felt threatened by prisoners. The only time I have felt unsafe has been in the presence of your staff." My voice was raised.

Mary put her hand on my arm. The officials all stepped away from us. They had a quick conference, and then the operations assistant warden said, "Okay, fifteen minutes, with an escort."

I turned to Mary and Susie and said, "See you outside." I couldn't believe the words that were coming out of my mouth.

I handed Mary my legal papers, walked back into the strip room, got my coat, and stepped into the compound, where there was one CO waiting to escort me. On the other side of the door were hundreds of women milling around. I realized that they had been waiting for me. As I walked past two buildings toward my unit, more and more inmates gathered and were following me.

I realized that I had to say something to them. They all wanted to say something and to touch me. Before I went into my unit, I turned at the door and faced the more than five hundred women amassed there. People were all talking and yelling.

I said, "I am going home today. I want to tell all of you that I have done over sixteen years and have been looking at another fifteen, and so I thought I might be buried alive in here. But I want you all to know that if my case has meaning, if it means something to you, I stand for hope. Let me stand for hope. Don't ever give up and don't lose hope that you all will be free. One day you will all be free. Fight for the living."

People started cheering and I was totally undone. I cried my way back into the unit. All 140 women were on the first floor lining the tier. People were crying and grabbing me. I went down the hall to my cell. I didn't really have anything to pack; I had just wanted to say good-bye and give people my thanks.

Jane said, "I told you! I love you, Susan."

I grabbed her and held on to her for dear life as long as I could; I didn't want to leave her there. But she pried me from her and pushed me out of the cell. I walked down the hall and spoke to every person who was standing and waiting to say good-bye. I got to Maureen and she was smiling an enormous smile. "You I will see in Jamaica."

"Right soon, I hope."

Pandemonium broke loose as I got to the front of the unit. Ms. Shaloub came out of her office. "Come on, let's go." She took my arm.

I turned to everyone standing there and yelled, "I love you all! Remember, freedom is a constant struggle." She moved me out into the crowd outside, and into the R&D building.

I had to sign papers and get my clothes and wait until they

were ready to let me out the door. Another woman had also been given a sentence commutation and was going to Houston, Texas, all by herself, with no spare clothes and no money beyond the exact amount to buy the fare. The prison personnel were going to drive her to the bus station in Danbury and then she would go to Penn Station in New York and get a bus to Texas. She was twenty-four years old and had been in prison since she was eighteen. She had never been to New York and was worried about traveling alone. She had four days until she had to report to the authorities in Texas. It would take her that long to get there, and so the plan didn't leave her much room to breathe.

I suggested to her that she talk to my friends outside in the parking lot and said we could take her to New York with us. The head of the records department, who had been called in overtime to do our paperwork, overheard me and said that would not be possible because we were both on parole and as soon as we walked out the door we would not be able to talk to each other, let alone drive to New York. I thought he was kidding, but they sent her out the door before I could speak further with her.

Then the same administrator handed me a piece of paper and said, "Sign it. These are the ten federal conditions of parole."

As I read them, they seemed as absurd to me as the Bureau of Prisons forms I had signed prior to transit saying that I promised not to escape. But the condition that flashed in front of me now was "no association with any ex-felons."

I signed the paper. Then I was done.

It was cold and starting to snow. My friends wanted to go home. It was fine with me. I put on my coat, stuffed the papers in my pocket along with a piece of BOP identification, and pushed open the door.

After more than sixteen years of prison, freedom was only a

memory. With each successive door I passed through, however, that state of being, that faded dream, grew upon me. I walked out of the Danbury Federal Prison for Women into an empty parking lot on a snowy afternoon. An hour earlier, as I sat on the other side of the fence and wall, that same weather had been depressing and uncomfortable, but now it looked pristine and dramatic. That afternoon, for the first time in more than sixteen years, I was not listed on the national four o'clock institutional count. I would not have to stand up and be counted. I was free of handcuffs, free of leg cuffs. I had a clear view of the horizon, and there were no helicopters buzzing overhead as I threw my hands toward the sky and shouted to my father's spirit, "Dad, I am free! We made good on the promise! I'm free!" I hadn't even realized that I had been holding my breath.

After sixteen years and three months I was released on parole, having been granted executive clemency by departing President William Jefferson Clinton. On January 20, 2001, at 4:00 p.m., I fell into the waiting arms of Mary O'Melveny and Susie Waysdorf. Mary and Susie were at the front door waiting to take me to Manhattan, where my mother, Bella, and friends were waiting for me. My mother had said, "I won't believe it until she is out and on her way."

But I could not leave until I walked around the parking lot to get a final view. I looked back from the other side of the wall, knowing that hundreds of women, whom I had left moments before, many of them dear friends, were crammed at the windows watching me, filled with their own longings. I waved, I saluted, and I jumped up and down as I stared past the razor wire and the distance between me and all of them. I wondered who of all those hundreds of women would make it out. Which of them would make it to the other side, to freedom? I made a snowball and packed it hard and threw it at the side of an empty prison truck. A man standing at the front entrance and cradling a shotgun in his arms scowled at me. "Get out of here," he shouted. At that moment, Mary and Susie drove their car up and Mary motioned to me to get in. Her grin was as wide as the open door. I hopped into the front seat with tears streaming down my face, and we drove out of the parking lot, down the big hill, and onto Route 37, which would take us to New York. Home.

Afterword

I WAS PART of the political left that grew out of the 1960s and I took up the radical choice of trying to help make a revolution. This period of history was a different time than the one that we are living in today. It was a time when I—and thousands of people like me—believed that "you're either part of the solution or part of the problem." And it was a time of massive civil conflict. Whether it was the FBI's infamous counterintelligence program (COINTELPRO) that led to the infiltration, deaths, incarceration, and silencing of rising activists within their social movements, especially African Americans and other people of color, or whether it was small groups of students or workers trying to physically stop the war machine by attacking the government, the two sides were locked in struggle. As a result of my own choices and actions, I became part of this narrative and ultimately a political prisoner.

The U.S. government does not recognize the existence of political prisoners in our country. The identity of political prisoners is concealed from the public and, consequently, their right to justice is denied. Today, many nations publicly recognize that the post–World War II era, especially from the 1950s to the 1980s, was characterized by legitimate conflict in response to social inequities that resulted in the imprisonment and death of men and women

across the globe. But not the United States. There are still scores of
political prisoners behind bars in America.

Going to prison blew my mind. It changed every idea that I
previously had and all of my relationships to my friends and family.
It destroyed every preconception I had about oppression and suffering, my own and others. It was a terrible, relentless, sixteen-year
existential nightmare. The work of staying alive in prison was
all-consuming. For long periods of time, prison life reduced me to
a grave state of nothingness. What was common to all the institutions I passed through was a brutal application of social control
and *loss of freedom*. I made lists to remember what I had lost.

One list went:

The power of control over my life

My connections to the past

My privacy

My memory

With time and age and lack of care, control over my own body

As these losses accumulated, I was stripped barer and barer, and
the world became smaller and smaller, narrower and narrower, my
very being diminished. Many times it drove me to utter despair because I was experiencing the loss cell by cell, emotion by emotion,
and memory by memory. And to feel that is enraging. I felt I was
being destroyed bit by bit.

To survive it, to hold fast, to keep a part of one's self free from
that process of disintegration takes an enormous effort. But people
do it. I did it; I resisted one moment at a time. All my life I had responded to injustice by asking how do I live with this and how can

I do something about it. What our society says about history and oppression and what the reality is remain so divergent. From an early age, I felt that my role was to expose that contradiction and to take a stand on one side of the equation—on the side of social justice. I made good decisions and many bad decisions along the way. I inherited the history of America and then I chose my path, as best I could, to be a part of the radical and very human thread of it. I went on an incredible and terrible American journey. I found the resistance that has always existed in American history. I found it in living in the most disenfranchised community in this country—the African American community. I found it in the solidarity that black women, one after another, gave to me in prison, whether it was throwing an orange into my cell, or giving me their turn in line to get medication, or when they and others stood up to authority, over and over again, to demand their dignity. I saw it as I was moved from the prison cells in the mountain ranges around Tucson, Arizona, to the green hills of Lexington, Kentucky, to the Washington, D.C., jail that "warehouses" thousands of black and Latino prisoners just blocks from the White House. It came to me when again and again someone inside or outside forced me to remember that I was not frozen in my worst or most extreme acts and that I could still create and resist and find my own humanity.

I survived, my thinking changed, my consciousness changed, and I got to the other side. I made it out. I am out only because of years of a movement's support, brilliant and unyielding legal help, astute political strategy, parents who never ceased fighting, and ultimately the mercy of a president. It is all of them that I must thank. Now I am consumed by the business of living. I am for the most part intact. I have a new life, including a family and work that has value. I am valued. And I am especially grateful that I was able to make good on my promise to my late father that I would get out of prison and one day take care of my mother. I have written this book because I am the exception to the rule: I was released. For the most part, our society does not believe in second chances. We say that we do, but the truth is that we don't. And yet we should.

Today, there are 2.4 million men and women in jail, the majority of whom are nonviolent offenders. It *is* possible to challenge our propensity to punish. It is possible to have mercy. We can.

Notes

Chapter 1: **Explosives**

1. **Assata Shakur (Joanne Chesimard):** Lifelong activist and continuous target of the U.S. government. Beginning in the 1960s, Shakur was a participant in the student movement and (as a member of the Black Panther Party and the Black Liberation Army) the struggle for black liberation. In 1973, at the height of the government's attack on the black liberation movement, state troopers ambushed Shakur, along with two other members of the BLA, on the New Jersey Turnpike. One trooper, Werner Foerster, and one of the men Shakur traveled with, Zayd Malik Shakur, were killed. Shakur sustained two bullet wounds and, along with her other passenger, Sundiata Acoli, was captured and indicted for first-degree murder. Her treatment, which included significant amounts of state-inflicted torture, incited public scrutiny. In 1979, members of the Black Liberation Army successfully freed Shakur from the Clinton State Correctional Facility for Women. After a period of living as a fugitive in the United States, Shakur was granted political asylum by the government of Cuba and has been living in exile there since 1984. Sundiata Acoli remains in prison.

2. **Mario Savio:** A founder of the 1964–65 Free Speech Movement (FSM), in Berkeley, California. The FSM was a student protest movement that demanded students' rights to free speech and academic freedom. It was an early divestment movement against the military-industrial complex.

3. **The Young Lords:** Founded as an anti-gentrification street gang in Chicago in the 1960s, the Young Lords evolved into a significant Puerto Rican nationalist organization with active chapters operating across the United States, organizing for Puerto Rican independence abroad and against the racist conditions of Puerto Rican people living in the U.S. Inspired by the ideology and actions of the Black Panthers as well as other radical community organizations, the Young Lords implemented neighborhood programs addressing community realities such as housing rights, education, nutrition, and protection from police violence. They influenced a generation of poets, musicians, and artists. In turn, they, too, became targets of and were subject to the systematic efforts of COINTELPRO to eradicate community organizations working toward the end of racial oppression and injustice. As a result, the Young Lords dismantled in 1976, only to resurface two years later wherein members established a variety of political community projects and continued to act in solidarity with activists and organizations fighting for Puerto Rican independence.

4. **Franz Fanon (July 20, 1925–December 6, 1961):** Revolutionary, psychiatrist, philosopher, recognized for his theories and analysis of the complex socio-political and psychological consequences of colonization and occupation. This theory, entrenched in Fanon's colonial experiences, first in his native

Martinique, then as a soldier in France during the Algerian war, and then as a practicing psychiatrist, produced his most highly regarded work, *The Wretched of the Earth.*

5. **George Jackson (September 23, 1941–August 21, 1971):** In 1960, at the age of eighteen, George Jackson was given a sentence of one year to life for stealing seventy dollars from a gas station. During his incarceration at the Soledad prison, he organized several groups, including the Black Guerilla Family. He was eventually appointed as field marshal of the Black Panther Party. On January 17, 1970, he, along with two other men, was charged with the murder of a prison guard. These three men became known as the Soledad Brothers. George Jackson authored two seminal and widely read books—*Soledad Brother: The Prison Letters of George Jackson* and *Blood in My Eye.* On August 7, 1970, George Jackson's younger brother, Jonathan, entered a courtroom armed with the demand that the Soledad Brothers be released. Jonathan was killed as he drove away from the courthouse. On August 21, 1971, armed guards at San Quentin prison assassinated twenty-nine-year-old George Jackson in an open courtyard under the auspices that they were thwarting his escape. It became common knowledge that this was a lie and that George Jackson had been assassinated in an effort to silence a voice that was eminently successful at publicizing the corrupt prison system and organizing incarcerated men and oppressed communities into political consciousness.

6. **COINTELPRO (Counter Intelligence Program):** A United States government operation established by FBI director J. Edgar Hoover to target, disrupt, and eradicate political organizations and individuals deemed as threats to U.S. national

security. Secretly active between the years of 1956 and 1971, until a group of radicals discovered the files during a break-in of FBI offices. From its inception, COINTELPRO operatives (FBI agents and police forces) were instructed to exploit their governmental power and resources to implement a series of illegal intelligence-gathering methods, including surveillance, infiltration, legal entrapment, physical force, and torture. The results of these actions dismantled radical organizations, caused the lifelong imprisonment of activists as a result of unprecedented sentences and the extra-judicial assassinations of many other activists, mostly people of color, who were gaining significant power during this period. Although COINTELPRO is no longer an official program, the methods once considered illegal during its period of operation have now been legitimized by the judicial system, affecting laws regarding torture, surveillance, imprisonment, and repression.

7. **Ernesto "Che" Guevara (June 14, 1928–October 9, 1967):** Well-known Argentinean revolutionary leader whose political consciousness initially arose in response to the poverty he observed during his travels as a doctor in Guatemala. Guevara eventually developed an established revolutionary ideology rooted in a convergence of Marxist principles and the direct experiences of U.S. imperialism in Latin America. He eventually met Fidel Castro and joined the struggle against the U.S.-backed dictatorship in Cuba, wherein he played a significant role in the ultimate victory. Guevara was then appointed to a number of significant governmental offices until he left Cuba in 1965 in an attempt to bring the revolutionary accomplishments in Cuba to the Congo and Bolivia. He was captured and assassinated in Bolivia by the CIA in 1967. Guevara still

remains one of the most prominent figures representing successful international revolution.

Chapter 3: **Detention**

1. **Bobby Sands (March 9, 1954–May 5, 1981):** Member of the Irish Republican Army, writer and commanding officer of IRA Prisoners of War. Bobby Sands was arrested and tortured multiple times before he died (along with ten others) in Long Kesh (the Maze) prison on day sixty-five of a political prisoner-led hunger strike. The hunger strike was in protest of brutal prison conditions, as well as a response to the retraction and elimination of the previously held, government-sanctioned status given to political prisoners, an assignation that had been won in IRA–British Forces negotiations that had granted said prisoner rights and privileges according to the Geneva Convention.

2. **Lolita Lebrón (November 19, 1919–August 1, 2010):** Life-long Puerto Rican Nationalist leader and hero who served twenty-seven years in Alderson prison for an armed attack on the U.S. House of Representatives on March 1, 1954. The attack was intended to publicize the struggle for Puerto Rican independence, Lebrón, along with Puerto Rican Nationalists Rafael Cancel Miranda, Andres Figueroa Cordero, and Irving Flores Rodriguez occupied the House and unloaded their weapons into a group of legislators discussing an immigration bill. All four were found guilty of attempted murder and sentenced to lengthy prison terms. The activists were released in 1979 after President Carter issued pardons to all parties involved. Lebrón resided in Puerto Rico until she died on August 1, 2010.

Chapter 4: **Conviction**

1. **Los Macheteros:** Radical Puerto Rican organization rooted in the historic traditions of resistance against European and American colonization. Initiated in the 1970s amid a country-wide movement for independence from U.S. colonization, Los Macheteros carried out a number of actions in both Puerto Rico and the United States including, most famously, a Wells Fargo Bank robbery, the money from which was used to buy toys for children in Hartford, CT and Puerto Rico. Los Macheteros were and continue to be a target of government repression and murder. Most recently, sixty-seven-year-old Avelino Gonzalez-Claudio, was arrested and sentenced to seven years in U.S. prison for his alleged participation in the Hartford Wells Fargo expropriation twenty-five years ago. Founder and leader Filiberto Ojedo Rios was hunted by the FBI for decades and was assassinated by U.S. forces in Puerto Rico in 2005 at the age of seventy-two.

2. **The Ohio Seven:** A group of activists engaged in the United Freedom Front, a clandestine organization founded in 1975 in solidarity with anti-imperialist struggles in Central America and anti-apartheid movements in South Africa. The Ohio Seven, two of whom are still incarcerated as political prisoners in the U.S. (Jaan Laaman and Tom Manning), carried out and were convicted on charges relating to a series of targeted bombings against the U.S. military and corporations.

3. **Black Liberation Army (BLA):** Originally formed as the clandestine armed wing of the Black Panther Party, the BLA ascribed to Marxist-Leninist ideologies of armed resistance, which pro-

posed armed struggle as a crucial element in the fight for liberation of oppressed peoples. The U.S. government effectively infiltrated and created internal strife within the Black Panther Party, thus causing an organizational split, leading the Black Liberation Army to break off as its own faction. As a result, the BLA succeeded the party in a series of bank expropriations and prison liberations, most notably that of the Brink's robbery in Nyack and the freeing of Assata Shakur. Many members were and are exposed to conditions of torture and unprecedented lifelong sentences within United States prisons.

Chapter 7: **Lexington High Security Unit**

1. **Dead wings:** Dead wings utilized single cells in otherwise empty areas within German prisons consigned for the particular detainment of captured members of the Red Army Faction (RAF) in 1970s Germany. In an effort to defeat the political movement, dead wings were developed to systematically destroy the solidarity between and the humanity of political prisoners. Captured activists were exposed to extreme conditions of state-funded, meticulously researched torture, including twenty-four-hour isolation (absolutely no contact with other humans), sensory deprivation, and both physical and psychological abuse.

2. **Stammheim Prison:** Built as a high-security prison in Germany in the early 1960s, Stammheim became famous when leaders of the Red Army Faction (RAF) were incarcerated in a special section built within its general structure in 1975 for the explicit internment of political prisoners. On October 18, 1977, a group of the imprisoned leaders were found dead. Prison

officials reported the deaths as suicides. One survivor, however, maintains that they were extra-judicially killed as political prisoners.

Chapter 8: **Litigation**

1. **The Wilmington Ten Conspiracy Case:** In 1971, Reverend Benjamin Chavis, Southern regional program director of the United Church of Christ's Commission for Racial Justice, was called to Wilmington, North Carolina, to lead a community of African American high school students who were attempting to boycott the New Hanover Public School System. The boycott developed in response to an upsurge in the occurrence of Klan-led racial violence resulting from an ill-conceived government effort to desegregate public schools. In that same year, police advanced on Chavis and nine young activists in the church that had become their headquarters. They were all accused of arson and were all given twenty-nine to thirty-six years in prison. In 1976, Amnesty International took up their case, publicizing Chavis and the youths as the first instances of political prisoners in the United States. After nearly five years in prison, the Wilmington Ten were all exonerated.

Chapter 10: **AIDs Epidemic**

1. **Robinson Randall,** *The Debt: What America Owes to Blacks,* New York: Plume/Penguin Putnam, 2000.